Politics
of Arms Control

The Role and Effectiveness of the
U.S. Arms Control and Disarmament Agency

Duncan L. Clarke

THE FREE PRESS
A Division of Macmillan Publishing Co., Inc.
NEW YORK

Collier Macmillan Publishers
LONDON

The Free Press
A Division of Macmillan Publishing Co., Inc.
866 Third Avenue, New York, N.Y. 10022

Collier-Macmillan Canada Ltd.

Library of Congress Catalog Card Number: 79-1955

Printed in the United States of America

printing number
1 2 3 4 5 6 7 8 9 10

Library of Congress Cataloging in Publication Data

Clarke, Duncan L
    Politics of arms control.

    Inlcudes bibliographical references and index.
    1. United States. Arms Control and Disarmament
Agency. 2. Disarmament. 3. Arms control. 4. United
States--Defenses. I. Title.
JX1974.C4842 1979   353.008'92   79-1955
ISBN 0-02-905700-0

To My Parents,
and to Cynthia, Amelia, and Xena

"Nothing in human life is more to be lamented, than that a wise man should have so little influence."

Herodotus

Contents

Part I
Setting

1 Introduction

ARMS CONTROL IS, by law, an integral component of national security policy, and the U.S. Arms Control and Disarmament Agency (ACDA) is a designated focal point for American arms control efforts. However, law and reality have coincided only sporadically and haphazardly. Vital defense program decisions have been made with only the most casual reference to their arms control implications, and ACDA has often been prevented from participating meaningfully in decisions directly affecting arms control. Concern about ACDA's effectiveness and its noninvolvement in key decisions led Congress to pass legislation in 1975 to enhance the Agency's policy role. In each of the three succeeding years additional legislation was enacted with a similar purpose. ACDA thereby acquired some important prerogatives, and in certain areas the distance between arms control policy and overall national security policy may have narrowed somewhat.

But—as illustrated by President Carter's 1977 nomination of Paul Warnke to become ACDA's fourth Director and chief U.S. negotiator at the Strategic Arms Limitation Talks (SALT)—it is uncertain whether the Agency will be able to exercise these prerogatives fully in the future. Never before had a Democratic or Republican President appointed an outspoken, liberal arms control advocate to either of those two posts, despite the widely held perception within government that ACDA is a uniquely "liberal" policy actor in the national security bureaucracy. Indeed, largely *because* of this perception, past Presidents always selected ACDA Directors who were moderate, "responsible," and Republican. Powerful actors within the executive branch and some influential members of Congress questioned both the legitimacy of ACDA's role in national security affairs and the wisdom of associating American foreign policy too intimately with arms control. Former Presidents avoided alarming these potential critics of arms control agreements by giving ACDA a low profile.

Not surprisingly, then, none of ACDA's first three Directors enjoyed ready access to the Chief Executive. Presidents Kennedy, Johnson, Nixon, and Ford—in varying degrees, to be sure—chose not to identify closely with "those arms controllers" in ACDA, who some regarded as "weak" on national defense. Consequently, ACDA could rarely aspire to a major policy role.

The Warnke nomination, discussed more fully in Chapter 13, diverged from past practice, provoking an acrimonious controversy that presented President Carter with one of the first serious political tests of his administration. In the early 1970s—with Soviet-American détente, the SALT I agreements, and several other significant arms control developments—arms control gained considerable receptivity in Congress. However, by 1977 there was increasing uneasiness about growing Soviet military might, Moscow's compliance with the SALT I accords, and Soviet assertiveness in various regions of the world. American officials no longer spoke of an era of détente. It was against this background that the Senate considered the nomination of an active proponent of arms restraint. While Warnke's conservative opponents questioned his negotiating ability, his consistency on defense issues, and the advisability of the ACDA Director's simultaneously holding the post of U.S. SALT Ambassador, their basic quarrel was with his philosophy. They were afraid that he would not be firm in dealing with the Soviet Union, that he might be disposed to "trust the Russians." In at least one instance, Warnke's patriotism was even called into question. Above all, his critics feared that this Director, unlike his predecessors, would have access to the President.

The Senate ultimately confirmed him to both the SALT and the ACDA positions, but the controversy did not fade away. Instead, Warnke became a symbol to conservatives of alleged U.S. timidity and weakness in the arms control field. His presence in the Carter administration served as a rallying point for those who opposed SALT II and other possible arms control accords such as a comprehensive nuclear test ban treaty. Hence, although ACDA's policy role within the executive branch improved in many areas under Warnke's leadership, it was by no means evident that history would judge his directorship as beneficial either for ACDA or, far more significantly, for arms control.

This book examines ACDA's policy role within the U.S. government as well as the conditions and factors that bear upon the Agency's effectiveness in implementing this role. "Effectiveness" refers to an actor's ability to influence policy outcomes, to create, shape, or importantly affect the policy environment. An actor who is thought to be effective by others within government is one who plays the policy game skillfully and successfully. "Policy" here refers not only to what ACDA and the rest of the national security bureaucracy actually do in the arms control field but also to what the Agency might aspire to accomplish. Hence my analysis is both descriptive and prescriptive. The study has a dual purpose and focus—(1) to detail the activities and to assess those factors bearing upon the effectiveness of a federal agency with an important mission, and (2) to place that agency for the purpose of analysis within its real political environment, namely, the larger American arms control policy process.

Determining a policy actor's effectiveness in carrying out its role within the decision-making process is an inherently plastic and judgmental exercise. At times even an agency's director may be unaware of how or why a particular decision was reached. Weighing the relative impact of bureaucratic, personal, and other influences on policy outcomes is a slippery undertaking. By what or whose standard is effectiveness to be judged? An executive branch official painfully aware of harsh internal constraints concludes that, considering these realities, his agency performed creditably. A congressman, employing very different criteria, reaches a contrary conclusion. In addition, effectiveness varies over time and changes with the issue.

It is essential to appreciate these limitations. Clearly, any attempt to ascertain conditions relating to an entire agency's effectiveness demands a certain humility. Nonetheless, at least for ACDA, we can acquire considerably more than just a "feel" for effectiveness. Indeed, a fairly precise picture can be delineated.

To begin with, much is known or knowable about ACDA. For example, we know that until 1976–1977 it was virtually excluded from policy decisions affecting conventional arms transfers and American commercial nuclear exports. We know further that ACDA lacks a powerful, well-financed public constituency; that its technical and scientific contracted research program has produced several notable achievements; and that the Agency has often played a prominent part in formal arms control negotiations with other nations. In these and many other areas an assessment of effectiveness is possible. Further, the fact that ACDA is a rather young (since 1961), very small organizational unit with an identifiable mission, facilitates analysis. Finally, people in government constantly judge agency, bureau, and personnel effectiveness. The 1975 legislation, for instance, was the direct result of a congressional perception that ACDA's effectiveness had declined. I merely suggest a more systematic framework within which an overall or net assessment of the Agency's performance might be conducted. While it is impossible to be more precise than the nature of the subject matter allows, there are sets of factors and conditions relating to the question of effectiveness that, when taken together, are illuminating. Those who are personally familiar with ACDA might differ, perhaps vigorously, with some of my conclusions, but all will agree, for example, that the President's confidence in ACDA's Director, the Agency's relationship with Congress, and the caliber of its leadership are among the key elements to be taken into account.

Questions concerning organizational change or the wisdom of proposed legislation affecting federal agencies must be weighed in light of an agency's political environment.[1] No examination of an executive agency should be *sui generis*. ACDA's operational environment is the U.S. arms control and national security policy process. A generous slice of that process is therefore examined. Although policy is also fundamentally affected by external, international developments—to which some reference is made—the book's focus is internal. While ACDA is neither the only actor in the arms control process nor the most important, here it is the touchstone, the lens through which the process is viewed. Only those aspects of the process that bear significantly upon ACDA's role are analyzed. The scope, then, is arbitrarily, yet necessarily, limited. Treatment of ACDA is intensive but not all of its many activities can be exhaustively explored. For instance, this book will discuss its negotiating role, external research program, and stake in arms control interest groups, but each of these subjects could, and someday probably should, be covered in separate studies. Finally, there are informational and chronological limitations. No study that seeks to portray a living organization operating in its actual milieu is possible without scores of frank, confidential interviews. Some information is bound to fall between the cracks. Subsequent studies will add to and refine earlier findings. Comprehensive coverage is restricted to the period from ACDA's establishment to the end of the Ford administration in January 1977. The early Carter administration is also addressed, but here extensive treatment is limited to ACDA's relationship with Congress.

As the study proceeded it had some modest policy spinoffs, usually subtle, occasionally specific (legislation). Before the work of scholars like Aaron Wildavsky, Richard Neustadt, Graham Allison, Morton Halperin, I. M. Destler, John Steinbrunner, Donald Warwick, and others, many academics had a certain disdain for, and preferred to stay aloof from, practical policy matters, especially if this meant immersing oneself in the actual policy process. While such sentiments persist, they have been frontally challenged over the past two decades by a flood of valuable scholarly work. Academics, because they are academics, have a talent for systematizing, conceptualizing, and experimenting with new analytic techniques. On the other hand, many government officials fault academics on precisely these grounds—alleged overconcern with methodological artistry and sweeping theoretical constructs, often with minimal regard to the "stuff" of policy. Academics have their own complaints about short-sighted, inflexible, in-basket-oriented bureaucrats.[2] What are needed are studies that are alert and sensitive to the value of systematic analysis, yet simultaneously grounded in the actual political setting, and that employ an approach suited to that mode of analysis.

In the spring of 1977, Congressman Jonathan Bingham (D–N.Y.), addressing the author, said "I am struck by the fact that you obviously have had a great deal of access to a great deal of information from within the Agency."[3] But the kind of information necessary for a study of this sort is not readily procurable. Public documents, while essential, are insufficient and even misleading. One must go to the actual participants. More than 250 formal interviews were conducted with past and present executive and legislative branch officials. Numerous informal contacts were made through personal discussions, telephone calls, and written communications. Emphasis was given to ACDA officials, from the Director to the working-level analyst, but interviewees represented most major components of the national security bureaucracy. Very few interviews would have been granted without my assurance that remarks would not be directly attributed to the source. For that reason, the reader will find many direct quotations, without citation, attributed to an "ACDA officer" or a "ranking State Department official." Other passages either lack source substantiation or are only partially substantiated. It must be assumed in these instances that the material is based upon confidential interviews.

Data reliability was, therefore, a primary concern. There was a sensitivity to what anyone who has served in government knows, that the policy process is characterized by the accidental, the confused, and, often, the inscrutable. The pitfalls are many. Some officials were reluctant to talk candidly, all saw only part of the action, others had memory lapses, several had obvious normative biases, and a few relayed inaccurate or misleading information. In weaving together thousands of fragments of information, an art form, there was a conscious effort to check and cross-check for reliability. Most, but not all, data came from more than one source. Many people were contacted more than once; one key official was interviewed six times. Informed individuals commented upon the study as it progressed. When there were differences of opinion, the author exercised his own judgment based upon all available evidence. Finally, I teach in Washington, where many colleagues, students, and friends serve or have served in government, several in the arms control field. They keep me "honest."

Each chapter reflects a set of interrelated conditions, developments, functions, or relationships bearing upon ACDA's role and effectiveness. An understanding of the Agency is possible only if all chapters are considered collectively. Furthermore, this is a study of both internal executive branch politics and executive/legislative relations. While Part II deals with the executive branch and Part III with Congress, the separation is not exclusive.

The next chapter discusses ACDA's historical, political, and legislative origins. Chapter 3 treats ACDA's "image" within government. The Agency is widely perceived as being "soft" on national security, which makes ACDA, and arms control generally, suspect to those who view arms restraint as inimical to the national interest. Part II (Chapters 4–11) details ACDA's place within the executive branch. Chapter 4 deals with the Agency's leadership and cohesion. By looking at all of ACDA's Directors between the years 1961 and 1978, this chapter also provides a general overview of ACDA's evolution. Chapter 5 addresses a vital consideration—the Director's link to the President. Chapter 6 explores ACDA's ability to gain a hearing and play a significant role in the arms control policy process, Chapter 7 its access to sensitive national security data. Chapter 8 treats the ACDA–State Department relationship as well as the question of ACDA's appropriate organizational location within the executive branch. Chapter 9 then analyzes three key Agency functions: negotiations, research, and public information. Chapter 10 treats a special subject directly related to ACDA—the General Advisory Committee on Arms Control and Disarmament—and Chapter 11 examines ACDA's size, budget, and personnel. Part III (Chapters 12–14) concerns Congress and ACDA's outside constituency. Chapter 12 examines arms control interest groups, while Chapter 13 elaborates ACDA's relationship with Congress. A novel and potentially important legislative attempt to increase the role of both Congress and ACDA in a crucial arms-control-related area through the use of an arms control impact statement procedure is analyzed in Chapter 14. Finally, Chapter 15 concludes the book by summarizing its findings.

Paul Warnke resigned the ACDA directorship on October 31, 1978, shortly before the publisher's deadline. It was still premature to draw firm conclusions about his long-term impact on the Agency and arms control. But it appeared appropriate, even mandatory, to add a short epilogue updating events and examining some of the larger issues raised by these events during the first two years of the Carter administration.

2 Origins

WITH THE POSSIBLE EXCEPTION of the abortive Baruch Plan (1946),[1] disarmament was seldom considered among the most urgent of America's foreign policy concerns in the 1945–1960 period. An Antarctic Treaty was signed in 1959, but not until the Partial Test Ban Treaty in 1963 was a significant arms control agreement concluded. The international environment of the Cold War period was inhospitable. Soviet–American disarmament negotiations often degenerated into propaganda exchanges, which gave the whole subject of disarmament an air of unreality and futility. Until 1955 international attention focused primarily on general and complete disarmament. While partial disarmament measures were discussed after 1955, the less ambitious, but promising, arms control approach to international tension reduction was still in its intellectual infancy. The pronounced nuclear inferiority of the Soviet Union throughout this period probably foreclosed the possibility that Moscow would seriously consider entering into major strategic arms limitations. And the then relatively primitive capability for verifying compliance with arms control accords also inhibited movement.

Government Organization for Disarmament

Government organization for disarmament reflected its low estate in policy circles. Disarmament issues were often handled by ad hoc groups. Except for a brief period from March 1955 to May 1957, there was little sustained, high-level, centralized direction of U.S. disarmament efforts; nor was any sizable staff assigned this function. From 1946 to March 1958 disarmament was handled within the State Department by the low-prestige Office of United Nations Affairs (later the Bureau of International Organization Affairs), and until 1955 the Department rarely assigned more than four professionals to disarmament. Defense Department (DOD) disarmament activities were usually managed by the Assistant Secretary of Defense for International Security Affairs. His office coordinated position papers with the Office of the Secretary of Defense (OSD), the Joint Chiefs of Staff (JCS), and other pertinent departmental offices.[2]

On March 19, 1955, President Eisenhower appointed Harold Stassen to head the new Office of Special Assistant to the President for Disarmament. Stassen had Cabinet rank. He was charged with conducting a review of U.S. disarmament policy and reporting his findings and recommendations to the National Security Council (NSC). It was expected that he would have direct access to the President, enjoy equal status with department heads, attend NSC meetings, and have budgetary autonomy from regular departments. In August Eisenhower authorized establishment of the interdepartmental Special Committee on Disarmament Problems, chaired by Stassen, and gave it primacy for coordinating disarmament policy. Stassen soon assembled a staff larger than any previous government disarmament group. More than fifty people were obtained from State, Defense, the armed services, the Central Intelligence Agency (CIA), and the International Cooperation Administration.

Stassen did in fact enjoy access to the President, and he played a central role in important disarmament negotiations. Eisenhower would often support Stassen in his frequent clashes with JCS Chairman Admiral Arthur Radford and Atomic Energy Commission (AEC) Chairman Lewis Strauss. During Stassen's tenure eight task forces were recruited on a consultative basis to examine such problem areas as aerial inspection and reporting, inspection and control of nuclear materials, and inspection and reporting methods for industrial production. These task forces reported their findings to Stassen's staff and, among other things, resulted in the first U.S. reference manual on disarmament inspection.

Predictably, Stassen met resistance from other bureaucratic actors. Secretary of State John Foster Dulles was particularly distrustful of Stassen's operation. Deeply skeptical about the wisdom of conducting disarmament negotiations with the Soviet Union, Dulles felt that if such talks must occur the State Department, not Stassen, should have that responsibility. Dulles took such a close personal interest in Stassen's activities that the Secretary himself often wrote the instructions to U.S. disarmament delegations. Growing uneasiness finally led Dulles to urge the dismantling of Stassen's office, which occurred in March 1957. Its functions were transferred to State, where Stassen was to work directly under the Secretary of State. The tension between the two men escalated to the breaking point when, on May 31, 1957, Stassen delivered an uncleared memorandum to chief Soviet negotiator Valerian Zorin. Dulles was furious and soon thereafter announced that Stassen had been reprimanded "with the President's approval." Whatever influence Stassen had retained prior to this incident vanished. His staff was cut in half, and he submitted his resignation in February 1958.[3] Thus ended the only serious attempt before 1960 to upgrade U.S. disarmament efforts functionally and organizationally.

Following Stassen's departure Ambassador James J. Wadsworth was appointed U.S. representative for future disarmament negotiations. At the same time, an advisory group to the Secretary of State on disarmament policy was formed. It included former U.S. High Commissioner for Germany John J. McCloy, former Secretary of Defense Robert Lovett, General Alfred Gruenther, and General Walter Bedell Smith. Responsibility for disarmament issues within State was transferred from the Bureau of International Organizations to the Office of the Special Assistant to the Secretary of State for Atomic Energy Affairs, where only twenty people were assigned to disarmament matters. This office was headed by a Foreign Service reserve officer, class four, whose junior rank reflected disarmament's lowly status. Though the office became the focal point for U.S. disarmament planning and staff work, it lacked adequate technical expertise and had insufficient manpower to organize or supervise detailed examination of issues.[4]

Throughout this period there was continued reliance on ad hoc groups. In the fall of 1959 a Boston attorney, Charles Coolidge, was asked to assemble a staff to conduct a review of disarmament policy. Senator Hubert H. Humphrey (D-Minn.) reflected a consensus view when he stated that the Coolidge report "was found to be useless [and] the Department had to begin to formulate a policy from scratch, only a few days away from high-level meetings with other nations."[5] For Humphrey and others this underlined the inherent shortcomings of an ad hoc approach to arms control and disarmament.

In September 1960, at the height of a presidential campaign that saw both Senator John F. Kennedy (D-Mass.) and Vice President Richard M. Nixon promising to upgrade the disarmament function, President Eisenhower announced the establishment of a U.S. Disarmament Administration located in the State Department. Staffed on an interdepartmental basis and under the Secretary of State's direction, it was charged with developing and coordinating U.S. arms control and disarmament activities. By March 1961 its staff numbered fifty-four.

Two other organizational developments in the second Eisenhower administration affected the policy process in the late 1950s and into the 1960s. After the Soviets launched Sputnik I in October 1957, Eisenhower announced the formation of the President's Science Advisory Committee (PSAC) chaired by James R. Killian of the Massachusetts Institute of Technology. In 1959 Killian was succeeded by George B. Kistiakowsky as Special Assistant to the President for Science and Technology. PSAC members included some of the nation's most eminent scientists, and the committee soon acquired a reputation for solid, objective analysis. PSAC's analyses counterbalanced those from the AEC and the Pentagon concerning preparatory studies for arms control negotiations and overall policy deliberations. Despite its small size, PSAC gained the confidence of President Eisenhower and played a leading role in the government's nuclear test ban discussions.

A second development was the creation of the Committee of Principals by Eisenhower in 1958. It became the formal vehicle for the formulation, review, and coordination of arms control policy and met more than thirty times between 1958 and 1961. Those usually in attendance at committee meetings included the President's Science Adviser, his Special Assistant for National Security Affairs, the Secretaries of State and Defense, the Directors of the CIA and the U.S. Information Agency (USIA), and the Chairmen of the JCS and AEC. Policy papers were generally first developed in a lower-level working group whose departmental membership mirrored that of the Committee of Principals. These papers were then discussed by the senior committee before going to the President.

The committee, however, did not bring coherent direction to policy, partly because it lacked strong presidential guidance. The central arms control issue of the day, a nuclear test ban, did not elicit unwavering White House support. Eisenhower was ultimately unconvinced that a test ban would, on balance, further American security interests. Perhaps influenced by the AEC, he questioned whether atmospheric testing constituted a grave health hazard. Additionally, there were sharp divisions of opinion among senior officials over the wisdom of a test ban. At the risk of oversimplification it can generally be said that by 1959, after Dulles's death, the State Department favored a test ban, as did the President's Science Adviser and the CIA. The JCS, DOD, and AEC were opposed. The effect of this division within the Committee of Principals was to halt movement toward a test ban. Even if the President had been more favorably disposed toward a test ban, the Eisenhower NSC system tended to deter most officials from going directly to the President on an issue. The Committee of Principals reached decisions through consensus, not voting. Eisenhower preferred, even insisted upon, agreement. When presented with conflicting views, he generally called for further study to resolve the matter. To go directly to the President on a disputed issue also risked alienating senior officials whose cooperation was essential.[6]

Establishment of ACDA

The Stassen incident prompted several members of Congress to question the effectiveness of U.S. disarmament efforts. Much of the criticism focused on organization. No one was more outspoken than Senator Humphrey, who chaired the Foreign Relations Committee's Subcommittee on Disarmament. Humphrey was at the heart of the process leading to ACDA's formation. He marshaled data, engineered political strategy and coordinated inputs from interest groups and individuals. Many years later he often proudly referred to himself, with considerable justification, as the father of the Arms Control Agency.

Humphrey's subcommittee issued several reports from 1957 through 1959 recommending improvements in the executive's organization for disarmament.[7] The Democratic Advisory Council—whose members included distinguished liberal Democrats like Eleanor Roosevelt, former President Truman, Adlai E. Stevenson, and Senators Humphrey and Kennedy—established a Committee of Science and Technology composed of sixteen prominent scientists and engineers. In the summer of 1959 some members of this committee, led by former Air Force Secretary Trevor Gardner and Harrison Brown of the California Institute of Technology, devised the idea of an agency to develop instruments and techniques for implementing arms control accords. The full Science and Technology Committee presented this notion for a National Peace Agency to the Democratic Advisory Council in December. The council warmly endorsed the proposal, President Truman calling it a "good statement."[8]

The concept of a National Peace Agency was, at this stage, very modest. It was to have only research, not policy, responsibilities. But because of its distinguished supporters and because the proposal came on the eve of the 1960 presidential primaries, it gained widespread attention. The first bill for a National Peace Agency was introduced in January by Congressman Charles Bennett (D–Fla.). The next month Senator Humphrey introduced an almost identical bill in the Senate. By March there were nineteen National Peace Agency bills, and several additional bills of a similar nature, and twenty-one other legislators had pledged their support. But most legislators had little interest, positive or negative, in the subject, and no legislative action was taken on the bills in 1960. Only a small but articulate liberal minority urged action on the matter.

That summer the nonpartisan National Planning Association issued a report detailing policy, personnel, and organizational deficiencies in U.S. disarmament efforts since 1945. Jerome Spingarn of that association, who later joined ACDA, consulted Senator Humphrey on the subject matter of the report. It was read by many who were in a position to influence the evolution of a disarmament agency.[9]

During the March New Hampshire Democratic primary Senator John F. Kennedy, a member of Humphrey's Disarmament Subcommittee, was harshly critical of the Eisenhower administration's treatment of disarmament. Kennedy charged that the nation had "no consistent, convincing disarmament policy." He called for a U.S. Arms Control Research Institute under presidential direction, which "could undertake, coordinate, and follow through on the research, development and policy planning needed for a workable disarmament program."[10] While all the early bills, including Kennedy's, envisaged a research-oriented agency (only Kennedy's hinted at a policy function), they were based on the conviction that the existing system was inadequate and that a separate agency would inject new life into the area.

THE RATIONALE

After Kennedy's election, proponents of the agency elevated their objectives. Many hoped that it would be a focal point for integrating arms control considerations into national security decisions thereby providing a needed balance to DOD and the AEC. Organizations are frequently established in order to address a neglected yet important concern. This is generally seen as a way to increase policy options by providing policymakers with otherwise unavailable alternatives and information.[11] Arms control had been neglected, and the organizational missions of the AEC and DOD did not naturally incline them to correct the situation.[12] Government scientific and technical expertise, except for PSAC, was monopolized by those actors least interested in arms control. Vital decisions were made without weighing their long-term arms control ramifications. A startling example of such a decision, which was to affect international stability profoundly, is cited by Gerard Smith:

> [The Atoms for Peace Program] was *the* classic example of a major decision taken without any consideration for its arms control implica-

tions. The . . . Atomic Energy Commissioners were advised after the event. Molotov later asked Dulles what in the world did the U.S. have in mind in proposing to allow stockpiles of weapons grade material to spring up all over the world. Dulles hadn't been advised of this fall-out from the proposed program.[13]

The only department that might have acted as an effective counterweight, the State Department, had neither the scientific capability nor the desire to do so. Indeed, ACDA's creation has been characterized as a "divestiture" by State.[14] A senior State Department official appearing before the House Appropriations Committee did not object to a statement that his department had no need for technical expertise in arms control because its province was strictly protocol and negotiations; Congress then denied State's $500,000 request for arms control research.[15] Secretary of State Dean Rusk opposed enlargement of State's arms control capabilities. He was to testify in 1961 that State was not equipped to conduct a large-scale research program, administer a control system under a disarmament agreement, or deal with the "wealth of technical, scientific, and military problems" in the arms control field.[16] Little wonder Senator Humphrey found that, when left to the State Department, arms control "encountered indifference and inertia; . . . it often became the victim of 'higher' departmental priorities."[17]

Before arms control could figure more prominently in foreign and national security policy, the personnel and organizational problems that had plagued American arms control efforts had to be faced. Inadequate interdepartmental coordination contributed to confusion and indirection. There was ample evidence, besides the Coolidge Report incident, to substantiate the findings of a 1961 Senate Foreign Relations Committee report that "U.S. preparedness involving control and reduction of armaments has not always been adequate."[18] When Henry Cabot Lodge was U.S. representative to the 1955 London disarmament conference, he found that "it was difficult to get a U.S. position."[19] Although the creation of Stassen's office had alleviated this problem, it recurred when his office was dismantled. The Geneva Surprise Attack Conference of 1959 further emphasized the need to move from an ad hoc to a broader-based, continuous, better-focused approach. When the U.S. representative to the 1960 ten-nation disarmament talks, Frederick Eaton, opened discussions with America's allies, he could not even convey a U.S. position, because DOD–State Department differences were unresolved. This brought pointed criticism from Senator Kennedy and others. Eaton later stated that there had been a "lack of adequate backup papers to support our position," and in fact, "the executive branch has never been adequately organized or staffed to handle the complicated problem of disarmament.''[20]

Matters were exacerbated by personnel problems at both senior and working levels. Secretaries of State had neither the time nor the inclination to give informed, coherent direction to arms control policy. The American negotiator often had insufficient standing to gain ready access to the highest levels of government. Sometimes he lacked the knowledge and experience to be effective even if he had had such access. After Stassen's resignation this problem became acute. It jeopardized not only systematic policy formulation but even the ability of the United States to respond to changing developments within ongoing negotiations. The discontinuity in senior American officials further aggravated matters. From 1945 through 1961 the United States was represented at seventy international meetings at which arms control or disarmament was discussed. At these conferences the Soviet Union's delegation was led by one of five or six experienced officials. During this sixteen-year period U.S. delegations were headed by sixteen different officials, and our negotiators were sometimes forced to meet Soviet professionals with a hurriedly recruited staff.[21]

Except for the brief Stassen era, the number and overall caliber of government professionals assigned to disarmament were inadequate. Foreign Service officers usually lacked scientific expertise, and their periodic rotation every two or three years made it impossible to build a corps of permanent arms control professionals. Nor were conditions propitious for attracting quality people. The low priority assigned to arms control by State and the military services meant that it was hardly a promising route to career advancement.[22]

While rectification of this state of affairs was uppermost in the minds of the proponents of an arms control agency, other considerations buttressed their case. Dean Rusk and Henry Cabot Lodge were to testify in 1961 that such an agency would favorably impress world opinion. Far more important, Kennedy, Humphrey, and others hoped that the agency would help the United States to survive in a radically altered international system. By the early 1960s many realized that growing Soviet nuclear strength meant, or would soon mean, that the traditional national response to outside threats—augmenting military might—while essential, could not by itself indefinitely guarantee or even necessarily enhance either national or international security. A much more permanent, professional, and directed organizational effort was required for coping with a nuclearized world.

The 1955–1960 period had marked the beginning of the end of an era in pursuit of the illusive and unattainable goal of general and complete disarmament. A more pragmatic partial approach began to gather momentum after 1957 with a series of technical and political conferences for limiting nuclear tests and with the Geneva Surprise Attack Conference. As the discussion moved from the ethereal heights of general and complete disarmament to the reality of more narrowly defined but negotiable issues, it was essential that arms control's growing political salience be matched by efficient government organization.

Another reason for a separate agency, established by legislation, was to give Congress more say in arms control policy and to improve its access to information and to executive officials. Senator Humphrey and others had complained that Congress experienced serious difficulty obtaining information from Stassen, inasmuch as, being a White House aide, he could plead executive privilege.[23]

KENNEDY AND McCLOY

President Kennedy's first State of the Union Message, in January 1961, stressed the urgency of arms control. A few days before, on January 2, he had appointed John McCloy as his Disarmament Adviser, charging him with responsibility for making recommendations to the President on U.S. policy and organization for disarmament. McCloy's appointment had been carefully weighed by Kennedy. He was an experienced, respected "establishment" figure in the mainstream of American national security policy. McCloy had advised past Presidents and was well known for his caution and prudence. Kennedy was concerned about the view that arms control and disarmament were naive and unrealistic. Arthur Schlesinger, Jr., reports that Kennedy "followed his customary practice of seeking a conservative to executive a liberal policy. The appointment of John J. McCloy . . . was thus a deliberate effort to prepare the political ground by placing disarmament in charge of a figure whose background unassailably combined the Republican party, the Pentagon, the Ford Foundation, the Chase Manhattan Bank, Cravath, Swaine & Moore, the Brook and the Links."[24] The feeling that arms control and disarmament were suspect, that they were somehow different from national security, pervaded the entire process leading to ACDA's formation. It was to follow the Agency in one form or another, with varying levels of intensity, throughout its history.

It was McCloy who enlisted the cooperation or at least the acquiescence of the heads of the affected departments. He was also a critical link in fashioning a supportive coalition of diverse agencies, congressmen, interest groups, and individuals. Virtually every department had some reason to object to ACDA's establishment. The JCS were inherently uncomfortable with the notion of disarmament. The State Department might have opposed the semi-autonomous status eventually given to ACDA. The Budget Bureau had a known aversion to the creation of new agencies. The AEC, DOD, and the National Aeronautics and Space Administration (NASA) could have vigorously resisted the new agency's proposed research facilities and coordination authority. The USIA might have contested the public information function included in the McCloy bill.

Some of these objections were raised. But McCloy's stature and persuasiveness, coupled with the support and friendship of Secretary of State Rusk and Defense Secretary Robert McNamara, overcame them. McCloy later remarked, "It was like walking through mud up to the knees. No one was too anxious to have this thing. I persuaded them."[25]

The staff of the Disarmament Administration, which had been hastily assembled during the fall political campaign, was assigned to assist McCloy. Three people worked particularly closely with him in drafting the original bill—Adrian Fisher, George Bunn, and Betty Goetz. All three were to join ACDA. Fisher became Deputy Director, and Bunn was General Counsel.

Despite Kennedy's deep personal interest in arms control, his concern about congressional opposition led him to have second thoughts about the agency. Thirteen years later McCloy stated that, "somewhat to my surprise, after I had been working here for some time on it, he came to me after having consulted the legislative leaders, and said he could not put this on his must list of legislation because he was not at all sure that such a radical type of legislation would be passed and didn't want to take risks."[26] McCloy was told that the legislation had to proceed on its own merits, without vigorous administration support. When Congress passed the legislation Kennedy reportedly thought its passage was a political miracle and ascribed it mainly to the personal efforts of McCloy and Humphrey.[27]

Kennedy's initial thought was to locate the proposed arms control unit in the Executive Office of the President to symbolize its importance. But Richard Neustadt persuasively objected that this risked conflict over policy coordination with the State Department. If the agency were headed by McCloy, Neustadt argued, it would have access to the President and influence at the Pentagon wherever it was situated. Neustadt, joined by

Edmund Gullion of the Disarmament Administration, therefore recommended that it be a quasi-autonomous unit attached to State. Kennedy approved the recommendation.

McCloy, it turned out, did not become ACDA's first Director. However, he was appointed Chairman of the President's General Advisory Committee for Arms Control and Disarmament. The original draft legislation had not called for such a body. The idea came from key members of Congress. A primary purpose of the committee was to keep a watchful eye on suspect arms controllers.[28]

On May 25, 1961, the President delivered a special message to Congress proposing the creation of a disarmament agency. On June 23 McCloy sent the final draft legislation to Kennedy, accompanied by an explanatory letter, and on June 26 Kennedy formally submitted to Congress McCloy's bill for a U.S. Disarmament Agency for Peace and Security. The McCloy letter, in setting forth the bill's purpose, addressed many of the problems Kennedy and others had noted in past American disarmament efforts. The agency was to provide an independent bureaucratic voice for arms restraint and should have "exceptionally broad competence, functions, and resources" so as "to bring its point of view and recommendations promptly to the highest level of Government." It was to have "primary," yet shared, responsibility for arms control. Authority must be shared because of the intimate relationship of arms control, foreign, economic, and national security policy. The Agency's policy role was broadly conceived. It was to participate in "the formulation of overall policy in areas importantly related to or affecting disarmament such as basic national security policies." The proposed legislation stressed that "disarmament considerations are so all-pervasive in scope and importance that the President must concern himself with these matters on a continuing basis." The agency was to coordinate and augment research and development in arms control. Finally, McCloy had argued internally that the agency must have authority, with State Department guidance, to conduct arms control and disarmament negotiations, that without this authority it would lose a crucial lever for influence. Hence its director was supplied with such authority.[29]

CONGRESS AND THE STATUTE

The administration bill was introduced, with cosponsors, in the House by Foreign Affairs Committee Chairman Thomas "Doc" Morgan (D–Pa.) and in the Senate by Hubert Humphrey. The Senate bill was first referred to the Government Operations Committee, but after considerable maneuvering it was sent to the more receptive Foreign Relations Committee. On the House side alone, seventy identical or similar bills were introduced.

The August hearings saw testimony from senior government officials and many distinguished citizens. A total of twenty-nine witnesses appeared before the Senate Foreign Relations Committee. None testified in opposition to the bill. The twelve interest groups testifying before the committee—including the Methodist Church, the Federation of American Scientists, and the United World Federalists—were all supportive. Only two organizations, the Daughters of the American Revolution and the American Coalition of Patriotic Societies, sent in opposition statements for the record.

The United World Federalists played a notable role. For instance, Sandford Persons of that group sent an informational packet on the bill to eighty-nine national organizations in July. Some of these organizations, like the Jewish War Veterans, the American Association for the United Nations, and the Amalgamated Meat Cutters, sent supporting statements for inclusion in the hearings. In addition to being a catalytic group among nongovernmental organizations, the United World Federalists performed a vital public relations service for Senator Humphrey's greatly overburdened staff. McCloy's office also benefited. The World Federalists made it possible for McCloy to appear on several television programs, and useful political information was fed to his staff.[30]

At the Senate hearings Secretary Rusk testified that the agency must not be just another bureau of State, indeed, it should have sufficient independence so that its director would have the stature to deal frankly with top U.S. officials and foreign representatives.[31] But Rusk, citing the Stassen-Dulles relationship, insisted that the agency be under the Secretary of State's direction, because negotiations are properly the function of the State Department and close policy coordination is essential. McCloy also emphasized this point—Stassen "did not necessarily have to report to the Secretary of State, . . . and it did not work out too well."[32]

Supporters of the bill had gathered a long list of distinguished retired military figures, including former President Eisenhower, who agreed to endorse the agency. McCloy later said that "without the support of these military figures . . . , I doubt that as strong a bill as was passed could ever have been enacted."[33] Though Defense Secretary McNamara warmly endorsed the legislation, former Defense Secretary Robert Lovett more accurately reflected the predominant Pentagon sentiment. Lovett warned that the agency "is going to be a Mecca for a wide variety of screwballs.

It will be a natural magnet for... the give-up groups.'' To curb the
''screwballs'' Lovett urged that Agency employees have the tightest security clearances in government.[34]

General Lyman Lemnitzer, Chairman of the JCS, stated that the Joint
Chiefs supported the proposal. But when asked by Senator Humphrey
whether their comments to McNamara had been favorable, he was eva-
sive. General Lemnitzer replied that they agreed with the ''general objectives,'' but that the JCS had ''made several suggestions'' and ''all of the
suggestions were not accepted.'' Lemnitzer indicated JCS uneasiness
about the Agency Director's being able to go directly to the President.
They felt that all agency recommendations to the President should be
filtered through the NSC. He further stated that McCloy had assured him
that, despite the bill's language, important matters would in fact be handled this way. McCloy promptly and forcefully denied that he had given
such assurances and defended the necessity of the director's having the
flexibility afforded by direct access to the President.[35] Clearly, and predictably, ACDA's forthcoming birth was not hailed as a joyous event by
the military services.

After some amendments and a cautionary note that the bill (H.R.
9118) ''does not reflect any intention that the United States give a higher
priority to disarmament than to defense,''[36] the House Committee favorably and unanimously reported out the administration's bill. It passed
the full House on September 12 by a vote of 290 to 54. The Senate
Foreign Relations Committee also unanimously reported the bill (S.
2180), but it attached several significant amendments, one of which was
crucial. The committee feared that the agency might encroach upon the
activities of existing departments, that unless it was an integral part of the
State Department, disarmament policy might not be fully coordinated
with overall foreign policy. Additionally, as Senator Humphrey subsequently observed, several committee members were ''concerned that
this Agency would be a haven for everybody who wanted to disarm
tomorrow morning.''[37] Therefore, the committee proposed that the
agency be placed ''within'' the State Department so that it would be
unambiguously under ''the supervision and direction of the Secretary of
State.''[38] A slightly modified version of this bill passed the Senate by a 73
to 14 vote.

On the Senate floor the conservative opposition, which included
Armed Services Committee Chairman Richard Russell (D–Ga.), argued
that the proposed agency would be insensitive to American defense needs
and duplicate the activities of the Departments of State and Defense.
Senator Barry Goldwater (R–Ariz.), convinced that we were ''developing

a new mother-love type of agency," offered an amendment that would have stripped it of any authority to conduct or contract for research. The amendment failed by just three votes (43 to 46), thereby narrowly preserving one of the agency's central purposes. Minority Leader Everett Dirksen (R–Ill.) then employed his unequaled eloquence in behalf of his own motion to rerefer the bill to the Armed Services Committee. It failed, however, 33 to 54.[39]

Differences in the two bills were resolved in the Conference Committee. The most important question was the status and location of the agency in relation to the State Department. But the Senate receded from its insistence that the agency be an integral unit of State. The language, which became section 22 of the Arms Control and Disarmament (ACD) Act,[40] made the Agency's Director "the *principal* advisor to the Secretary of State *and* the President on arms control and disarmament matters." (Emphasis added.) While he had "primary" government responsibility for arms control and disarmament, in carrying out his duties he is "under the direction of the Secretary of State." Hence ACDA became, in law, a quasi-independent entity whose Director, in his capacity as arms control adviser, could go directly to the President. But policy coordination was to be ensured, and suspected disarmers tethered, by linking ACDA closely to State.[41]

The Agency's name, the Arms Control and Disarmament Agency, was also a compromise between the Senate's Arms Control and Disarmament Agency for World Peace and Security and the House's Arms Control Agency. Disarmament was a long-term normative objective, arms control the present reality. The Conference Committee's report stated: "The sequence of the words in the title indicates that arms control is the first step toward the ultimate objective of disarmament."[42] Years later Senator Humphrey said that the word "disarmament" was inserted as a kind of "moral imperative." He added, "The problem is . . . that people get frightened when you say disarmament."[43]

The conference report was approved without amendment by the House (253 to 50) and by unanimous consent in the Senate. President Kennedy signed the ACD Act into law on September 26, 1961.

The act reflected an uneasy balance between the desire to have a vigorous, distinct voice for arms restraint and a determination that the arms controllers themselves be restrained by "responsible" elements symbolized by the State Department. Congress was not taking any chances with a concept that had yet to prove meritorious. While an "ultimate goal of the United States is a world which is free from the scourge of war," arms control and disarmament policy "must be consistent with national security policy as a whole'' (ACD Act, section 2). Wherever the word "disarmament" had appeared in the administration bill, it was usually replaced with "arms control and disarmament," which was defined to mean (section 3[a]) "the identification, verification, inspection, limitation, control, reduction, or elimination, of armed forces and armaments of all kinds under international agreement," including necessary international control systems and the strengthening of international organizations.

Defining arms control and disarmament solely in terms of "international agreements" may seem restrictive. The administration draft had contained the phrase "international agreement or measure" which implied somewhat more latitude. But striking out "or measure" did not meaningfully constrict ACDA's scope of inquiry or jurisdiction. The legal definition of arms control and disarmament, as opposed to harsh bureaucratic political realities, has not been confining in practice. A reading of the whole act, especially in light of the subsequent history of the Agency, reveals that, for practical purposes, the words "possible future" might be read before "international agreement" (which itself is undefined), thereby largely negating the hint of restrictiveness.

What Congress did intend to monitor and constrain carefully were actions or agreements that *obligated* the United States to limit its armaments. Hence Congress inserted a proviso in section 33: "That no action shall be undertaken under this or any other law that will obligate the United States to disarm or to reduce or to limit the Armed Forces or armaments of the United States, except pursuant to the treaty making power of the President under the Constitution or unless authorized by further affirmative legislation." Apart from its legal rationale, and assuming its constitutionality (which is not entirely beyond debate), the proviso's political rationale is sound. As George Bunn argues, no major arms control agreement "is likely to receive the continuing support of public opinion—which it needs to be lasting—if it ignores Congress altogether."[44]

The Agency received four "primary functions." The least important, considering the Agency's subsequent history, is the preparation and operation of "such control systems as may become part of the United States arms control and disarmament activities" (section 2[d]). What this meant in practice for many years was that ACDA periodically led a small team of inspectors to the frigid Antarctic to verify compliance with the Antarctic Treaty. The two SALT I accords established a joint Soviet–American Standing Consultative Commission to monitor compliance with the agreements and the chief U.S. representative on the commission has been an ACDA officer. Other arms control agreements also include various control systems. While the phrase "control systems" was conceived rather narrowly in 1961, and while it is not without ambiguity, a reasonable case can be made that it incorporates such activities as SALT monitoring, although that authority, arguably, can also be gleaned from other sections of the ACD Act. But in reality the CIA, because of its unique capabilities, has dominated the monitoring of arms control agreements.

ACDA was also given responsibility (section 2[c]) for the "dissemination and coordination of public information concerning arms control and disarmament." The McCloy-drafted bill had specifically stipulated that there be an Office of Public Affairs, but that provision was eliminated by Congress. This hardly encouraged the Agency to adopt a highly visible public profile. While ACDA did eventually establish such an office, it pursued an extremely cautious public affairs program.

A third enumerated function (section 2[a]) is the "conduct, support, and coordination of research for arms control and disarmament policy." The Director (section 31) is charged with acquiring "a fund of theoretical and practical knowledge concerning disarmament." To facilitate this, section 31 directs him:

> (1) to insure the conduct of research, development, and other studies in the field of arms control and disarmament; (2) to make arrangements (including contracts, agreements, and grants) for the conduct of research, development, and other studies in the field of arms control and disarmament by private or public institutions or persons; and (3) to coordinate the research, development, and other studies conducted in the field of arms control and disarmament by or for other Government agencies.

Section 31 (a–m) then details the appropriate subject matter areas for research. In effect, anything remotely related to arms control or disarmament is researchable.

Congress placed heavy emphasis on the research function, because the field had scarcely been defined, yet alone thoroughly researched. The House Foreign Affairs Committee even instructed the Director to engage in research "to the maximum extent feasible."[45] Research expenditures were to dominate ACDA's budget throughout its early years.

The fourth major function (section 2[b]) is the "preparation for and management of United States participation in international negotiations in the arms control and disarmament field." Congress inserted "management" in place of the word "direction," which had been in the administration's version. This was in deference to State's traditional prerogatives in negotiations and in recognition of the need for close coordination. Furthermore section 34(a) states that, "under the direction of the Secretary of State" the Director "may," in exercising his authority, "consult and communicate with or direct the consultation and communication with representatives of other nations." The House report elaborates on the congressional intent: "The Agency staff is expected to carry the responsibility of backstopping negotiations and to work intimately with appropriate political desks of the Department of State. The Agency will, however, have the action responsibility on all disarmament matters."[46]

Years later, when ACDA sought a greater voice in the weapons acquisition process, the Pentagon was to assert that the Agency's policy role was legally confined to those matters directly related to ongoing or impending international negotiations. But there is little in the ACD Act or its legislative history to support this view. Congress purposely linked ACDA's Director to the Secretary of State, fully recognized State's negotiating role, and jealously guarded its own right to approve arms control obligations undertaken by the President. However, the scope of ACDA's policy purview was expressed broadly. It is inconceivable that Congress intended the "principal" arms control advisor to the President and Secretary of State to be limited to current negotiations. As a 1974 House Foreign Affairs Committee report states, "The charter of the Agency is broad, if permissive rather than specific. It permits the Director and Agency to do anything relevant to arms control which is acceptable to the President and Secretary of State—in recognition that any arms control activity falls within the sphere of national security and foreign policy."[47] Section 31(j) gives the Director extensive authority to study "the national security and foreign policy implications of arms control and disarmament proposals." Sections 2 and 33 authorize him to make arms control and disarmament policy recommendations to the President, the Secretary of State, and other executive branch officials. Section 2 further states that ACDA must be so positioned in the executive branch that it can "assess the effect of these recommendations upon our foreign policies, our national security policies, and our economy." ACDA's ability to examine some areas clearly relating to arms control was to be severely curtailed, as we shall see, but this was because of political and bureaucratic resistance and was not attributable to the language of the ACD Act.

Four other sections of the Act, all reflecting some degree of congressional caution about arms control, should be mentioned. Section 26 permits the President, with the advice and consent of the Senate, to appoint a General Advisory Committee to advise him on matters affecting arms control, disarmament, and world peace. Section 50 requires ACDA to submit an annual report to Congress about its activities. Anticipating the problems ACDA was soon to encounter in establishing its legitimacy as an actor in the national security bureaucracy, section 35 authorized the President to institute procedures for coordinating arms control activities with affected departments and for resolving differences of opinion. Section 45 responds to the concern of Robert Lovett and many members of Congress that ACDA might attract "screwballs." It prescribed detailed security requirements for ACDA employees: Security standards "shall not be less stringent" than those in "agencies having the highest security restrictions."

Conclusion

The establishment of ACDA like most political events was the outcome of compromise and balancing of competing interests. There is a distinct tension in the ACD Act. On the one hand, there are expectations that the Agency will be active and, presumably, effective across a wide policy spectrum. On the other hand, ACDA is curbed—most notably by being "under the direction of the Secretary of State"—from fully realizing these expectations. The Agency was ordained to be, and is, a junior actor. It was almost certain then, as time passed, that ACDA's more vocal and expectant supporters would be disappointed in its policy performance.

Within the executive branch ACDA cannot by itself always ensure that arms control considerations are adequately integrated into relevant aspects of national security policy. To do this, ACDA requires the support or acquiescence of senior actors. When such support is withheld, its advice is ignored or rejected—or, worse, ACDA is excluded from the policy action altogether. And ACDA's ability or even, at times, inclination to speak with an active, independent voice has been questioned.

As important as the law is, the ACD Act and judgments about ACDA's effectiveness must be weighed in light of executive and legislative *political* realities since 1961 (which we next examine). Doing this does not exempt the Agency from criticism. But an appreciation for the real constraints imposed by the political environment does lead to a more balanced appraisal of Agency performance. It might then be said, for example, that despite an often hostile climate ACDA has been an important voice for arms restraint, and it has on numerous occasions demonstrated greater independence from other agencies, including State, than might have been expected. Though it must often rely on senior actors,

ACDA, with only a relatively few exceptions, has generally been the point man for arms control. That is, it has usually been the first to advance executive arms control proposals, several of which are now binding international agreements. No other agency has arms control as its exclusive mission. While it is a secondary actor, ACDA's superb analytical assets have often helped tip the scales in favor of the bureaucratic coalition supporting arms control, and its technical research has made many tangible contributions. ACDA's relationship with Congress has not always been satisfactory, but Congress's role in arms control policy would almost certainly be diminished without the Agency. U.S. preparation for arms control negotiations is today thoroughly professional. Much of the credit goes to ACDA and its corps of trained experts. By the early 1970s arms control finally became a significant component of American foreign and national security policy. Its greater respectability and acceptance is due in no small measure to the professionalism of government arms control specialists. One searches in vain for the "screwballs."

③ Image

An ORGANIZATION often projects an "image" rooted in its perceived mission. Sometimes it has several images. Image may change over time and vary with issues or personalities. Outsiders may see the image differently. Still, a predominant image frequently emerges. For example, the Department of Energy (DOE), which before the fall of 1977 was the Energy Research and Development Administration (ERDA) and before that the AEC, is considered an advocate of civilian nuclear power and the export of nuclear technology and materials. The Army Corps of Engineers builds dams, everywhere. Treasury is the guardian of fiscal responsibility. State puts a premium on good political relations with other nations. DOD's DDR&E (Director of Defense Research and Engineering) is committed to developing new weapons technology.

ACDA's missions are the furtherance of an arms control perspective within government and negotiating arms control agreements. The Agency does not invariably equate national strength with rising levels of armaments. While conceding that arms are necessary, ACDA asserts that both national and international security can be enhanced through sound, balanced, adequately verifiable controls on weaponry. An essential mission of the military services is the development, deployment, and utilization of weapons. For DOD, then, and for some other organizational units, ACDA is, ipso facto, suspect. ACDA officers, sometimes pejoratively called "arms controllers," are considered "soft" on national security. Though ACDA vigorously, even heatedly, denies this, the image persists.

Within the national security bureaucracy one must be thought "strong," particularly when dealing with the Soviet Union. While the Pentagon is usually exempt from suspicion, those outside DOD must be sensitive to this prevailing norm. One State Department analyst has said, "There is *definitely* a 'tough guy' stance adopted by those in the national security bureaucracy, especially in State." To some degree ACDA, too, must adjust to avoid being isolated. A respected senior ACDA official said that he would never want to be labeled an arms controller. Arms controllers are considered weak, hence ineffective. There is a tendency to assume the expected bureaucratic tone in order to gain acceptance. This certainly does not imply submission to the Pentagon on substantive issues, but it is a precondition for playing the policy game. Also, there is a genuine conviction within ACDA that if arms control is to be feasible and viable it must be seen throughout government as congruent with overall foreign and national security policy. This is facilitated through outward acquiescence to shared modes and norms.

Every ACDA director has repeatedly and publicly downplayed ACDA's differences with Defense while stressing that arms control, properly conceived, strengthens national security. William Foster always asserted that his Agency was "as much concerned with maintaining the national security of our nation as any other department . . . in Government."[1] Fred Iklé, the Agency's third Director, after defining ACDA's "primary mission" as assuring that American security needs "are met at the lowest possible level of armaments," went on to say, "There is a feeling among the public and to some extent among Government personnel that arms control means weakening the defenses of the United States. . . . ACDA [must] make clear that our job is to *enhance* national security . . . and that arms control agreements, properly negotiated, can and do make our country safer and often at less cost."[2] Paul Warnke's opening statement at his 1977 nomination hearings quoted the ACD Act to the effect that arms control "must be consistent with national security policy as a whole." He vowed that this would be his "key principle."[3]

But the Agency cannot easily shed its "arms controller" image because, fundamentally, ACDA's essence *is* the limitation of armaments. Arms control is inherent in what ACDA is. This directly threatens the interests and missions of other actors. It is not always possible to specify how this impairs the Agency's effectiveness, but there is agreement both within the Agency and outside that it is a factor. Every ACDA officer has his "image story."

ACDA confronts a certain dilemma, often scarcely visible, yet at times poignant. It may be necessary to flee or appear to flee the Agency's *raison d'être* in order to have an effective voice within the executive branch. But the flight can proceed only so far, lest ACDA's very rationale for existence be pointless. The question on many issues, a question of style as well as substance, is, What balance should be struck between the unwanted extremes of being thought of as arms controllers (associated with epithets like naive, idealistic, and screwball) and bedding down with the JCS?

Early Problems

Most of ACDA's activities from 1961 to 1963 concerned immediate or foreseeable arms control issues, especially the Partial Test Ban Treaty. However, some attention was given to general and complete disarmament (GCD). Because of this, ACDA was to spend much of the 1960s trying to convince critics that GCD was dead and, inferentially, not worth the early attention it had received. Talk of GCD seemed to confirm the suspicions of conservatives and contributed to the passage of restrictive amendments to the ACD Act in 1963.

John F. Kennedy's February 1, 1962, letter of transmittal accompanying ACDA's first annual report to Congress stated that the United States would seek a comprehensive disarmament treaty that spring at the Eighteen Nation Disarmament Committee's (ENDC) meeting in Geneva. Much of the committee's work that year concentrated on GCD, and ACDA played an important role in developing the U.S. proposal presented on April 18.[4] ACDA sponsored contracted research in this area, and several Agency publications dealt with disarmament, including its first official publication.[5]

Opinions differ as to the sincerity of the U.S. proposal and ACDA's efforts in its behalf. Most believe that expectations were low, that it was intended largely for propaganda purposes. Few senior ACDA officials were optimistic, though some were more hopeful than others. As one in this latter group said, "It seemed in the first years that the horizons were open. This interest was partly a function of the period."[6] GCD never got off the ground, but ACDA's critics did. The aftermath was felt for several years. A decade later William Foster recalled that, "We . . . had a good deal of mud slung at us over that one."[7]

The GCD venture aroused an already alarmed military. Within the Air Force during that period the mere possibility that arms control or disarmament might prove feasible was cited to support rapid development of multiple, independently targetable reentry vehicles (MIRVs). In 1963 General W. Austin Davis, commander of the Air Force's Ballistic Systems Division, asserted that ACDA's presence portended eventual negotiated limitations on the number of deployed offensive missiles;

MIRV, he argued, must be well along before that occurred.[8] There are
two (printable) derogatory epithets worse than arms controller: disarmer
and, worse, unilateral disarmer. Both were bandied about when ACDA or
arms control were discussed. A colorful characterization of JCS attitudes
at this time was given in congressional testimony by retired Air Force
Major General Dale O. Smith, Special Assistant to the JCS for Arms
Control from 1961 to 1963:

> The underlying arms control philosophy governing ACDA is that our
> nuclear armaments by themselves cause world tensions and thus must be
> reduced, even unilaterally. The military view is that world tensions are
> caused by international political differences and that our nuclear arma-
> ments provide the deterrent and protection necessary in this unstable
> environment. Thus the two philosophies are diametrically opposed and a
> constant under-the-table conflict is in process between ACDA and
> JCS. . . . Mr. McNamara has consistently leaned in the direction of
> ACDA rather than supporting JCS.
>
> In the words of General Power, the United States is attempting the
> exercise of trying to dress and undress at the same time. . . . ACDA
> should be abolished forthwith.[9]

Congress, too, was unhappy about GCD, and ACDA bore the brunt of
its criticism. In 1963 ACDA employees were "nutball people" to Congressman Craig Hosmer (R–Cal.). Others accused ACDA of wanting to
regulate hunting rifles. Congressman William Bray (R–Ind.) charged the
Agency with "studying reasons for the free world to surrender to the
Kremlin." Senator Thomas Kuchel (R–Cal.) reported that his mail indicated that "thousands of Californians remain firmly wedded to the following fantastic fairy tales: that the Arms Control Agency can and will
disarm the United States. . .; that the law establishing the agency consti-
tutes treason [etc.]."[10] Treason is exactly what a young ACDA attorney
was accused of when he briefed a Republican senator in 1963 on the
Partial Test Ban Treaty. He was told, "Because of your low level in the
Agency you probably don't realize that you are committing treason."

ACDA's image clouded its relations with Congress throughout the
remainder of the Kennedy and Johnson administrations, although the
Agency had entirely washed its hands of GCD by 1963. Congressional
criticism inhibited an active public affairs program, and ACDA's contracted research was carefully monitored. In 1965 some legislators erroneously accused ACDA of complicity in Secretary McNamara's decision to close several bases in their states. In 1968 Congressman Hosmer,
in recommending that the Agency be stripped of all negotiating responsibilities, stated, "I voted for ACDA. . . . I believe it is a good idea to

collect all the people who are of that mind in one place where you can keep an eye on them. "[11] Reflecting on the 1960s, ACDA's Executive Secretary commented that his "first five or six years with the Agency was largely an exercise in apologetics, designed to reassure some member of Congress or the general public that what we were engaged in was not treasonous or dangerous. "[12]

Changed Attitudes and Image

William Foster could remark in 1971 that "the thing that most impresses me is the change in the attitudes towards arms control." His successor, Gerard Smith, citing the regular inclusion of references to possible SALT limitations in the annual posture statements of Secretaries of Defense and Chairmen of the JCS, agreed that arms control "has become respectable."[13] By the early 1970's arms control lost much of its prior stigma. Several agreements had been negotiated. SALT became a major foreign policy concern of the Nixon administration and a cornerstone of Soviet–American relations. GCD was only a bad memory. Disarmament was seldom mentioned, much to the chagrin of its few devotees like former Senator Joseph Clark (D–Pa.). The watchword was pragmatic arms control.[14] To be sure, the relatively optimistic atmosphere of the May 1972 Moscow summit soon vanished. The SALT Interim Agreement on Strategic Offensive Arms sparked a lively and continuing debate across the entire strategic policy spectrum; overall Soviet–American relations suffered a series of setbacks after 1972, and there was growing skepticism about the prospects for a SALT II agreement; some supporters of arms limitations wondered aloud if arms control had really become a cover for escalating armaments levels; the second Nixon administration crumbled ignominiously; and doubts about ACDA's effectiveness led to a thorough congressional investigation of the Agency in 1974. But while arms control has had its ups and downs, it has joined the real world. The novelty is gone. It is taken with the utmost seriousness.[15]

There is little support today outside the Pentagon for the notion that ACDA is jurisdictionally restricted to international negotiations. When Paul Nitze expressed his belief that arms control does not relate "to the design of our own defense posture," McGeorge Bundy retorted that arms control "is really an element of all arms policy," and he was joined by Gerard Smith and Fred Iklé, neither of whom had ever considered themselves confined to international negotiations.[16]

A substantial majority of Congress would agree with Senator Claiborne Pell (D–R.I.), Chairman of the Foreign Relations Committee's Subcommittee on Arms Control, Oceans, and International Environment, when he said, "It is sometimes thought that arms control and national security are separate objectives. This subcommittee does not believe that ... Arms Control is a vital ingredient of national security policy and good, solid arms control measures can enhance national security."[17] There is controversy over whether particular proposals, agreements, or actions constitute "solid arms control"; about how to define national security; and about who is best qualified to hold positions of responsibility in the national security bureaucracy. But few legislators denounce arms control qua arms control. This was evident during Paul Warnke's stormy 1977 Senate confirmation hearings, which witnessed, as at least six senators on both sides of the question noted, a clash in "philosophy" or approach to national security. Arms control per se was not attacked by Warnke's opponents (though his more fervent supporters might deny this). Rather, his views or alleged views on arms control and defense were scrutinized.[18] During this debate all but one or two newly elected senators demonstrated a basic understanding of arms control and its relationship to foreign and national security policy. Indeed, Congress's grasp of arms control, weaponry, and executive branch processes in the defense field has vastly improved since the 1960s.[19]

Arms control's greater acceptability has affected ACDA's image. ACDA is now a recognized actor with a legitimate function. Exactly what this function should be in some areas is a subject of continuing controversy, but the legitimacy of an arms control perspective is widely, though not yet universally, acknowledged. Fears that ACDA might advocate sweeping disarmament have virtually disappeared, but the arms controller label lingers. ACDA's image, for many, remains one of softness and fuzziness on defense. Henry Kissinger, "with almost total derision," referred to ACDA officers as "arms controllers."[20] Kissinger once phoned Gerard Smith on an arms control question to ask, "Will your people back up the President?" Smith was shocked and responded, "Of course, we're part of the government." On several occasions Secretary of Defense Melvin Laird went directly to the White House, both on specific issues like the anti-ballistic missile (ABM) and on defense budgetary matters, with charges that ACDA was "disloyal," that is, not a good team player.

The arms controller image becomes more trenchant on issues that, like SALT, endanger the missions or budgets of other actors. Ironically, though, ACDA's SALT image in the 1973–1976 period, following the

1973 "purge" of the Agency—discussed in the next chapter—changed so dramatically that it was widely viewed, even in the Pentagon on several SALT issues, as being "hawkish." This period, however, was a deviation from the norm that prevailed prior to 1973 and after 1976.

ACDA lost an important SALT I policy assignment partly because of its image. National Security Study Memorandum (NSSM) 28, issued on March 13, 1969, called for a comprehensive study of possible U.S. strategic arms limitation options. ACDA was assigned to coordinate the study. But both the White House and the Pentagon questioned ACDA's reliability, and the latter adamantly refused to cooperate with working groups chaired by arms controllers. ACDA lacked the political weight to move the study along, and in June it was relieved of what might have become a leadership role. Gerard Smith's heading the SALT delegation also contributed to tension between Kissinger and the delegation. One NSC staffer said, "Henry probably always harbored suspicions about a delegation led by the Director of the 'dove agency'. . . . Kissinger was paranoid and Byzantine." John Newhouse relates:

> Smith's role was one of several reasons that the delegation was regarded with suspicion, and occasionally with open hostility. Smith had the respect of the Washington community; he was a competent negotiator with a good grasp of the issues. His only apparent weakness, however, was critical: To direct both ACDA and the SALT delegation is compromising, certainly in the view of the White House or any agency that takes exception to ACDA's position on any SALT issue. However unfairly, Smith was seen as ACDA's man at SALT, chiefly concerned with extending the range of what might be negotiable. As such, he lacked the full confidence of the White House (and the Pentagon).[21]

After the conclusion of SALT I, ACDA continued to experience image problems. For example, the ACDA officer who headed the U.S. representatives on the SALT Standing Consultative Commission, though he held that position by presidential appointment, was still suspect to the military. When a senior ACDA official delivered a speech at Pepperdine University in 1972, he had to defend the Agency against charges by Richard Perle of Senator Henry Jackson's (D-Wash.) staff that the ACDA-led delegation had deliberately ignored White House instructions.

In some other areas, like nuclear proliferation and mutual and balanced force reductions (MBFR) in Europe, image has less salience. Most nuclear proliferation issues do not challenge either the defense budget or the missions of the military services. Hence ACDA often finds itself allied with the Office of the Secretary of Defense (OSD), DOD's Office of International Security Affairs (ISA), and the JCS. The State Department's internal orientation on nuclear-proliferation-related issues has generally been divided, but all Secretaries of State have been concerned about it and have sided with ACDA on many issues. In addition, ACDA possesses acknowledged expertise in the area and a long tradition of dealing with the problem. Disputes certainly arise, but many of them are with the Department of Energy (DOE). DOE murmurs about narrowly focused arms controllers, yet its positions on many nuclear proliferation issues do not gain presidential backing. ACDA can often count on the President's support as well as powerful congressional allies.

Concerning MBFR, a Foreign Service Officer (FSO) on assignment to ACDA alluded to various confidence building measures (CBMs) then being discussed with reference to Central Europe: "The JCS and DOD view anything coming from ACDA with suspicion and say, 'What can you expect from arms controllers?' " He added, "Ironically, if they were smarter, they'd seek us out more often and they'd likely find that we often *agree* with the hardliners. Then they could turn around and say, 'Look, even those arms controllers are critical of these CBMs.' " He agreed, however, as did other ACDA officers, that image is not a pressing problem. This is so for four reasons: (1) Through 1978 senior American officials evinced little enthusiasm for MBFR. The ultimate implications of these talks extend beyond arms control to the very future of Europe, which suggests why the U.S. stance has been extremely cautious. Not being a very live issue, ACDA cannot be threatening. (2) Though ACDA has introduced most of the proposals for faster movement on MBFR, Agency people tend to share much of the skepticism of other departments. (3) MBFR requires careful, time-consuming coordination and consultation with NATO allies, some of whom are notably reluctant to rush toward force reductions. This enhances the feeling that MBFR is hardly an urgent matter. (4) The executive policy process for MBFR, at least through 1976, was relatively stable, with a rather high continuity of personnel. This encouraged close personal relations which, combined with the other factors, mitigated image problems.

Security

The stringent security provisions of the ACD Act were partly grounded in a belief that arms controllers, because they are casual about national security, must be held to the highest security standards. In fact,

ACDA's security record has generally been excellent, certainly better than DOD's. ACDA is well aware of its image and knows that lax security could destroy the confidence of other departments and the President. During an open congressional hearing in 1963 an ACDA official inadvertently disclosed highly classified data about U.S. nuclear weapons. A security officer was then acquired to prevent any recurrence. Adrian Fisher, the Agency's Deputy Director throughout the 1960s, remarked, "We had to operate cautiously in the area of security" because ACDA was considered a "bureau for beatniks."[22]

ACDA has never had an important public constituency, and it began to enjoy more outspoken congressional support only in the 1970s. Actors seldom leak their positions if they have no outside following. Unlike ACDA, the military services have public prestige and influential congressional allies. These allies are likely to be well informed of the military's views, especially when the JCS fear their position will not be accepted by the President.[23]

From 1969 through 1972 security remained tight, although the White House harbored suspicions about ACDA. General Alexander Haig, Kissinger's chief NSC deputy, once called Gerard Smith to accuse an unidentified ACDA employee of leaking classified information to a senator for the purpose of defeating Senator Jackson's amendment to the SALT Interim Agreement. The senator denied Haig's allegation. Only once during this period was there evidence of an ACDA employee's going to Congress without authorization. He was fired.

During the troubled 1973–1976 period, when the Agency acquired a more conservative hue and experienced severe morale problems, security, in the sense of the safeguarding of classified information, apparently remained intact. However, some ACDA people of both liberal and conservative persuasion did speak privately with outsiders about sensitive internal Agency matters. Referring to this type of leaking, a well-positioned Agency official said, "In the past we've been one of the tightest outfits in government. Today (1976) ACDA is a sieve." That ACDA did by this time have influential friends in Congress probably contributed to the willingness to leak such information, but if there had not been a concern within the Agency that its mission was in jeopardy (plus widespread unhappiness with Deputy Director John Lehman's administrative and personal style), it is unlikely that even this form of leaking would have been significant. The Agency had powerful critics as well as friends on the Hill, and conservatives were at least as active as liberals in passing sensitive information during this peiod. Said one senior

ACDA official, "If it [ACDA] was a sieve, it stemmed from the anti-arms control elements within the Agency leaking materials to the disservice of arms control."

ACDA's unusually strict security caused some administrative inconvenience. Until 1975, when Congress eliminated the problem by amending section 45 of the ACD Act, whenever ACDA contracted with a research organization having full DOD clearances the Agency could not accept them. Instead, time and money were spent on a separate clearance investigation even when the researcher used only DOD classified material and the contracting organization had worked under DOD clearances for many years.[24] On a variety of other matters the ACD Act requires that ACDA contractors and prospective employees be cleared by DOE even if they already have full clearances from another department. The House passed a bill in 1977 to end this needlessly duplicative effort, but legislation was averted by a written ACDA–DOE agreement designed to mitigate the problem.[25]

Part II
The Executive Branch

4 Leadership and Cohesion

AN ORGANIZATION'S VITALITY depends on the quality and nature of its leadership. And this hinges upon elusive, yet crucial, personality traits of the senior officials—their complementarity with other people, values, operating styles, and sensitivities. Our focus here concerns the two individuals who set the tone for the Agency, the Director and Deputy Director.

The leaderships's operating skill within the bureaucracy and its willingness to play the policy game often determine organizational effectiveness. This is particularly so for a small unit like ACDA, which, for all its analytical capabilities, lacks the bargaining levers of more senior actors. Given an opportunity and choice to participate in a policy issue, ACDA, like other actors, must decide whether or not to play the game and, if so, how assertively. Even the President must determine how much of his capital or reputation he wants to expend or risk on an issue. Real costs are incurred if one acquires a reputation for losing. Additionally, in presenting its case ACDA—like other national security agencies—must usually indicate at least general identification with widely shared values and perceptions. To assume a solitary stance sharply at variance with prevailing norms is to run a high risk of alienating senior actors who might then shun the Agency altogether.[1]

Congressional supporters of ACDA like Congressman Jonathan Bingham have urged the Agency to be an aggressive "advocate" for arms control within the executive branch. Agency spokesmen, while acknowledging their advocacy role, have also been conscious of the bureaucratic perils of excessive zeal. Philip Farley reminded Congressman Bingham of ACDA's negotiating responsibilities: "when one negotiates, one negotiates on behalf of the President and the total executive branch position."[2] Similarly, when an official testifies before Congress he does so as a representative of the entire executive branch. To some degree ACDA must be perceived by other bureaucratic actors as a loyal "team player" if it is to be effective.

But there are also inherent pitfalls in this "to get along, one goes along" approach. First, it places ACDA in an awkward position vis-à-vis its liberal supporters in Congress, who, by the early 1970s, were asking and sometimes requiring it to become a more *public* arms control advocate as well as a congressional informant in certain national security areas (see Chapters 9 and 14). Compliance with such demands risked alienating those senior officials whose good will was essential. Noncompliance ensured continued pressure from those legislators whose backing was invaluable and who argued, with considerable justification, that ACDA's very rationale for existence disappears if it fails forcefully to argue the case for arms control.[3] Also, that case may never get a proper hearing if ACDA is timid or habitually in league with, say, the Pentagon. On major questions there are always those advocating an essentially "military decision" or those advocating the interests of foreign nations. An aggressive arms control advocate can shift the spectrum of debate, sometimes making the more moderate positions of certain State Department officials, NSC officers, or Pentagon civilians appear more reasonable in comparison. On many issues, if ACDA does not push the case for arms control, no one will. Finally, a very cautious or conservative leadership might invite intra-Agency tension. Weak advocacy on truly vital issues or consistent identification with traditional competitors could be seen by lower-level ACDA personnel as jeopardizing the Agency's essential mission.

There are, then, conflicting sets of cross-pressures affecting a decision whether or not to make an assertive plea for arms control. The balance struck depends upon personalities and subject matter as well as an assessment of numerous factors that are often in flux. Either course of action, caution or spirited participation, entails costs and benefits.

This chapter also examines Agency cohesion. The personality traits, styles, and preferences of the leadership can decisively influence the sense of commitment its employees feel toward the organization. Differences of opinion can strengthen an organization, yet there should be a core area of agreement about its essential mission and purpose. Without such agreement, a vital ingredient for agency effectiveness will probably be either absent or diluted, namely, loyalty to the organization and its leaders. Except for ACDA's earliest years, when some senior military officers in the Agency were actively hostile to arms control, this was never a serious concern. But from 1973 until the Carter administration ACDA's cohesiveness was shaken. Internal tensions were considerable.

The chapter examines an important period in ACDA's history that followed an incident widely referred to within the arms control community as "the purge."

Leadership

President Kennedy felt that the first head of a somewhat suspect ACDA should be someone who would quiet the fears of conservative critics. He settled on a businessman named William C. Foster, a lifelong Republican and former Deputy Secretary of Defense whose background and prior government service cast him as an eminently solid, respectable, and above all safe choice. Foster had been one of the most active members of the Gaither Committee, which reported to President Eisenhower in 1957 on the nation's defense posture. After the issuance of the report, Foster had repeatedly and publicly urged greater sacrifices for a strong defense posture. The following year Foster, who had an active interest in arms control, led the American delegation to the conference on the prevention of surprise attacks at Geneva.

Foster guided ACDA through its difficult formative years when arms controllers were often likened to the plague. He was hardworking and sincere and, contrary to the expectations of some, he became, in the words of one who knew him well, "a convert" to arms control. Indeed, on some issues he was quite zealous, even emotional, to the point of straining personal relations. He clashed personally with General Earle Wheeler, among others; he sometimes took setbacks personally; and at times he adopted what one official described as a "bulldog stance" even when that was unproductive. His tenacity, though, was an important factor in moving the government toward a Non-Proliferation Treaty.[4] Except for this treaty, however, which by the mid-1960s dominated much of his time, Foster—despite his commitment to arms control—was not one to take the initiative in moving new issues to the fore. Many important functions were delegated to Deputy Director Adrian Fisher.

Fisher had a quick and easy grasp of complex security issues. Whereas Foster had difficulty dealing with the bureaucracy, Fisher interacted comfortably with the military, OSD, Secretary Rusk, the White House, and Congress. He was often the chief U.S. negotiator at Geneva. Sometimes he acted as de facto director (when Fisher was at Geneva, others occasionally assumed this role).

Outside the nuclear nonproliferation area the Agency was not an aggressive arms control advocate. Several factors contributed to this cautious stance, including prevailing attitudes toward ACDA and arms control, the closed and generally unreceptive nature of the Johnson foreign policy system, the central arms control role of McNamara and ISA, and a reluctance on the part of ACDA's leadership to take bold (and bureaucratically hazardous) initiatives. "ACDA," said Fisher, "always faced the problem of not raising too much hell so as to avoid being crowded out of the act."[5] For instance, in 1967 ACDA decided not to press the MIRV issue after its officers evidently concluded that objections to MIRV could threaten an ABM ban in the forthcoming SALT negotiations. Even in 1968, when MIRV's threat to strategic arms control became clearer, ACDA chose not to risk its credibility in what would almost certainly have been a losing fight.[6]

ACDA's second Director, Gerard Smith, was a Republican attorney with years of experience in the arms control, atomic energy, and national security fields. During his varied career he had held such posts as chief political adviser to the 1955 Atoms for Peace Conference, Director of State's Policy Planning Staff, and Special Adviser to the Secretary of State for MLF Negotiations. His party affiliation, government career, and appointment as SALT Ambassador were elements in ACDA's generally enhanced policy role during the first Nixon administration.

Smith's SALT duties, however, called him away from Washington for prolonged periods of time. Day-to-day concerns were handled by Deputy Director Philip Farley. Like Fisher, Farley had extensive government experience in national security affairs, good personal relations with other departments, and a firm grasp of arms control issues. But, though able and diligent, Farley could not have the standing of a Director. ACDA's weight in some instances would have been greater in interagency circles if it had been more regularly represented by its highest-ranking officer.

Like their predecessors, Smith and Farley (except for SALT) downplayed the advocacy role. They were especially cautious in their congressional and public relations. Kissinger's tight policy control deterred all bureaucratic actors from taking independent initiatives, and it was virtually unthinkable that an ACDA Director could speak out publicly with any degree of latitude. But it also appears that the leadership's inherent temperament was cautious. The noteworthy exception—within the executive branch—was SALT, where ACDA took on the Pentagon with enthusiasm. Its analysts regularly dissected OSD/JCS studies, and its analyses were highly valued by the NSC staff. Said one NSC staffer, "ACDA went not only for the jugular but the capillaries too."[7] Ironically, or tragically (or, more portentously, predictably?), some of those who had most actively advocated the arms control perspective were driven out of the Agency in 1973.

On some issues the cautious approach was tactically prudent. ACDA stopped pushing for a MIRV flight test moratorium when the administration was no longer receptive to the idea. This irritated some congressmen and outside observers, but it was a wise decision. Similarly, ACDA remained silent about the fall 1971 Cannikin nuclear test in Alaska when it could not realistically be halted. Indeed, Cannikin may have been viewed as actually improving the chances for an ultimate comprehensive test ban. An NSC staffer remarked, "We should have abstained too. Some of us fought too hard against Cannikin and we may have damaged our stock with Kissinger."

In other areas a more aggressive stance might have been helpful—naval limitations in the Indian Ocean and chemical weapons are possible examples. But the most critical neglected area was nuclear nonproliferation. It drifted without high-level attention by ACDA or anyone else while SALT consumed the bureaucracy's arms control efforts. A respected ACDA expert in the nonproliferation field lamented, "Farley did not push very hard here. He was a 'team player.' "

After Smith's resignation and the decision of the White House to replace several top ACDA officers, which became evident by January 1973, the Agency was without a Director (Farley served in an interim capacity) for six months before Fred Iklé was confirmed by the Senate in July. The position was offered to Harold Agnew, Director of the Los Alamos Scientific Laboratory (and perhaps to others as well), but he rejected the offer.[8] Prospective candidates for the office may not have relished the task of heading an agency which was at that time out of favor with both the Nixon White House and the influential Senator Henry M. Jackson (D–Wash.), who had urged the personnel changes.

Fred Iklé, a former consultant to the Jackson-chaired Subcommittee on Arms Control of the Senate Armed Services Committee, was acceptable to the Senator. He was a social scientist who had taught at MIT and written widely on arms control and foreign policy matters. He certainly was not considered a wild-eyed arms controller. Iklé had never served in government, except in a consulting capacity. Before coming to ACDA he had headed the Rand Corporation's Social Science Department.

Iklé inherited an extremely difficult situation. In the summer of 1973 the Agency's morale was shattered, its budget had been slashed, its contracted research was cut in half, many staff members had left, its congressional supporters were irate, and Senator Jackson and the Nixon

White House had made it unmistakably clear that they expected ACDA to take a more conservative line on SALT. Iklé worked hard, often late into the evening and on weekends. He personally rewrote many ACDA studies. He had a fine mind and mastered the complexities of pressing arms control issues. Iklé often fought for ACDA's interests particularly vis-à-vis State and ERDA. His commitment to arms control was sincere, though more cautious and selective than that of his predecessors. And more than either Smith or Foster, he made special efforts to improve and maintain relations with Congress.

ACDA's Director was no longer U.S. SALT Ambassador, so Iklé, unlike Smith, could devote full time to Washington-based policy concerns. Unfortunately, however, several factors combined to inhibit ACDA's overall effectiveness. Iklé's more cautious approach to SALT, which inclined ACDA increasingly to ally with the Pentagon, severely strained relations with Kissinger and the State Department. This substantive clash was aggravated by Iklé's strained personal relations with Kissinger (and some others as well). Additionally, he did not (and could not) have the kind of status that often comes only after high-level government service. A member of State's Policy Planning Staff remarked, "Iklé doesn't have Smith's prestige. Who's Iklé? You could step on him and he'd yell 'ouch.' "

Henry Kissinger made the change from academia to government, but it was more difficult for Fred Iklé. Though it is hard to envisage anything more Byzantine than academic politics, many scholars have trouble making the transition to the politics of government bureaucracy. Iklé was interested in ideas and intellectual refinement. He was not a skilled bureaucratic operator. On this there was universal agreement.[9] There was also a broad, though not quite unanimous, consensus that Iklé was a weak administrator. His defenders argued, with considerable merit, that some of the complaints about administrative style reflected dissatisfaction with his conscious encouragement of different perspectives, especially on SALT. But the complaints came from all parts and levels of an agency that underwent three reorganizations in less than three years and represented a variety of concerns.[10]

These problems were not counterbalanced by the Deputy Director. After the purge, FSO Owen Zurhellen held that post for a year. Zurhellen had no background and little interest in arms control and did not immerse himself in substantive issues. He was succeeded by John Lehman, a former Nixon NSC staffer who later served on the MBFR delegation. With the possible exception of Paul Warnke, no official in the history of the Agency aroused more controversy. The mere mention of Lehman's name often elicited an automatic, sometimes emotional, response. The Senate Foreign Relations Committee, after heated debate, narrowly reported out his nomination by a 9-to-6 vote. Senator Pell, whose subcommittee passed on ACDA's budget authorization, had called several people in the Agency and the State Department but failed to find anyone supportive of Lehman's nomination.[11]

Lehman felt his "chief qualification" for the position was his "knowledge of the way to get things done in the Government."[12] It was hoped that his familiarity with bureaucratic political mores would offset Iklé's weaknesses in this regard. Some ACDA officers did cite specific instances when Lehman opened blocked channels or facilitated Agency involvement. But others—sometimes citing the identical instances—criticized his performance. However, with few exceptions, and then only among some who shared his conservative views, there was wide agreement within and outside ACDA—often including conservatives—that his abrasive operational style was frequently counterproductive. His manner of dealing with people, particularly those with whom he disagreed, contributed far more to his generally negative reputation than did his normative views.[13]

Many ACDA and State Department officials, though they exempted two or three people from the indictment, concurred with Farley when he wrote in 1974 that "it is difficult to see what the present top officers below the Director bring in the way of special skills, experience, or *motivation*."[14] An analyst in State's Politico-Military Affairs Bureau, referring to specific ACDA officers with SALT responsibility, said: "Most of them aren't 'anti-arms control,' they just don't try very hard." A Kissinger staffer at State added, "People are now annoyed if they have to deal with ACDA. That is, ACDA is so much in bed with Defense that those who do favor arms control feel awkward going to ACDA. . . . Consequently, we don't give ACDA's papers the kind of weight they might otherwise receive."

Criticism of this sort focused mainly on the SALT area, where Iklé's earnestness about arms control was widely questioned, and on certain officials beneath the Director. However, a case can be made that ACDA had some effectiveness as a SALT advocate in that the frequent resistance by Iklé and Lehman to Kissinger's proposals achieved its purpose: President Ford ultimately elected not to endorse Kissinger's SALT II position. Iklé favored a SALT agreement, but not on Kissinger's terms.

Apart from SALT, Iklé was at least as ardent an advocate as Gerard

Smith. When caution was exercised, it was often for good reason. No one was interested in truly sweeping MBFR; arguably, more limited measures might have received greater attention, but the general bureaucratic and international climate was not promising. Besides, one of the reasons Congress amended the ACD Act in 1975, requiring the submission of arms control impact statements in conjunction with authorization and appropriations requests for certain military programs, was to enhance ACDA's role in the weapons acquisition process. Yet Iklé utilized this authority reluctantly for fear of alienating those departments whose cooperation was important to ACDA. But everyone agreed that this legislation placed ACDA in an awkward position. ACDA's hesitancy about its new authority partly reflected problems inherent in the legislation itself and, much more important, the bureaucratic realities of the Ford Administration (see Chapter 14).[15]

ACDA's more conservative tone extended to conventional arms transfers, where by 1976 three of the nine analysts working in the area were military officers. One of the six civilian analysts said, "Few of us are either optimistic or even interested in arms control in the conventional area. ACDA doesn't oppose an arms sale unless there are *very* compelling reasons."[16] Of the arms transfer requests referred to the Agency, it objected to about 5 percent. In 1976 it objected to sixty-seven proposed transfers and was overruled only three times.[17] Those who are disturbed about burgeoning international arms traffic might reasonably expect ACDA to have more concern, or at least interest, in the problem. But, until Paul Warnke's directorship, this did not occur. Still, Iklé's relative inattention to the area made him no different from past Directors. Few have invested time in what may be the least promising arms control field. Indeed, though because of congressional action, ACDA's role did improve. Iklé personally welcomed legislation that sought to enhance ACDA's voice.

In some areas Iklé was quite active. More than other Directors, he frequently made his case public. He openly objected when he thought others were poaching on ACDA's territory.[18] The unilateral U.S. declaration renouncing the option to develop "mininukes" was due in large part to his personal efforts.[19] In 1974–1975 he testified successfully against the Army's request for appropriations to produce binary weapons.[20] According to one congressional staffer, Iklé was "single-handedly effective" in stopping that program.

But Iklé gave highest priority to nuclear proliferation. He deeply believed nuclear proliferation threatened world peace and that the United

States could lessen the danger. After the 1974 test explosion in India he increasingly went public with his concerns, perhaps hoping thereby to prod the government to take the matter more seriously. When Iklé objected to a public reference Kissinger made concerning peaceful nuclear explosions, Kissinger promptly acknowledged that he had misspoken. Within the State Department there was a difference of opinion over the U.S. stance toward a French-South Korean agreement under which France was to build a chemical reprocessing plant in South Korea. Iklé asked Kissinger to pressure Seoul into abrogating the agreement. It was canceled in 1976 after Washington expressed concern. Words like "courageous" were used even outside the Agency to characterize Iklé's efforts for nonproliferation. The remarks of an NSC staffer suggest both the strengths and the limitations of Iklé's advocacy:

> He was as hardline on nonproliferation as he was with SALT. This is the only area I'd give Iklé an "A." His pressure was very influential in getting Kissinger to take nuclear proliferation seriously. Right after the Indian explosion, all the pressure came from Iklé. We NSC guys held back. Iklé preempted us.
>
> But, ironically, because of strained personal relations between Iklé and Kissinger, Kissinger at first reacted negatively to Iklé's urgings. While Iklé's concerns were very legitimate . . . the initial result— because it came from Iklé—was counterproductive.

Paul Warnke's experience in national security affairs was extensive. He was the Defense Department's General Counsel in 1966–1967 and Assistant Secretary of Defense for ISA from 1967 to 1969. Though at the urging of many Democratic legislators like Senator Humphrey President Carter named Warnke Director, he twice rejected the office. He accepted when Carter personally asked him to reconsider and then only after the President agreed that, like Gerard Smith, he was also to be U.S. SALT Ambassador.[21] His Deputy Director, Spurgeon Keeny, was ACDA's Assistant Director for Science and Technology under Smith. Warnke's appointment represented the first time that a prominent and publicly outspoken arms control proponent, widely perceived as a liberal, was named Director. It was clear from the intense Senate debate over his selection that he would face close and continuous scrutiny from congressional conservatives. It was also evident that any assessment of his ability to function well within the bureaucracy and with Congress would have to consider how his actual performance related to his initial arms controller image, whether or not a picture of responsible advocacy was projected.

Cohesion

THE PURGE

At the May 1972 Moscow summit meeting President Nixon and Secretary Brezhnev signed the two most significant arms control accords theretofore concluded between the superpowers. Though Gerard Smith was with the American delegation in Moscow, he was excluded from the negotiations. Later Smith was "disinvited," according to a senior official, from attending a gala Kissinger briefing of Congress on the SALT agreements. Throughout the long negotiating process Kissinger had often denied him access to tightly guarded policy developments. These factors, and perhaps others, led him to inform the White House in July of his intention to resign; his formal resignation was submitted in October. Yet Smith firmly believed that, while not ideal, the SALT Interim Agreement limiting strategic offensive arms was sound. (The ABM Treaty provoked little controversy.) Senator Jackson felt differently, and during the Senate hearings Smith bore the brunt of much of Jackson's displeasure with the Interim Agreement.

Since at least the early 1960s his senatorial colleagues had considered Senator Jackson among the two or three most knowledgeable and influential members of Congress in national security affairs. Never suspected of arms controller leanings, Jackson was initially cool to the establishment of ACDA and the Partial Test Ban Treaty, though he eventually supported both. He declined Nixon's offer in 1968 to become Secretary of Defense but led the administration's fight for the Safeguard ABM system in 1969. His views were at first accorded considerable weight by the Nixon White House. But when the President decided to conclude the two SALT agreements his relations with the White House deteriorated.

Jackson's dissatisfaction with the Interim Agreement was primarily twofold. He objected to giving the Soviets a quantitative advantage in intercontinental ballistic missiles (ICBMs) and submarine-launched ballistic missiles (SLBMs), and he asserted that the agreement inadequately addressed the possibility that the Soviet Union might be able to threaten the survivability of U.S. ICBMs. He was also incensed that the JCS representative on the SALT delegation, Air Force Lieutenant General Royal B. Allison, would testify in support of agreements Jackson found gravely defective.

General Allison had been the JCS liaison to the interagency group coordinating the U.S. SALT position under the Johnson administration. He had the confidence of the Joint Chiefs as well as civilian officials and was widely regarded as able and diplomatic. During the lively hearings of the Senate Armed Services Committee, Jackson sought to elicit Allison's criticism of the Interim Agreement and the administration's supporting rationale. But Allison, both because he was a loyal administration spokesman and because he genuinely supported the agreement, refused to do so. Jackson was particularly irked when the General asserted that the Minuteman force would remain secure throughout the agreement's five-year duration. After Allison's testimony, Jackson phoned Admiral Thomas Moorer, JCS Chairman, and demanded Allison's removal from the delegation. Admiral Moorer, who was pleased in every respect with Allison's performance, reluctantly informed the General of Jackson's position. Reportedly, Jackson promised to block any assignment or promotion for the General requiring Senate action. Allison and Jackson then met privately. Jackson apparently accused him of joining "the ACDA crowd of disarmers." Humiliated, despite a distinguished career, General Allison resigned from the service.[22] A senior official who had worked closely with Allison remarked, "This *must* do serious damage to the likelihood of getting top-flight military people to work on arms control."

After the administration accepted a Jackson-sponsored amendment declaring that it was the sense of the Senate that future SALT accords be based on the principle of numerical equality, Jackson agreed to back the Interim Agreement. Jackson and Nixon then met to discuss SALT and ACDA, perhaps on September 30 following the signing of the Interim Agreement, when they were alone in the White House Rose Garden. It was surely important for the administration to reestablish relations with Jackson, who had, after all, finally backed the Interim Agreement. Nixon also faced reelection in a few weeks. It is reasonably clear that the Senator urged Nixon to replace the old SALT team with more conservative people and to split the role of ACDA Director and SALT Ambassador. Nixon agreed.[23]

On November 21, 1972, Senator Jackson delivered a speech before NATO's Military Committee in which he said, "Now, minimum deterrence is the orthodoxy of the arms control community that planned and negotiated the American side of the Moscow accords." Jackson, of course, knew this to be false. U.S. strategic doctrine and posture under the Nixon administration, as under the Kennedy and Johnson administrations, was anything but minimum deterrence. The Director of ACDA certainly did not subscribe to minimum deterrence, as Jackson was well aware.[24]

At that time the highest-ranking American officer on the Military Committee, the Deputy to the Chairman, was Lieutenant General Edward Rowny, U.S. Army. General Rowny, who was acquainted with the

Senator, succeeded General Allison as JCS representative on the SALT delegation. He was definitely acceptable to Senator Jackson.[25]

Except for the conservative Paul Nitze from OSD, the entire membership of the SALT I delegation was replaced. Career diplomat U. Alexis Johnson was named SALT Ambassador. Johnson had no prior background in arms control, nor had he shown particular enthusiasm for it. Numerous officials within the bureaucracy associated with SALT I were replaced by more cautious individuals. For instance, former ACDA official Ronald Spiers of State's Politico-Military Affairs Bureau was replaced by perhaps the strongest SALT critic in the Department, Seymour Weiss.

"Operation Compliance," as Adrian Fisher called it, became apparent to ACDA by late December 1972, when the Agency was ordered by the White House and the Office of Management and Budget (OMB) to slash its budget by one-third and to fire specified officials. Farley was instructed not to reveal that this was anything other than a joint ACDA–OMB agreement. When Farley sought an explanation for the dramatic budget reduction, a White House aide said only, "You know." A call to General Alexander Haig at the NSC failed to clarify this response. Finally, Farley was told that the White House did not want the next Director to select his own Deputy. In March, White House press secretary Ronald Ziegler announced that thereafter ACDA would be merely a "research and staffing organization" rather than a negotiating agency.[26] But even this description of ACDA's fallen state overemphasized the diminished role prescribed for the Agency since its contracted research budget was severely cut.

The White House accepted the resignations of only five or six political appointees, but this constituted one-third of the small Agency's ranking leadership. By the spring of 1974 only four of ACDA's top seventeen officials were still with the Agency. One left the following year, and another, the government's foremost nuclear nonproliferation expert, was originally on the White House's termination list but was retained after Farley pleaded his case. Several of the seventeen were scheduled to leave about that time, and their departure was unrelated to the White House directive. Also, Farley was asked to remain. But some who were neither fired nor otherwise slated to leave, including Farley himself, subsequently left, partly because of the changed political climate within the Agency. This was also the case with several lower-level people, some of whom went to other agencies.

In December 1972 ACDA had 219 employees. When Iklé became Director the next July, the number had fallen by more than 25 percent to

162—an all-time low since the very early years. In addition, OMB eliminated forty positions that had been authorized by Congress (from 244 to 204 authorized slots). ACDA was able to cushion the blow somewhat for civilians, the core of the Agency, by releasing fifteen military officers and thirteen FSO's, but the impact was still considerable. Equally consequential was the psychological impact it had on the remaining civilian professionals.[27]

Prior to the White House directive, ACDA had asked OMB for a budget of $10.75 million for Fiscal Year 1974, an increase over its $10 million FY 1973 authorization. Instead, OMB allotted ACDA only $6.7 million for the coming fiscal year. The actual cut was even greater, as ACDA continued to pay the $1 million annual administrative costs of the SALT negotiations, though it no longer headed the delegation. Congress restored some of the funds so that the final budget for FY 1974 was $8 million, a 20 percent reduction from the previous fiscal year. Almost half of this decrease came in contracted research, which fell from almost $2 million to $1.1 million. In the summer of 1974 Iklé essentially asked for a full restoration of these budgetary and personnel cuts for FY 1975. Congress complied, so that by the spring of 1975 ACDA's personnel complement and budget approximated what they had been in December 1972.[28]

Until 1975, however, ACDA was variously handicapped.[29] Lack of funds prevented needed research in the nuclear proliferation area. ACDA's systems analytical capability relied heavily on active-duty military officers. When their numbers declined, the Operations Analysis Division was understaffed. SALT activity was affected. In the spring of 1974 an ACDA officer with SALT responsibility said: "This year and last we have been seriously understaffed in a number of key SALT areas. . . . There are several things ACDA simply does not have the manpower to do."

It might be argued that what happened to ACDA after the November 1972 election was not unique. Nixon was determined to reduce what he considered to be an excessive number of Democrats in the bureaucracy. Throughout government in 1973 those political appointees thought to be associated too closely with certain constituencies or programmatic interests were fired. The obsession about "loyalty to the team" extended to State, Defense, and other departments. A system that discouraged dissent, demoralized professionals, and isolated the President affected the entire executive branch.[30]

But the impact on ACDA was so severe that the word "purge" is entirely appropriate. Imagine OMB ordering a one-third reduction in DOD's budget in one year! Also, while most of the ACDA officials asked to resign were Democrats, White House suspicions of disloyalty were especially intense regarding suspected arms controllers, regardless of party affiliation. When Farley was informed he could stay on, a White House staffer explained that it was felt he would be "loyal" to the White House and not give his first allegiance to the Director. Secretary of Defense Melvin Laird's repeated accusations of ACDA disloyalty had fallen on receptive ears.

INTRA-AGENCY TENSION

In the wake of the purge, ACDA gained some Republicans and several Jackson Democrats. Many were personally acceptable to Senator Jackson or his close aide, Richard Perle. Perle was well known for his extensive executive branch sources of information, aggressive operational style, and conservative foreign and national security policy views. He was also among the most prolific "leakers" of information to the press and had an established relationship with some conservative columnists.[31] Lehman and Perle were personal friends and retained their close association throughout Lehman's tenure at ACDA.

A more or less identifiable Jackson clique soon formed within the Agency. Its prominent members held several of the senior positions, but it was also represented at the working level, particularly in the SALT and SALT verification areas. One ACDA analyst who claimed membership in the Jackson group listed several people whom he said were in "the Jackson underground."

Lehman's general orientation on national security issues was evident long before he came to ACDA. At his nomination hearing Senator Pell remarked that "from what your colleagues feel about you, the general feeling is that you would not be pushing the cause of arms control."[32] Particularly in SALT Lehman did, indeed, come to identify closely with Pentagon positions. Shortly after leaving ACDA, Lehman expressed his views on SALT. He stated that verification problems were "a particular weakness of the SALT I accords." Minimizing the threat posed to the Soviet Union by U.S. forward-based nuclear systems in Europe, Lehman criticized "some senior officials of the Ford Administration" for their alleged insensitivity to the "real" balance in forward-based systems. And praising the cruise missile as a theater system, he felt it was "foolish in the extreme to foreclose any of these promising stabilizing weapons systems options in the present SALT context."[33] These are perfectly legitimate views. However, before the purge, their most ardent proponents would normally have been expected to come from the Pentagon, not ACDA.

Below the Deputy Director, the Agency's next leadership level also took on a more conservative hue by the fall of 1973. Two of the four Assistant Directors and the General Counsel were considered less enthusiastic about arms control than their predecessors. Experienced FSO Leon Sloss, who served as Acting Director (after having been an Assistant Director) from January 1977 until Warnke's confirmation that spring, had opposed the ABM Treaty when he was at State.

Fred Iklé demanded prompt high-level attention to nuclear proliferation. But he was not in the forefront of those seeking expeditious negotiation of a SALT II accord; nor did he find negative implications for arms control in the changing U.S. strategic doctrine enunciated by Secretary of Defense Schlesinger. Schlesinger's doctrine, adopted by the President, placed greater emphasis on counterforce targeting and accurately targeted weapons systems capable of providing the President with improved confidence in ordering limited nuclear strikes. Shortly before entering government Iklé had deplored what he considered to be excessive U.S. reliance on mutual assured destruction. He therefore welcomed Schlesinger's relative shift away from countervalue targeting. However, legislators like Senator Thomas McIntyre (D–N.H.) and most of the outside arms control community, including Gerard Smith, were highly critical of the new doctrinal emphasis. Smith argued that the Schlesinger–Iklé approach weakened deterrence, fueled the arms race, strained the budget, assumed an unlikely degree of rationality in nuclear war, and was—in any event—unnecessary, because the President already had adequate counterforce options. Whatever the relative merits of this debate, Iklé's position effectively meant that there was little executive branch opposition to Schlesinger's program.[34]

Within ACDA there were different SALT perspectives, but the predominant tone set by Iklé and Lehman was far more conservative than it had been. The Agency frequently allied with DOD on such things as the cruise missile, verification questions, and certain terms of negotiation. This left Kissinger without the kind of ACDA support he had previously enjoyed.[35] Much of the analysis buttressing Kissinger's position came from former ACDA officials now with State. An NSC staffer said, "Iklé is to the right of the JCS on SALT. . . . Yes, I am serious about this—to the right of the JCS." Kissinger staffers and many others in State, ACDA, and even Defense agreed.

Iklé's defenders argued that his critics were the real problem. All he wanted was a sound, verifiable agreement, not arms control at any price.

"They [State] think good arms control is accepting the Russian position.
If ACDA has changed [its SALT image], it's largely because the *Russians* have changed. . . . Kissinger wants *agreement* more than viable
arms control. He wants agreement to further détente. He's too anxious."
Iklé's critics denied these assertions, though they felt that when even the
supposed arms controllers allied with the military, Kissinger had ample
reason to be anxious about world peace. The net result of ACDA's SALT
posture was to weaken the coalition favoring more rapid movement toward agreement. Said one ACDA SALT official who often differed with
Iklé and Lehman, "Good policy requires that someone be on the left
flank, for obvious reasons. Kissinger and the President need an arms
control agency, not just one more weapons advocate."

The first chief of Iklé's most controversial organizational unit, the
Verification Division of the new Verification and Analysis Bureau, came
to the Agency from the government's foremost weapons advocate,
DDR&E. Prior to the establishment of the Verification Division, verification questions were addressed by analysts with full-time functional responsibility for specific substantive issues. Hence the SALT or nuclear
test ban analysts examined verification problems associated with SALT or
test ban agreements. But Iklé made verification a separate activity.

According to a ranking member of the Verification Division, there
were four reasons for its establishment: (1) to better examine the adequacy with which existing and possible future arms control agreements
could be verified; (2) to "keep ACDA honest" via a distinct entity "with
no vested interest in a particular treaty;" (3) image—"Iklé wanted to
create the impression around town that ACDA [would no longer] push
treaties for their own sake with little sensitivity to verification;" and (4)
"ACDA was not a player in the verification game [within the intelligence
community], and this could be an opening wedge." The Verification
Division dealt with a variety of issues, though much of its attention was
directed at SALT. Iklé regularly asked for its input.

Predictably, it sparked controversy from the moment of its creation.
For some, it was a jurisdictional threat. The CIA resisted Iklé's attempt to
move into an area it considered the exclusive preserve of the intelligence
community. Within ACDA, too, its activities were sometimes resisted.
For instance, Iklé directed it to analyze the verification problems of the
Threshold Test Ban, but ACDA's Robert Buchheim, whose bureau had
primary responsibility for this agreement and who chaired the interagency
group for the test ban, resisted the intervention. Buchheim and many
others did not consider verification a separate specialty. It should, they
argued, be returned to the respective functional units, as Agency organi-

zational structure should reflect the fact that verification questions are inherently inseparable from other substantive arms control issues.

Nor was the Verification Division seen as a disinterested, neutral party. Many in State characterized its members as "politically obtuse Cold War ideologues." Throughout much of ACDA there was concern that the Division, in stressing verification *problems,* overemphasized the risks of arms control instead of the opportunities. The CIA took issue with what it considered to be the worst-case assumptions this group consistently made about Soviet behavior in general and treaty compliance in particular.

The ideological tension between CIA analysts and some members of the Verification and Analysis Bureau was considerable. One member of the Verification Division said, "The CIA is a peacetime operation, and it assumes we live in a friendly world where people don't deceive you. The assumptions they make about Soviet behavior concerning verification are absolutely erroneous." An officer in the Verification and Analysis Bureau who often jousted with CIA analysts derided "that CIA–INR mafia," which refused to "face reality." One officer from this Bureau was an adviser in 1976 to a widely publicized group of Sovietologists and SALT critics headed by Richard Pipes of Harvard. This group was temporarily brought into government by Director for Central Intelligence George Bush to contest a competing team of analysts led by a National Intelligence Officer from the CIA. Both groups assessed future Soviet intentions and military capabilities, a subject periodically addressed in National Intelligence Estimates.[36]

Views of Soviet behavior held by some members of the Verification Division were, in fact, pessimistic.[37] The Division regularly assumed, according to one of its members, that Moscow would try to violate agreements. CIA analysts, however, say that, while the military services might hold such *a priori* assumptions, an intelligence organization charged with providing policymakers with accurate information can ill afford to base assessments on preconceived views that frequently lack credible substantiating evidence. It would, they add, be equally foolish to presume Soviet compliance. The only intellectually honest course is to base estimates on "the facts."

ACDA has a vested interest in seeing that arms control agreements are reasonably verifiable. Otherwise the probability of noncompliance would increase dramatically, thereby discrediting all arms control efforts. In areas like nuclear proliferation, ACDA has always been the most insistent proponent of stringent verification standards. But, with very few exceptions—such as large-yield above-ground testing of nuclear devices—no arms control agreement can be verified with complete certainty. Nations conclude arms control agreements if they believe that, on balance, their respective national interests will thereby be enhanced and the agreement can be adequately verified. Among the numerous factors affecting perceptions of adequacy are a nation's past record of compliance, the degree of risk posed by possible violations, ability to respond to violations, commonality of interest in the agreement, and whether the political benefits of a treaty compensate for lessened verifiability. A final national decision about the adequacy of verification is virtually always a political judgment; that judgment might be quite different, depending upon the subject matter or region under consideration.

Although ACDA must be interested in verification, it must also be an advocate for arms control. Undue concern about the usually inherent verification problems might incline the Agency to deemphasize the benefits of an agreement. There will always be those who will stress verification limitations. But those believing that the overall advantages of a proposed agreement outweigh the limitations will not always have a champion, particularly if ACDA fails to take the initiative.

An official ACDA publication prepared, ironically, by the Verification Division states, "New and more comprehensive arms control agreements are likely to pose greater challenges to our verification capabilities. But these are challenges we should be prepared to accept. If the uncertainties of the future are real, the opportunities for arms control are also real."[38]

A major complaint about ACDA's verification activities under Iklé was that their collective effect was to encourage neglect of "the opportunities for arms control."[39] There was considerable agreement with the view of a Kissinger State Department aide that ACDA's "Amrom Katz and Manfred Eimer are the two top government people on the *limitations* of aerial reconnaissance. That is, they insist on an unrealistically high standard of verification for what may only be reasonably verifiable. Hence ACDA takes the role that the JCS always takes."

The leadership's more conservative stance was mostly felt in SALT and SALT verification. It also affected MBFR and conventional arms transfers, but with less consequence. Similarly, the Agency's interest in Indian Ocean arms control might have been greater under a different leadership. ACDA had little interest in pushing for a nuclear-weapons-free zone here (or in any other region). It fully concurred in the conclusion of a 1976 NSC study that this was an inappropriate time to seek a naval arms limitation agreement in the region with Moscow. Finally, despite considerable congressional opposition to building a U.S. base on the Indian Ocean island of Diego Garcia, Iklé and his Deputy testified that the base would not exacerbate international tensions or harm prospects for future arms control in the area.[40]

Organizational effectiveness is impossible without motivated personnel. Employees must, as Morton Halperin states, "believe that what they are doing makes a difference . . . ; that the organization's efforts are appreciated and that its role in the scheme of things is not diminishing."[41] After the purge, in 1973–1974, Agency morale reached an all-time low. There was a pervasive sense of undeserved punishment and diminished importance. This feeling was articulated by Gerard Smith, "while I was aware that military officials have often been cashiered for failure, this purge is the first case I know of where arms control officials were cashiered after a success." Smith further stated: "To be an expendable member of the bureaucracy as well as an arms controller is indeed to be in double jeopardy. . . . Now all officials working on arms control realize it is somewhat hazardous duty."[42]

Morale also suffered from the unexpected, dramatic changeover in personnel. "In the absence of continuity," Louis Gawthrop says, "there is a very high probability that one or several organizational maladies will appear among operating personnel: apathy, alienation, demoralization, or aggression."[43] All of these "maladies" were witnessed at this time.

Morale improved by 1975 with the restoration of personnel and budget levels, a lower employee turnover rate, and for some a growing sense that ACDA still had a significant role to perform. But ACDA was never as cohesive as it had been before the purge. Until the Carter administration there was a distinct ideological split within the Agency, which affected feelings of loyalty to the organization and interpersonal relationships. Those who did not identify with the influentially (but not numerically) dominant Jackson group were convinced that it was subverting ACDA's *raison d'être*. Morale was further aggravated, according to many, by John Lehman's harsh intra-Agency operating style. Finally, Iklé's three reorganizations of the Agency contributed to the atmosphere of uncertainty and impermanency.

ACDA was reorganized for a fourth time in less than four years when Warnke became Director in the spring of 1977. Among other things, the Verification Division was abolished, as was the Verification and Analysis Bureau. Verification was returned to the functional bureaus and divisions, while those conservatives who had not resigned were reassigned to less prominent positions. Congressional conservatives promptly charged that Warnke had "purged" the Agency. A piece by William Safire in the *New*

York Times, which asserted that Warnke had activated an "ideological hit list" and had fired several "verifiers" who were civil servants, was widely circulated.[44] In fact, no civil servants were asked to leave, and only one political appointee (a liberal Democrat) was fired despite the change in administration. Some of the most conservative officers, including the former head of the Verification Division, elected to stay on.[45] Many conservatives, of course, did choose to leave in light of the changed political climate. Most went to other departments. By mid-1977 Warnke was receiving warning signals from both the left and the right. That summer conservative members of Congress, fearing that the verification function had been downgraded, were successful in amending the ACD Act to require the Director to report to Congress in specified instances on verification matters (see Chapter 13). Liberals, on the other hand, were grumbling that some conservative political appointees from the past administration were still there. But there was no purge. ACDA's budget and personnel increased while the leadership transition was entirely normal.

5 The President: Confidence and Access

The real organization of government at higher echelons is not what you find in textbooks or organizational charts. It is how confidence flows down from the President.

Dean Rusk

THE PRESIDENT'S CONFIDENCE is the *sine qua non* for effectiveness in the executive branch. Without it one can, at best, have only a secondary or tertiary impact on high policy. Presidential confidence appears to encompass at least three essential components: (1) It is personal. Presidents interact with people. Confidence is conferred upon individuals, not organizations. Presidents often have or acquire views about an entire department or subunit within a department, and these views can significantly affect his relationship with its leadership. But the ultimate effect of such perceptions can be profoundly influenced by the personal rapport, or lack thereof, between the department's leadership and the President. (2) The President must believe that subordinates are capable of effective performance, that they have the will, professional ability, and political sagacity to perform creditably. (3) Confidence flows only to those considered loyal and responsive.[1]

There is a distinct reciprocal relationship between having the President's confidence and gaining access to him. With presidential confidence, a senior official's prospects for securing access to the Oval Office improves. Without confidence, access is difficult or impossible. Nonaccess guarantees that a senior official cannot personally engage the attention and interest of the supreme policymaker. Simply put, this means that

61

he is not a central actor in the policy process. Access, then, is critical to overall effectiveness.

Access to the White House may or may not improve if the President personally shares an interest in the substantive functions for which a senior official's department has principal responsibility. If he enjoys the President's confidence, their shared interests can facilitate access. Without this confidence, particularly if substantive jurisdiction in the area is shared with other bureaucratic actors to whom the President may turn, access is unlikely to be enhanced.

Presidents, of course, substantially determine the nature and scope of advice they receive by their individual styles, norms, political appointees, and decisions about whom they will see.[2] Modern Presidents have differed considerably in how widely they have sought advice in the national security field and in their own personal involvement with issues. But all recent Presidents have obtained their most vital national security advice from a select number of senior advisers: the Assistant for National Security Affairs (Special Assistant for National Security Affairs before 1969), the Secretary of State, the Secretary of Defense, (often) the Secretary of the Treasury, the Director for Central Intelligence, and the JCS, especially the Chairman. Occasionally others will play an important role, but these six are usually the key advisers.

For a junior actor like ACDA to join this inner circle is exceedingly difficult—particularly when it has image problems, is "under the direction of the Secretary of State," and lacks both institutional weight and a public constituency. Furthermore, from Kennedy to Ford, no President had a close personal relationship with ACDA's Director. It is evident, then, that none of ACDA's Directors from 1961 through 1976 had the kind of presidential confidence necessary for easy access to the White House. A decision to go to the President is a serious matter even for Cabinet members. Richard Neustadt compares it to a decision to go to war.[3] For ACDA's Director, that option is legally and theoretically open. Politically, it has seldom been comfortably exercisable or, at times, exercisable at all. Said one Director by way of understatement, "None of us [ACDA Directors] could pick up the phone and talk with the President."

Factors like image and public constituency, while not immutable, are not readily altered. Nor can legislation supportive of the Agency bring presidential confidence where none has existed. But Presidents come and go. If a new President wants arms control *and* is willing to have the Director as a principal adviser, ACDA's role within the executive branch will improve. This will be most likely to occur if, perhaps even before he took office, the President has had a personal relationship with the individual who assumes ACDA's directorship.[4]

Kennedy and Johnson

William Foster's relationship with President Kennedy was not close, and his access to the White House was limited. When he did see the President, Foster was often accompanied by Secretary of State Rusk. It was Rusk who generally set forth the issue, while Foster might fill in some details. This was so despite Kennedy's deep concern about averting nuclear holocaust. Only after Kennedy assumed office did the United States finally present an entire draft treaty for a nuclear test ban. Kennedy personally directed U.S. efforts toward the Partial Test Ban Treaty. He involved himself in the minutiae of the negotiations, pressured the bureaucracy, and acquired considerable expertise on the subject. His commencement address at the American University in June 1963, where he announced a U.S. moratorium on nuclear atmospheric testing and the beginning of discussions with Moscow, is one of the most stirring presidential pronouncements on world peace.[5]

Vietnam dominated Lyndon Johnson's foreign policy and demanded most of his time. He indicated little interest in arms control during the first years of his presidency. In 1965 he rejected a recommendation to curb nuclear proliferation.[6] Only late in his administration (1967–1968) did Johnson begin to concern himself with nuclear proliferation matters and SALT. But the Soviet invasion of Czechoslovakia in August 1968 put a damper on arms control. The SALT talks were postponed, the JCS were unreceptive to any arms control proposal, Senate ratification of the Non-Proliferation Treaty was delayed, and Johnson—by then a lame duck President—would not spur the bureaucracy to grapple with arms control issues.

When Johnson did seek arms control advice he went to his Secretaries of Defense and State as well as his Special Assistant for National Security Affairs, not William Foster. Foster's access to Johnson was even worse than under Kennedy, and by 1968 ACDA had virtually no communication with the White House. What little access existed was provided by Dean Rusk and, to some degree, by ACDA patron Vice President Hubert Humphrey, who sometimes offered his good offices to facilitate entry into the Oval Office.[7]

Nixon–Ford–Carter

During the 1968 presidential campaign Richard Nixon indicated an interest in arms control and spoke of the general complementarity of DOD and ACDA objectives: Both sought the enhancement of national security. When, on January 29, 1969, President Nixon announced Gerard Smith's appointment as ACDA Director and U.S. Ambassador to the forthcoming SALT negotiations, he also stated that ACDA's role and status were being "upgraded," that ACDA's functions were among "the most important" of his administration, and that Smith would "have direct and ready access to the President."[8] Although ACDA quickly lost an important SALT assignment it had received in March, the Agency experienced new life from 1969 to 1972. ACDA played an unprecedented role in national security affairs. Internationally, there was considerable activity in the arms control field. Nixon followed SALT closely during his first administration. According to Smith, "No President prior to Nixon would have dreamed of getting so deeply involved in an arms control negotiation as to wrestle with a chairman of the CPSU [Communist Party of the Soviet Union] over agreed ceilings on the depth and diameter of concrete silo launchers."[9]

But Smith did not enjoy the promised "direct and ready access" to the President. He recalled the frustration this engendered: "[I]t used to be a rather lonely business and a somewhat unequal struggle to be contesting for the president's arms control mind with Mel Laird. He, a powerful Republican politician (who had voted against ACDA) and a close intimate in the presidential official family—I was what Henry Kissinger in his more benevolent moods would call a bureaucrat and at other times a technician."[10] America's chief SALT negotiator never had sufficient time alone with Nixon to talk frankly about SALT. This, plus charges of "disloyalty" from Laird and later the White House, were referred to by senior ACDA officials as among the most disturbing aspects of their government service. And Fred Iklé, Smith's successor, had even less access—virtually none—to Nixon.

There were at least three reasons for Nixon's lack of confidence in ACDA's Director. (1) There was no personal rapport between Smith and Nixon and, if possible, even less between Iklé and the President. Nixon barely knew Iklé, and the Director's obscurity was ensured when the Nixon White House failed to issue any kind of statement on or after the occasion of his appointment. (2) Nixon considered ACDA people "woolly-headed," lacking the toughness thought necessary for dealing with the Russians. One senior official said, "Nixon saw ACDA as a sort of EPA [Environmental Protection Agency] of national security; he liked and trusted 'idealistic' environmentalists about as much as 'naive' arms controllers. ''[11] Nixon received confirmation for his opinion when the SALT Interim Agreement came under attack from Senator Jackson and others. Indeed, just months after that agreement was approved by Congress ACDA was cleansed of its senior "arms controllers." (3) By 1970 Kissinger dominated the foreign policy bureaucracy, particularly SALT, and he gradually gained near-monopoly access to the President. ACDA was hardly alone in complaining about nonaccess. Destler remarks that Nixon limited "the charmed circle to one man. The result must be one of the shorter 'lines of confidence' in bureaucratic history.''[12] Smith and Iklé did see Kissinger, but access to the Secretary of State, while essential, is no substitute for personal contact with the President.

Iklé's line to the White House improved under the Ford administration. Gerald Ford, though attentive to some arms control issues, did not involve himself in the subject as completely as some of his predecessors. President Ford's advisory system and personal style were, however, far more open than Nixon's. In late 1975 Secretary of State Kissinger lost his title as Assistant for National Security Affairs to his deputy, General Brent Scowcroft. Also, Ford's appointment that year of his friend Donald Rumsfeld as Secretary of Defense loosened Kissinger's nearly exclusive hold on national security advice. While the ACDA Director still lacked either a close relationship with the President or easy access to the White House, by 1975 Iklé was occasionally seeing the President. Sometimes he was accompanied by Kissinger or Scowcroft, and at other times he met with Ford on a one-to-one basis.

Few recent Presidents manifested a more comprehensive concern for arms control in the first year in office than Jimmy Carter. His inaugural address called for the eventual elimination of all nuclear weapons. The new President's first interview, just a few days later, was devoted to arms control. The U.S. SALT proposal presented to the Soviets, and rejected by them, in the spring of 1977 had received Carter's close personal attention. Carter announced in January that U.S. overseas sales of conventional arms would henceforth be subject to "very tight restraints." By the fall it was evident that "very tight" would at best translate into more or less tight, but by 1978 the United States had, for the first time, defined a national policy for conventional arms transfers. In early 1977 the United States and the Soviet Union set up several working groups to address a broad range of arms control issues. A complete review of American policy in the nuclear proliferation area was completed in the early spring. It was followed by a major presidential policy pronouncement, and in

March 1978 the President signed the Nuclear Nonproliferation Act. In January 1977 Carter called for proceeding "quickly and aggressively" toward a comprehensive test ban on "all nuclear devices" and ordered an NSC review of the subject.[13] This immediately pitted ACDA, with some NSC and State Department allies, against ERDA, DOD, and the JCS. The familiar questions were contested: Could it be adequately verified? Should peaceful nuclear explosions be covered? Would it unduly retard U.S. nuclear weapons development? The bureaucratic infighting was described by one participant as "particularly brutal." Then, that spring, Carter personally intervened, making it clear that he had already decided that there should be a comprehensive test ban. The question was how to negotiate it.

President Carter's early interest in arms control was apparent. Less evident were the prospects for successful conclusion of sound arms control agreements. Evaluation of Carter's arms control policy must await the passage of time. The same must also be said of Paul Warnke's relationship with Carter. During the presidential campaign Carter said that ACDA had been "gutted" and had to be "revitalized."[14] Then he repeatedly and vigorously defended his nominee for ACDA Director and SALT Ambassador. Especially after the nomination of Theodore Sorensen as Director for Central Intelligence had to be withdrawn, Warnke's nomination was widely perceived as a crucial political test for the new President, and Carter personally consulted with key senators about it. An apparent concern of Warnke opponents was that he *would* have a close personal relationship with the Chief Executive. At the first press conference of his administration, Carter said: "I know Mr. Warnke very well. I have met with him several times. . . . I have complete confidence in him. . . . I believe his views are well considered by me. I have accepted them." A few hours before the Senate vote to confirm, Carter repeated before a national television audience his "complete confidence" in Warnke. When Warnke was sworn into office on March 14, Carter lavished praise on his new Director and indicated that he had "weathered . . . unwarranted criticism." He also announced that Warnke would accompany Secretary of State Cyrus Vance to Moscow on March 28 for SALT discussions with Soviet leaders.[15]

From all appearances Warnke began his tenure with the full confidence of the President. During 1977 he saw the President on several occasions and played an active policy role. By 1978 Carter was referring to ACDA as "the focal point" of his administration's arms control efforts.[16] But whether the bitter controversy over Warnke's nomination—which did not abate after his confirmation—Warnke's outspoken advocacy for arms control, his subsequent performance, or international events would ultimately work to his advantage or disadvantage was not yet apparent by mid-1978. One thing was clear, however. Although the President's confidence in the Director enhanced ACDA's voice in executive circles, it certainly did not insulate Warnke from conservative congressional critics. Indeed, it made this formidable group even more skeptical about the SALT II negotiations. What they found most disturbing was that, for the first time, an ACDA Director actually had the President's ear on a regular basis. And this Director, many were convinced, was a classic "arms controller."

⑥ Hearing on Policy Issues

The effectiveness of any agency serving in essentially a staff role is a function of the degree to which it is listened to.

Elliot Richardson

Persuasion requires not just logic but a hearing, and some are more listened to than others.

I.M. Destler

To AFFECT POLICY a bureaucratic actor must be heard. It needs a forum in which to express itself. The President is the most important listener, and for ACDA a receptive Secretary of State is vital. But this chapter focuses more on other listeners and forums: ACDA's place in the overall foreign policy system, its informal ties with other actors, and membership on formal interagency committees.

Most really fruitful hearings tend to be informal and personal. Official interagency committees are appropriately characterized by Harold Seidman as "crab grass in the garden of Government institutions. Nobody wants them, but everyone has them."[1] But their critics have not devised adequate substitutes. They can perform a useful coordinating role. Interagency committees are not ideal mechanisms, but they may be more significant for lesser agencies like ACDA than for senior actors. Without them ACDA's opportunity for a hearing would diminish or sometimes disappear altogether.

The adequacy of ACDA's hearing on policy issues relates importantly to the extent to which an issue challenges the perceived missions of other actors. Hence, certainly before 1977, ACDA was largely excluded from the weapons acquisition and conventional arms transfer processes, but it fared better in relatively less threatening areas like nuclear proliferation. We shall examine aspects of ACDA's policy role in the major arms control issues from 1961 to early 1977 and its search for a better hearing. ACDA's ability to win allies is also discussed. "In policymaking," says Graham Allison, "the issue looking *sideways* is commitment: how to get others committed to my coalition."[2] Allies are doubly important for a non–Cabinet-level agency like ACDA; without them it cannot prevail.

1961–1968

ACTORS AND COMMITTEES

Unlike President Eisenhower, Presidents Kennedy and Johnson chose not to rely heavily on the NSC and a formal, routinized NSC system.[3] Instead, their foreign policy systems were informal and ad hoc. Kennedy's key arms control advisers were Defense Secretary McNamara, Special Assistant for National Security Affairs McGeorge Bundy, the President's Science Adviser Jerome Wiesner, Secretary of State Rusk, and, to a lesser degree, Chairman of the JCS Maxwell Taylor. Johnson's circle of senior advisers was much narrower, with McNamara and Rusk being the most important.

Before joining the Kennedy administration, McGeorge Bundy had been a member of the Harvard–MIT seminar group, which in 1959–1960 had studied problems related to a nuclear test ban treaty. Though he left defense budgetary matters to McNamara, Bundy was receptive to arms control and intervened at crucial moments in the test ban deliberations. Carl Kaysen of Bundy's staff was particularly active in prodding the bureaucracy and forcing arms control issues.

During the latter years of the Eisenhower administration James Killian, Jr., George Kistiakowsky, and the President's Science Advisory Committee (PSAC) played an active role on test ban and other arms control issues and reviewed high technology programs of the AEC, DOD, and CIA. They often blocked programs that did not meet their approval, and PSAC provided the only body of expertise on military research and development outside the Pentagon.[4] Jerome Wiesner, Kistiakowsky's successor, was an active force for arms control, particularly the Partial Test Ban Treaty. He often carried the technical argument against the Pentagon in meetings with the President. PSAC, however, began to decline in influence as McNamara, OSD, and Bundy assumed active roles. The decline accelerated after 1963 as President Johnson's Special Assistant for Science and Technology, Donald Hornig, had neither a close relationship with the President nor a strong interest in arms control.

Except for Hornig's staff assistant, Spurgeon Keeny, who had a joint appointment with the NSC staff, PSAC had no significant role in internal SALT matters in the late 1960s. However, during the Nixon administration a 1969 PSAC report highly critical of the battlefield utility of biological weapons was adopted by DOD's Office of International Security Affairs (ISA) and read by Deputy Secretary of Defense David Packard who then took it to Defense Secretary Laird. It was a key factor in Laird's subsequent support of the Biological Warfare Convention. Although Nixon's Science Adviser, Lee DuBridge, reportedly supported a U.S.-Soviet MIRV moratorium in 1970, PSAC played no significant arms control role and was eventually abolished by Nixon.[5] President Ford spoke of reestablishing a body similar to PSAC, but it never came about.

Next to the President, no one had a greater impact on arms control than Robert McNamara. He took on the JCS; he enjoyed presidential confidence; except in the nuclear proliferation area, Dean Rusk invariably deferred to him on arms control matters; and McNamara had able assistants like John McNaughton and an aggressive ISA which supported the test ban, SALT, and the Non-Proliferation Treaty while opposing the Sentinel ABM. Without such a powerful and welcome ally, ACDA could have gone virtually unnoticed. McNamara, however, when announcing a freeze on the level of U.S. strategic forces or making some defense cutback, though conscious of the relevance of such moves to future arms control, rarely used an arms control rationale publicly to explain his actions. Rather, they were generally ascribed to cost-effectiveness in order to avoid alienating a Congress thought to be cautious about arms control. But McNamara, who backed the Partial Test Ban Treaty over opposition from the JCS, had a deep interest in arms control, which seemed to grow stronger the longer he was in office. Once at a Committee of Principals meeting, Arthur Schlesinger recalls, after an ACDA official objected to a proposed arms control measure, alleging that it threatened U.S. security, McNamara responded, "If I'm not afraid of it, I don't see why you should be. You take care of disarmament. Let me worry about the national security of the United States."[6]

The new ACDA had difficulty establishing itself during the Kennedy years. William Foster remembered that "in the very beginning, it was a struggle to maintain the semi-autonomous nature of ACDA and to be accepted as a participant in basic decisions."[7] Resistance was such that Kennedy issued an executive order in 1962 calling for full policy coordination and cooperation with ACDA, requiring departments to keep it "fully and currently informed on all significant aspects of United States arms control and disarmament policy and related matters, including current and prospective policies, plans and programs."[8]

ACDA's success in gaining an adequate hearing, except in nonproliferation matters, did not improve in the Johnson administration. It was often shut out of arms control policymaking. McNamara's private relations with the President frequently meant that other actors could not make orderly inputs before Johnson had formulated his own opinions. ACDA often was not consulted until after the fact. It learned of the use of chemical agents in Vietnam after their introduction and found out about the ABM decision after it was made. And Bundy's successor, Walt W. Rostow, concentrated on Vietnam and seldom involved himself in arms control.

The formal interagency coordinating committee for arms control during the Kennedy–Johnson era remained the Committee of Principals. Though personalities changed and Foster began attending meetings in 1961, basic membership carried over from the Eisenhower years. In 1963 the ACDA Director and the JCS Chairman acquired full official membership, and such others as John McCloy, Robert Lovett, and Ambassador Arthur Dean were sometimes in attendance. Foster could request a meeting of the Committee by going to its Chairman, Dean Rusk. It had a working group, the Committee of Deputies, headed by ACDA's Adrian Fisher, whose membership paralleled that of the senior Committee except at a lower level. The Committee of Deputies was somewhat more active than the Committee of Principals. Fisher usually called its meetings, and he was supported by ACDA's staff, which could set the agenda for the Committee of Principals and could initiate interagency studies—something virtually impossible in the Kissinger years.

The Committee of Principals received specific directives from Kennedy and played a useful coordinating role on test ban deliberations. But after 1963 the committee gradually atrophied. It held fifteen meetings in 1964–1965 but only three in 1966. A former ACDA official said, "From 1963 on, it played an exceedingly minimal role. Its meetings were an excuse for doing nothing, they were pro forma. It wasn't involved at all in the Outer Space Treaty, played virtually no role concerning the Non-Proliferation Treaty, and it generally recommended few, if any, really new or constructive positions. This formal mechanism was rarely used." The Committee of Deputies did coordinate the government's 1968 SALT preparations, but the senior committee was only perfunctorily involved.

PARTIAL TEST BAN TREATY

Upon assuming office Kennedy directed the acceleration of nuclear test ban efforts, and five days after his inauguration State's Disarmament

Administration appointed a panel to review technical aspects of a test ban. U.S. activities were interrupted in September 1961, the month ACDA came into existence, when the Soviet Union began the first in a series of atmospheric tests. Pressure immediately mounted for a resumption of U.S. atmospheric testing. Britain asked Kennedy to exercise restraint and, internally, Wiesner, U.N. Ambassador Adlai Stevenson, the State Department, and USIA opposed resumption. But McNamara, the JCS, and the AEC urged the President to respond to the Soviets. They were soon joined by an unexpected ally, William Foster. Privately and publicly Foster argued that unless U.S. testing resumed it might be thought that the Soviets had gained important advantages, and this could dim prospects for a test ban because, among other things, the Senate might not consent to ratification. Kennedy announced the resumption of U.S. tests in March 1962.

ACDA then assumed a central role in interdepartmental test ban deliberations, which continued until Kennedy's June 1963 American University speech just a month before the treaty was initialed in Moscow. The Agency also became a prime articulator to Congress of new scientific developments tending to minimize the risks of a partial test ban. In April 1962 an ad hoc committee was formed to consider a U.S. negotiating stance. It was chaired by either Fisher or ACDA's Assistant Director for Science and Technology, Franklin Long. Also represented were officials from OSD, State, CIA, the JCS, and the AEC. The group met regularly until July, when U.S. test ban positions were considered by the Committee of Deputies and then the Committee of Principals. In August the United States had two draft treaties, a comprehensive and a partial test ban, for presentation before the Eighteen Nation Disarmament Committee (ENDC). The Soviet Union rejected both, but the 1962 partial test ban draft was to form the basis of the subsequent treaty. ACDA had major responsibility for this draft.[9]

NON-PROLIFERATION TREATY

From the summer of 1963 until the Nixon administration, ACDA was denied a significant voice in every important policy area except nuclear proliferation. ACDA was the first to propose a Non-Proliferation Treaty, which by 1964–1965 dominated ACDA's attention. The Agency's persistence was a key factor in bringing the treaty to fruition. But it ultimately emerged because it addressed the increasingly evident crisis of global dissemination of nuclear explosive devices and, additionally, because the treaty did not threaten the missions or budgets of DOD or the AEC.

The principal opposition came from State Department supporters of an MLF (multilateral force), a proposal for sharing nuclear weapons with NATO, which Washington pushed with uneven enthusiasm until it was finally killed by President Johnson in December 1964. MLF proponents were concentrated in State's European Bureau and Policy Planning Council. Few were more supportive of the MLF than Gerard Smith, who was Special Assistant to the Secretary of State for the MLF.[10] Backers of the MLF felt that American pressure on West European allies to foreswear nuclear weapons would prove counterproductive, whereas nuclear sharing (or the appearance of it) would strengthen NATO's commital posture and bolster alliance cohesion. This group was joined by some partisans of European unification, who saw the Non-Proliferation Treaty's safeguard sections as a threat to the European Atomic Energy Community (EURATOM). Gerard Smith even asserted that the MLF was a pragmatic nonproliferation measure: "The MLF will . . . increase the number of states with fingers on the safety catch, rather than on the nuclear trigger."[11]

Treaty proponents, along with the Soviet Union, considered the MLF's demise a precondition to progress on curbing nuclear proliferation. When it did die, internal opposition to the Non-Proliferation Treaty largely expired with it. Dean Rusk had not been an MLF enthusiast, and he lent his support to the Non-Proliferation Treaty. DOD's views on the treaty ranged from neutral to positive, while the AEC, which had been an obstructionist on the Partial Test Ban Treaty, became ACDA's firm ally. The AEC was especially helpful in working out the safeguard provisions.

OTHER ARMS CONTROL ACTIVITIES

In other areas ACDA's voice was muted or unheard. Foster's 1963 meeting with Soviet Foreign Minister Andrei Gromyko opened the way to an agreement restricting the placement of weapons of mass destruction in outer space. But, except for ACDA's Sidney Graybeal, who was privy to the data and negotiations, the Agency had no role in the Outer Space Treaty negotiations (1967), which were handled by U.N. Ambassador Arthur Goldberg with State and Defense Department support. There is little evidence that ACDA had a say in the initial 1962 decision to institute a chemical defoliation program in Vietnam. In any case, the one-year-old Agency may have been reluctant to question the military seriously on the issue. The Pentagon monopolized decisions on the use of chemical agents in Southeast Asia; ACDA had no role in the decision to introduce tear gas in Vietnam; and information on such things was closely held in the Pentagon away from a suspect ACDA. When ACDA learned of these programs it was, in fact, disturbed but could not obtain a meaningful hearing or affect battlefield decisions.[12]

The story was similar concerning conventional arms transfers. A 1967 staff study for the Senate Foreign Relations Committee reported: "One thing is clear . . . the Arms Control and Disarmament Agency . . . does not sit at the high table when decisions on the sale of arms are made."[13] Only after the issuance of this study did ACDA sit on some interagency bodies with responsibility in this area. But consultation with ACDA was sporadic and totally inadequate. Throughout this period ACDA had virtually no impact on U.S. arms sales or military assistance policy.

Finally, the Agency had a limited, yet not insignificant, role in SALT. Some time after the Soviet rejection of Johnson's 1964 offer for a nuclear weapons freeze, McNamara established a small group to examine U.S. negotiating positions for possible strategic arms limitation talks. Included in this group were a JCS representative, OSD's Paul Nitze and Paul Warnke, State's Raymond Garthoff, and Adrian Fisher from ACDA. The SALT idea was quietly broached with the Soviets in late 1966 and pressed in January 1967. ACDA officials were involved in these early initiatives.

In selecting a SALT negotiating team there appears to have been a conscious effort to minimize ACDA's role in order to avoid antagonizing the JCS, whose support was essential. General Earle Wheeler, Chairman of the JCS, had a low regard for arms controllers and was engaged in a bitter personal feud with Foster. In 1968, following an encouraging signal from Moscow, some initial staff work was done by the Fisher-chaired Committee of Deputies, but the JCS was uneasy about working with this ACDA-led body. In July a DOD group was formed in ISA headed by Morton Halperin. Halperin worked with some ACDA analysts and others in trying to draft a U.S. SALT position that would gain the military's approval. But in acting as essentially an agent for this group, ACDA aroused JCS suspicions, which resurfaced in 1969. A coordinated proposal was produced, which had been processed through the Committee of Deputies and was accepted by both the Committee of Principals and President Johnson, but talks were postponed when the Soviets invaded Czechoslovakia.[14]

1969–1977

ACDA AND THE NIXON–FORD NSC SYSTEM

As originally envisaged in 1969, the Nixon NSC system was to be considerably more regularized and systematized than the Kennedy-

Johnson systems. More actors were to be brought into the decision-making process through an elaborate system of senior NSC committees, all but one of which were chaired by Assistant for National Security Affairs Henry Kissinger. Major policy decisions were generally to be preceded by the issuance of a National Security Study Memorandum (NSSM), which would incorporate departmental inputs and be so structured as to present the President with a choice of policy options from which to choose. If the President decided to elect an option his decision was to be announced via a National Security Decision Memorandum (NSDM).[15]

In 1969 and, to some extent, 1970 the system functioned roughly as designed. By late 1970, however, Nixon and Kissinger often disregarded advice from below, and some decisions were kept from other senior officials. In so doing, the 1969 announced objective of ensuring a full and open hearing for a variety of views and options was undermined. Nonetheless, the proliferation of fixed-membership coordinating committees was a definite improvement for ACDA over the abolished Committee of Principals. ACDA's attendance at such committee meetings meant that its overall hearing on many issues, certainly at lower levels, improved. A more structured system also encouraged congressional committees to query Kissinger or Smith—"was ACDA present at this meeting?" ACDA and others had great difficulty obtaining an adequate high-level hearing throughout much of this period, but without membership on key NSC committees and participation in the production of NSSMs and other NSC studies ACDA's situation would have been far worse.

At first the NSC met frequently—thirty-seven times in 1969. But in 1971 it met only fifteen times, and by Nixon's last year in office it convened infrequently. When arms control was discussed, ACDA's Director and, usually, Deputy Director were in attendance. The NSC was not a decision-making body. Indeed, at times Nixon and Kissinger made their decision even before it met. Rather, its meetings tended to be pro forma. It discussed issues already thrashed out at lower levels, it was used to give consensus and legitimacy to particularly difficult decisions, and it was occasionally a court of appeal in a Kissinger-dominated system.

During the first Nixon administration, apart from Kissinger, there were two principal SALT foci within the White House staff. One was Helmut Sonnenfeldt and his assistant, William Hyland. Sonnenfeldt was very close to Kissinger and handled day-to-day SALT matters, including cables to the delegation. In this capacity he often worked closely with ACDA Deputy Director Philip Farley, who chaired the SALT Backstopping Committee.

The other SALT focus was the NSC's Program Analysis staff, most of whose members had systems analytical backgrounds. It conducted analyses for Kissinger and coordinated interdepartmental SALT studies. One member of this staff commented that "Sonnenfeldt was even more conservative than Kissinger, and he had a negative attitude towards AC-DA. . . . Everyone in Program Analysis [except one] thought the Safeguard ABM was ridiculous. . . . We didn't have the ideological baggage of a Sonnenfeldt and came to a position on the basis of 'hard' analysis; hence, we were sometimes called 'liberal.' '' By at least early 1971 virtually all SALT-related studies requested by the Program Analysis staff went out to both OSD and ACDA. Usually they would go through three or four drafts and be monitored by the NSC staff, often in coordination with the working group of the Verification Panel.

The Verification Panel was the senior NSC coordinating committee for SALT and some other arms control issues. It was chaired until November 1975 by Kissinger, and its regular membership included the Under Secretary of State, Deputy Secretary of Defense, Chairman of the JCS, Director for Central Intelligence, the ACDA Director and, during the first Nixon administration, the Attorney General. The membership of its working group roughly paralleled that of the senior committee but at a lower level, and it was chaired by an NSC staffer. ACDA's working group representative at the time was Spurgeon Keeny, though Farley also frequently attended; both were active in its deliberations. Keeny met with Kissinger and, occasionally, Nixon. Initially the working group dealt largely with substantive issues—strategic systems, their interactions, and the ramifications of possible negotiating options. But the positions of its members were well known, and its function soon became largely procedural. It critiqued conflicting departmental analyses and reworked them, kept dozens of papers flowing, and set schedules and deadlines for studies.

SALT studies and NSSMs generally went from the working group to the full Verification Panel which, in the words of a participant, "was more substantive and was very much Henry's platform." The panel often met at least two or three times before each SALT I negotiating session and monthly when SALT was in session. Though final decisions were not taken here, it made important changes in policy studies, and debate was lively. From the Verification Panel a study might go to the NSC for pro forma treatment before it went to the President for decision.

The most active committee was the Senior Review Group, which had met 130 times by 1972. ACDA was not a member of this body, but when it considered arms control-related issues—like chemical weapons or the

Conference on Security and Cooperation in Europe—either Smith or Farley was generally in attendance.

During the nineteen months of the second Nixon administration most of the formal NSC mechanisms fell into disuse. A besieged President increasingly conferred only with Kissinger; the NSC was rarely convened; Kissinger's dominance was described by many as virtually monarchial; and even when the Verification Panel did meet, both supporters and opponents of arms control complained that they were denied an adequate hearing. Access to Nixon was virtually impossible. Access to Kissinger was sometimes not much better. From November 1, 1973 to June 1, 1974, Kissinger was out of the country eighty-eight days.[16] Senior Pentagon officials fared little better than Fred Iklé in seeing Kissinger during this time, and important arms control matters were neglected. Iklé's frustration is captured in his testimony before the Commission on the Organization of the Government for the Conduct of Foreign Policy (Murphy Commission), where he noted, despite the ACD Act's injunction that ACDA's Director be "the principal adviser" to the President and the Secretary of State on arms control, and despite President Kennedy's 1962 executive order affirming this:

> In actual practice over the years . . . the role of ACDA has become diluted to a significant extent, accompanied by a marked increase in the number and level of officers in other agencies charged with arms control responsibilities. . . . The result has been for the President, the Secretary of State and other concerned officials to look to their own staffs for their primary advice on arms control, while looking to ACDA for research and analysis and more general services.[17]

The principal targets of Iklé's criticism were, of course, Kissinger and the greatly expanded arms control role of the State Department after he became Secretary of State. Kissinger retained his NSC position until November 1975, but primacy was given to his secretarial responsibilities. Brent Scowcroft directed the NSC staff and, in November 1975, became President Ford's Assistant for National Security Affairs. But the locus of power shifted to State. The NSC staff never regained its former authority.

In the first twenty-one months of the Ford administration the NSC met thirty-one times, and thirty-five new NSSMs were issued.[18] Access to the President was easier, and Kissinger's unique SALT dominance ended in 1975. But while the Verification Panel's working group remained fairly active, the senior group and other NSC committees met infrequently throughout the September 1973–January 1977 period. When the panel did meet, Iklé and Lehman attended. Several senior officials complained that the Verification Panel's inactivity adversely affected both SALT and MBFR coordination. An ACDA official in November 1976 summarized this view: "The entire arms control process has become very ad hoc. There has been a systemic problem: no central management of national security; it's fragmented."

SALT

The origins of the Verification Panel go back to ACDA's problems with NSSM-28 in 1969. Early that year an interagency SALT group was formed, chaired by Farley. Much of its work was done by analysts who had participated in the Johnson administration's August 1968 proposal. ACDA urged rapid movement lest delay foreclose such possible measures as a MIRV test ban. But Nixon and Kissinger had no commitment to past proposals or those officials associated with them, nor were they inclined to proceed hastily before conducting their own studies. NSSM-3 examined overall U.S. strategic posture, and, in March, NSSM-28 authorized ACDA to initiate SALT preparations and chair all interdepartmental working groups. But, as we have seen, the Pentagon refused to cooperate with a SALT process led by arms controllers. ACDA was powerless to move the process along, and this came to a head at an NSC meeting in June 1969, where JCS Chairman Earle Wheeler castigated ACDA for the quality of a study's verification analysis. Stalemated, Gerard Smith suggested on June 30 that, in light of General Wheeler's position, a high-level Verification Panel be created. Kissinger quickly accepted the idea and used the Panel to consolidate his control over SALT.[19]

Kissinger's SALT control was nearly total until 1975. He and Nixon regularly held certain SALT matters very closely, and even senior officials were cut out of crucial "backchannel" discussions between Kissinger and Soviet officials. For example, Smith was not consulted beforehand about the announced May 1971 breakthrough in the SALT I negotiations, and key sections of the May 1972 Interim Agreement apparently had not been fully considered by other senior officials. Concerning the Interim Agreement, Chief of Naval Operations Admiral Elmo Zumwalt later lamented that, although the JCS had technically been consulted about the number of SLBM submarines to be allowed the Soviet Union (62), the JCS did not participate in a meaningful way in that decision.[20] Said one senior ACDA official, "Kissinger had everybody buffaloed. I hope this country never again gets into that kind of jam."

Kissinger's SALT position, though undiminished, came under growing criticism during the second Nixon administration. In 1974 a Sub-committee of the House Armed Services Committee expressed concern about "the amount of restraint exercised by the Secretary over all players," and it worried that "varied input into the policy-making process may . . . be stifled by this control." It also noted that Kissinger's attention to the Middle East "resulted in the absolute grinding to a halt of the [SALT] negotiations."[21] In June 1974, after the JCS refused to support a SALT agreement coupling an extension of the Interim Agreement with limitations on MIRV deployments, Senator Jackson called a closed hearing to inquire into the degree of DOD and JCS participation in SALT matters. The Joint Chiefs made it clear that they had not been fully consulted on several key issues.[22]

Despite Kissinger's style, ACDA had an active SALT role during the 1969–1972 period because of, among other things, Smith's heading the delegation, membership on interagency SALT committees, and, perhaps above all, ACDA's technical and analytical capabilities, which Kissinger and the NSC staff found useful. The Agency had several scientists with years of experience in the area. Its Operations Analysis division was one of the largest systems analysis shops outside the Pentagon. Hence the Agency routinely participated in NSC SALT studies and NSSMs; in its SALT role it eclipsed the State Department, which lacked the analytical resources to compete.[23] Apart from Smith and Farley, ACDA's SALT analyses were directed and rather closely controlled by Spurgeon Keeny and his Science and Technology Bureau. Keeny was sometimes supported by ACDA's Weapons Evaluation and Control Bureau (WEC), but, as a top Keeny aide said, "On SALT you played 100 percent for Keeny or you didn't play."

Though ACDA was more active than State, the two cooperated and were usually allied (often with the CIA) on vital issues. The close ACDA–State association was facilitated by Secretary Rogers's good relationship with Smith, Rogers's support for the SALT activities of State's Politico-Military Affairs Bureau, a general doctrinal harmony on SALT between the two units, and excellent rapport between Smith and State's senior SALT delegation representative, Raymond Garthoff.

In SALT I ACDA and State argued for zero ABMs; both opposed mobilizing U.S. land-based ICBMs; in 1971 ACDA and some in State sought unsuccessfully to gain the inclusion of forward-based nuclear systems in SALT; and, joined by the CIA, they argued for a broad-scoped accord and against exotic ABM systems. In 1969 and early 1970 ACDA unsuccessfully sought a ban or at least a moratorium on MIRV flight testing. And ACDA not only favored including SLBMs in the Interim

Agreement but, initially, wanted to freeze the number of Russian SLBM submarines at a level less than our forty-one.[24]

Smith often sharply disagreed with Defense Secretary Laird, yet their relationship was generally cordial. But Smith tended to be closer to the JCS than to many in DOD. ACDA (and the CIA) clashed fiercely with DDR&E, which was charged with major SALT responsibility as ISA's influence declined. The JCS never took a SALT initiative as they considered it "inappropriate," as one military officer put it, to do a first draft on an arms control paper. A senior ACDA official commented that "the military knows what war is all about; ironically, some in the JCS thought that certain SALT accords could be in the U.S. interest." This same official colorfully decried the "naive engineers" in DDR&E who "assume that if Moscow isn't structuring its strategic forces like we are there is something fishy and nefarious. They have no political sense."

Following the conclusion of SALT I, until about 1975, ACDA's SALT role declined. After its 1973 "purge" the Agency saw its budget slashed and acquired new leadership, and some top SALT analysts departed. More important, Iklé and several of his senior officials were far more cautious about SALT than either Smith or Kissinger. ACDA increasingly allied with the Pentagon against Kissinger. Hence, in the words of an ACDA official, "since Henry was king at least until Rumsfeld came along, he tended to ignore us."

ACDA's internal organization for SALT (and other functional areas) was altered several times under Iklé, and there was some flux and diversity in SALT responsibility. This was consciously encouraged by Iklé, who ran ACDA's SALT operation much as he had reportedly operated when he was at the Rand Corporation. He preferred exposure to different points of view, even if it caused some confusion about lines of authority. Of course, Iklé and Lehman played the central role and were generally perceived by their associates as well as those outside the Agency as "conservative" on SALT. Several other senior ACDA officials and some working level analysts, all of whom joined the Agency during this period, shared common perceptions that, for example, Kissinger was too eager for a SALT II agreement, that most cruise missiles could not be reliably verified and—partly because of this—should not be candidates for arms control, and that the CIA habitually underestimated Soviet strategic capabilities. Many of the views of this dominant group were, however, challenged by the analyses of others like Sidney Graybeal, who headed the U.S. representatives at the Standing Consultative Commission and also held the title of Special Assistant for SALT. Graybeal's "staff" consisted of one secretary, which severely handicapped his effectiveness.

However, he was frequently supported by James Timbie's Strategic Affairs Division and, at times, by others within the Agency.

In 1975 Kissinger's SALT sovereignty ended with the appointment of long-time Ford confidant Donald Rumsfeld to Defense. James Schlesinger had been able, articulate, and the intellectual equal of Kissinger. But Schlesinger never shared Kissinger's close relationship to Presidents Ford and Nixon. Not only did Rumsfeld enjoy presidential confidence, but as a former Republican politician he was very aware of the upcoming presidential primaries, where Ford's main opponent came from the conservative wing of the party. There were many, apparently including Kissinger, who felt that, between December 1975 and February 1976, the United States might have had a SALT II accord if Ford had not been concerned about possible conservative criticism that he had "overruled Defense on SALT." Ford, of course, did not move to negotiate a new treaty. When Ronald Reagan did make SALT a political issue in the primaries, Kissinger's position was further weakened.[25]

As Kissinger's hold slackened, ACDA and others became more active. By this time ACDA's 1973 budget cut had been restored, and its personnel situation had stabilized. Relations with State remained poor, but Iklé was on cordial terms with several high-ranking Pentagon SALT officials, and ACDA's frequent alliance with the military reinforced the anti-Kissinger SALT group. One effect, in retrospect, of ACDA's SALT posture was to help kill a SALT II agreement in the Ford administration. ACDA's stance, though, was only one factor—and probably a relatively minor one—in this outcome.[26]

In 1977 Warnke assumed his place on the formal committees of the new Carter NSC system. He attended NSC meetings and meetings of the new Special Coordinating Committee when SALT matters were discussed, while other ACDA officers were represented on this latter committee's SALT working group. ACDA continued to chair the interagency SALT Backstopping Committee and the U.S. Commissioner on the Standing Consultative Commission remained an ACDA official. More important, Warnke appeared in 1977 to enjoy good working relations with two major SALT principals below the President, Secretary of Defense Harold Brown and Secretary of State Cyrus Vance.

NUCLEAR NON-PROLIFERATION

Following the Senate's ratification of the Non-Proliferation Treaty (1970), virtually no high-level attention was given to the problem of nuclear proliferation until 1974. President Ford did not really concentrate on it until 1976. Throughout much of this period SALT dominated the arms control bureaucracy and claimed much of Kissinger's time. Smith, too, being chief U.S. SALT negotiator, could devote little attention to other matters. Hence, even within ACDA, nuclear proliferation was the preserve of lower-level officials. Apart from SALT, Kissinger had numerous other concerns, and his consequent inattention to nuclear proliferation meant that this vital policy area drifted. But like a minefield in a shipping lane, it was bound to cause an explosion.

Farley did not aggressively press the urgency of nonproliferation issues with Kissinger; he did question the wisdom of relying on private corporations rather than the government for uranium enrichment activities, only to be told that the Nixon administration had already decided to use private firms (a decision later to be widely regretted). Also, tightening procedures for international control over nuclear exports necessitated some hard bargaining with European allies, especially West Germany and France, and Kissinger was apparently reluctant to strain relations over the issue. In 1971 ACDA examined the possibility of extending the concept of regional nuclear-weapon-free zones beyond that delineated in the Treaty of Tlatelolco (for Latin America) to other populated areas of the world. But there was little interest in this either at high levels or in other departments.[27] Before Iklé, two senior ACDA analysts were almost alone in the nuclear proliferation field, though their work later proved invaluable when proliferation became a lively issue in 1974. These two analysts played a prominent role in a 1972 NSSM concerning nuclear proliferation. It resulted in a NSDM that largely incorporated their proposals, especially concerning the need for a nuclear suppliers' conference. Implementation of this NSDM, however, was stalled by key officers in the AEC and State, and a suppliers' conference was postponed until the Ford administration.

The inevitable explosion literally came with India's nuclear test in May 1974. This evoked widespread congressional concern and press commentary. The very next month President Nixon announced that the United States would conclude agreements with Egypt and Israel for nuclear cooperation and construction of nuclear power plants. These two events prompted congressional hearings, which resulted in important nuclear proliferation legislation by late 1974.

In public testimony that year Iklé failed to allay congressional concern that key agencies had been excluded from the U.S. agreements with Egypt and Israel. He said it was a joint interdepartmental decision and that ACDA was involved in working out the safeguard provisions. But

Iklé avoided saying that he had personally endorsed the decision and admitted that it had not met a crucial ACDA criterion for U.S. nuclear exports: that recipient countries be located in a region free from latent or actual hostilities. In fact, the decision was made exclusively by Nixon and Kissinger. ACDA was not meaningfully consulted, nor, apparently, was DOD or the AEC. Indeed, Iklé believed that Egypt and Israel should at least have been required first to sign the Non-Proliferation Treaty. Despite the congressional furor, Kissinger did not give much personal attention to nuclear proliferation until several months after the Indian explosion. Senator Abraham Ribicoff (D–Conn.) later complained that it was not until his March 9, 1976, testimony before the Senator's Government Operations Committee that Kissinger even made a statement devoted entirely to nuclear proliferation. And President Ford's important October 1976 policy statement was the first presidential declaration exclusively concerned with nuclear proliferation since Nixon's brief statement accompanying his 1969 submission of the Non-Proliferation Treaty for Senate ratification.[28]

From 1974 to 1976 ACDA goaded the executive branch into giving priority attention to nuclear proliferation. ACDA had primacy here in two senses: It was a catalyst for action, and its analytical expertise was unsurpassed. But in a deeper policy sense ACDA was not, and never can be, the leading actor. That distinction always goes to more senior departments, in this instance, State. Still, ACDA contributed importantly to American nonproliferation efforts. It had central authority for preparing the U.S. position at the Non-Proliferation Treaty Review Conference (1975) and coordinated some significant interagency studies. ACDA was fully involved at all levels in the comprehensive Fri Report, which formed the basis of Ford's October 1976 policy pronouncement. The report was the product of an NSC ordered study headed by ERDA's Deputy Administrator, Robert Fri. It focused in large part on domestic nuclear activities, many of which had international implications, and this was the first time the domestic nuclear fuel cycle people in ERDA conferred meaningfully in this area with those, like ACDA, concerned with global proliferation. The final product reflected many ACDA positions, including opposition to U.S. and foreign commercial nuclear reprocessing plants. The Agency also acquired, with support from Congress and the White House, some jurisdiction in certain domestic nuclear activities.

Several factors combined to permit ACDA to play a significant role.

1. A series of events highlighted the threat of nuclear proliferation to international security. In the two years following the 1974 Indian blast and the U.S.–Egypt and U.S.–Israel nuclear agreements, Kissinger's se-

cret promise (neither Iklé nor Schlesinger was consulted) to transfer the nuclear-capable Pershing missile to Israel was aborted when it became public; Pakistan, South Korea, Taiwan, and South Africa moved closer to a nuclear weapons capability; the nuclear "deal of the century," with profound implications for future nonproliferation efforts, was concluded between West Germany and Brazil; and defective American and international safeguard procedures heightened prospects for illicit diversion of fissionable material to foreign countries and terrorist organizations.

2. These events alarmed Congress. Numerous hearings were held, and important legislation was passed (see Chapter 13). Said one ACDA analyst, "More than anything else, congressional interest helps ACDA. This 'noise' gives us leverage we otherwise wouldn't have. We can now say, 'Look, we know there are problems with this position but Congress is forcing our hand.'" And by 1976 candidate Jimmy Carter had made U.S. nonproliferation policy a campaign issue, which gave it special urgency to the Ford administration.

3. Kissinger and the President, albeit belatedly, turned their personal attention to the matter. They ultimately elected many of the ACDA-supported options. Iklé's poor personal relationship with Kissinger was a liability, but the two did meet often on nonproliferation issues.

4. Iklé—who possessed acknowledged expertise in the area—was supported by a small but outstanding group of ACDA analysts, one of whom was widely considered the government's foremost authority on nuclear nonproliferation. Equally important, the working-level analysts had good personal relations with their counterparts in other departments, substantially offsetting Iklé's difficulty in this regard.

5. Except for ERDA and one State Department office, ACDA's efforts did not jeopardize departmental missions or budgets. Image problems were therefore minimal. "To oppose U.S. antiproliferation efforts is like opposing motherhood," said a Pentagon official. With the looming threat of nuclear proliferation, ERDA's congressional support dwindled, as did its bargaining position within the executive branch. Effective January 1975 the AEC was split into the ERDA and the Nuclear Regulatory Commission (NRC). ERDA was subjected to restrictive legislation, and Congress later even abolished the AEC's perennial patron, the Joint Committee on Atomic Energy. DOD remained neutral, and both Kissinger and Ford rejected key ERDA recommendations, including its support for U.S. nuclear reprocessing facilities.

6. Fred Iklé was an aggressive, even abrasive, advocate who was convinced that nuclear proliferation demanded immediate attention. He hounded senior officials. When they delayed concentrating on the problem he went public to sound the alarm. Even his harshest critics praised

his efforts here and agree that he was instrumental in compelling the executive branch to take the problem seriously. Many believed it was too late to retard the spread of nuclear weapons, but Iklé and his analysts were convinced that much could be done at least to mitigate the danger and that, at any rate, the U.S. must make the attempt. Also, the Agency's internal differences on SALT did not spill over into this field. As a Kissinger staffer remarked, "This is the one area where ACDA's liberals and conservatives can work together."

7. Throughout the Ford administration ACDA chaired the ad hoc Nuclear Proliferation Backstopping Committee, the main interagency coordinating body, and the Agency participated in all other inter-departmental groups dealing with the issue. The NSC staff, ERDA, CIA, ISA, JCS, and several State Department offices were also represented on the Backstopping Committee. While a Kissinger staffer characterized ACDA's chairmanship of this committee as "a sop to ACDA; the real policy action is with State"—it did meet often and performed a useful coordinating function at a time when the formal NSC system had fallen into disuse.

Before 1976 ACDA was largely excluded by the AEC/ERDA from American commercial nuclear export policy. In October 1975, after de-tailing ACDA's struggle to move into this area, a senior ACDA official said, "ERDA 'goes bananas' here. We need a formalized role via legislation to get in." Since the Atoms for Peace era under Eisenhower the AEC had been the most enthusiastic supporter of an expansive nuclear export program and had successfully resisted ACDA's attempts to link that program more closely with U.S. nonproliferation policy and interests. ACDA often experienced difficulty obtaining adequate and timely data on U.S. nuclear exports. Dixie Lee Ray, AEC Commissioner in 1973 and 1974, and then Assistant Secretary of State for Oceans and International Environmental and Scientific Affairs (OES) until June 1975, accused ACDA of "meddling in areas where they don't belong. . . . They're try-ing to cover up their ineffectiveness in controlling conventional arms. It's conventional arms that are killing people not nuclear exports."[29]

Primary responsibility for licensing exports of nuclear materials and equipment, along with related regulatory activities, was transferred from the defunct AEC to the new NRC by the Energy Reorganization Act of 1974. Executive branch procedures for implementing this legislation were detailed in President Ford's February 1976 executive order.[30] The NRC owed its existence partly to a congressional perception that the AEC had actively pushed nuclear exports without sufficient sensitivity to accompanying risks. Congress therefore made the NRC, as its name indicates, a regulatory commission with considerable legal independence from the executive branch. The commission was vested with authority to approve or deny export licenses—though its decisions could be overridden by the President—as well as to monitor them based on its assessment of their impact on U.S. international security; at the core of this conception of security is an overriding concern about nuclear proliferation. But the NRC never denied a nuclear export license application during the Ford administration. Indeed, except in two instances, involving Spain and India, its five commissioners always unanimously approved such applications. Not until April 1978 did the NRC reject its first nuclear export request (by India). But this decision survived barely a week before being overruled by President Carter.[31]

When the NRC received an application a copy was forwarded to State, which then focused executive branch activity on the matter. Under the Ford executive order State was required to forward a copy to other concerned agencies, including ACDA. Within thirty days ACDA and other departments transmitted their views to State, which then sent the official executive branch position on the matter to the NRC. State dominated the process, though at the staff level the NRC maintained close contact with actors like ACDA. The NRC and ACDA also interacted on a variety of international safeguard issues, and ACDA sat on an interagency committee chaired by the Commerce Department when nuclear exports were discussed.

In the State Department several offices, and in politically sensitive cases even the Secretary, might be involved. OES, especially its Office of Nuclear Energy and Technology Affairs, had primary authority for negotiating U.S. civilian nuclear agreements with recipient nations and principal overall responsibility in the nuclear export area. Many of its officers were former AEC employees who interacted easily with ERDA, the NRC, and private industry. OES, which was worried that the NRC might "interfere" in foreign policy, was especially concerned that the United States honor its commitments to supply nuclear materials to established recipients. In this regard, one State Department officer characterized the OES–ERDA relationship as "a generic one." Another State Department official said:

> If one were to oversimplify, one would be inclined to view OES's driving force as . . . perpetuating America's image as a reliable nuclear supplier almost to the extent that occasionally they appear to be utterly oblivious to U.S. nonproliferation concerns. Obviously, supplier reliability is important, yet it is simply amazing how that office has glossed over details of agreements for cooperation or reactor sales that would have serious consequences for our nonproliferation objectives.

The regional bureaus were involved, and so too, occasionally, was the Policy Planning Staff. Often the regional bureaus tended to assign a higher priority to the maintenance of good diplomatic relations (favoring the application request) than to general nonproliferation objectives. The Politico-Military Affairs Bureau and its Office of Nuclear Policy and Operations were very active in the civilian nuclear area and sometimes allied themselves with ACDA against OES, ERDA, and the regional bureaus.

By 1976 interdepartmental coordination in the nuclear export field had improved, and an NRC official found ACDA to be "a devil's advocate. It's quite active in questioning nuclear export licenses." But ACDA's role was not yet secure, and important problems remained. For example, until April 1976 ERDA did not consult other departments concerning the retransfer of nuclear material from country X, which had an agreement with the United States, to a third party. As late as September 1976 the General Accounting Office (GAO) reported that the NRC was still not "fully involved" in the approval process for such retransfers. ACDA apparently acquired a very modest role in cases of retransfer only by December.[32]

Sweeping legislation was introduced in 1976 which, if enacted, would have given ACDA a specific jurisdictional mandate concerning U.S. nuclear exports. In early 1977 the Carter administration asked Congress to consider legislation that, *inter alia,* contained a statutory requirement forbidding the NRC from granting an export license until the executive branch first certified that its issuance would not be inimical to U.S. security interests. The bill required the participation of State, ACDA, Defense, Commerce, and ERDA in this decision. Then, in March 1978, President Carter signed the Nuclear Nonproliferation Act (PL 94-242), which established ACDA's considerable authority in the nuclear export field. Carter had given early priority to nuclear proliferation and issued an important presidential policy statement in April 1977. Under his administration the State Department retained and probably enhanced its leading role. State chaired the Interagency Group on Nonproliferation and headed the U.S. delegation to the London nuclear suppliers' group meetings.[33]

MUTUAL AND BALANCED FORCE REDUCTIONS (MBFR)

Though there were earlier low-level studies, White House involvement in MBFR was signaled by the issuance of NSSM-92 in April 1970, which examined issues pertaining to possible negotiations for the reduction of forces in Europe. Government MBFR activity increased over the next year and then escalated rapidly following two events in May 1971: Moscow indicated its interest, and Senator Mike Mansfield (D–Mont.) introduced a resolution for the unilateral reduction of U.S. forces in Europe. Official interest in MBFR was roughly proportional to the "Mansfield threat," and an arms control argument (among others) was employed to counter it. The administration asserted that Mansfield's proposal would destroy the prospects for sound, mutual and balanced European arms control. Later, as Mansfield's efforts were beaten back and détente became increasingly strained, little high-level attention was given to MBFR. No senior policymaker was genuinely interested in markedly reducing U.S. forces, and neither Smith nor Iklé was eager for significant MBFR. Hence, MBFR took on a certain histrionic air. ACDA analysts, well aware of this, often remarked that they were shuffling papers merely to give the impression of activity.

Most proposals for more rapid movement came from ACDA, but the Agency tended to share the common consensus that NATO's cohesion should not be jeopardized by sizable U.S. troop reductions. There were differences of opinion within ACDA, but the predominant tone emanating from the Director's office and the Agency's International Relations Bureau, headed and largely staffed by FSOs, was cautious. Interdepartmental differences did arise, but because of shared perceptions and considerable continuity of personnel in this area, they were usually not intense.

Under Smith, ACDA contributed to all interagency MBFR studies, though Melvin Laird was very uneasy about its participation. A senior ACDA official during that period felt that the Agency's voice might have been greater but added, "This is an example of a phony option. Nixon and Kissinger have already decided they don't want force reductions. Therefore, it doesn't really matter *what* ACDA's voice is."

ACDA's formal hearing improved somewhat in 1973 when Iklé, after some bureaucratic jostling, secured ACDA's chairmanship of the MBFR interagency backstopping committee for the negotiations that began that year. The meetings of the backstopping committee and the other interagency MBFR group, the Verification Panel working group, were generally cordial and consensual. The OSD, JCS, State Department, and CIA were also represented on both groups. The backstopping committee supported the U.S. delegation and occasionally performed other functions. For example, although Kissinger was often out of the country from late 1973 to mid-1974, it was essential that NATO present a unified negotiating stance. Since the NSC system broke down in his absence, the ACDA-chaired backstopping committee essentially drafted the U.S. position, in consultation with NATO, which Kissinger subsequently approved. Usually, however, such policy matters were handled by the Verification Panel's working group and the full panel. After Kissinger became Secretary of State the Verification Panel met irregularly, and high-level attention to MBFR was episodic. Under Warnke in 1977 ACDA participated in the MBFR meetings of the Carter NSC's Special Coordinating Committee and its working group. However, there was scant evidence in 1977 or 1978 that Carter intended to give serious consideration to significant MBFR.

CONVENTIONAL ARMS TRANSFERS

From the Eisenhower through the Ford administration the United States was without a global conventional arms transfer policy. The State Department, with primary jurisdiction over military exports, had no clearly delineated foreign policy objectives to guide military sales. Many officials felt (and feel) that a general across-the-board policy would be imprudent and probably infeasible, inasmuch as arms transfers are instruments for implementing U.S. foreign policy vis-à-vis specific nations and regions where circumstances vary considerably. Furthermore, it is argued that arms sales, being an integral component of overall policy toward a nation or region, should not be considered apart from other foreign policy concerns. Not surprisingly, then, the State Department defended its policy authority against outsiders who, it was feared, might be insensitive to larger foreign policy implications.

Within State, the Under Secretary of State for Security Assistance has broad oversight in this area. Two units in the Politico-Military Affairs Bureau—the Office of Munitions Control and the Office of Security Assistance and Sales—have primary responsibility, respectively, for licensing commercial sales and for government-to-government sales and transfers. The regional bureaus, which report to the Under Secretary of State for Political Affairs, play a crucial role. Generally, as the importance of the transfer decision increases, so too does the influence of the regional bureaus and the Under Secretary of State for Political Affairs. As State's usual concern is with a decision's impact on diplomatic relations, there is a distinct bias in favor of arms transfer requests. Internal evaluative criteria exist (can the level of technology be absorbed? too costly? impact on regional stability?), but they are applied flexibly depending upon the perceived significance of the recipient and the region. Intradepartmental differences do, of course, arise, usually between the

Politico-Military Affairs Bureau and the regional bureaus, with the former tending toward more restraint. Of the regional bureaus, an ACDA anaylst remarked, "These guys would give 'their' countries anything they want."

Sometimes the Defense Department does not take a stand on an arms transfer decision either because its senior officials are uninterested and there is a diversity of perspectives at lower levels or because DOD often defers to State, especially when it has a vigorous Secretary. Yet DOD has generally supported an active arms sales policy. Particularly since 1973, though, this stance has been importantly modified regarding: (1) items for sale on our "critical items list," which DOD considers to be in short supply for our own armed forces, and (2) certain technologically advanced items that the military would prefer to keep in U.S. hands, partly for security or technological intelligence reasons.

Several Pentagon offices may participate in arms transfers. They include the Assistant Secretary for ISA, ISA's regional bureaus (which tend to identify with their counterparts in State), and the military services whose professed role is restricted to implementing the policy decisions of others. Most important is the Defense Security Assistance Agency, whose Director is also a top ISA official and thereby has policymaking and policy-implementing responsibilities. This agency manages all U.S. foreign military sales decisions and controls all data relating to matters like the status of arms deliveries, payments, and pending negotiations. Its influence is considerable, particularly when policy guidance is minimal or vague. Both Congress and the executive branch are largely dependent on the Defense Security Assistance Agency for information concerning all but the most politically sensitive foreign military sales.

The President's involvement is usually indirect, for example, via general policy guidance toward a country or region or through involvement in the budgetary process concerning levels of assistance to important recipients. Normally, as a Senate staff study reports, he "does not make decisions on individual sales, or even the total sales level to recipient countries."[34] There are exceptions. President Nixon personally approved key sales to Iran; every recent President gave special attention to Israel's requests; and in 1977 President Carter indicated his intention to be more directly involved in this area.

Where is ACDA? That is precisely what some congressional committees were asking by the mid-1970s. Of four separate studies of the policy process in this area done, respectively, by congressional staffers, the State Department, an independent analyst, and the General Accounting Office, not one even *mentioned* ACDA.[35] Virtually nothing of concrete, lasting value has been accomplished regarding the international control of conventional weapons. The United States has concluded no arms control agreements in this area since before World War II. The bleak prospects for conventional arms control partly explains ACDA's low estate. Agency Directors, before Paul Warnke, were disinclined, unless prodded by Congress, to spend time where there was little likelihood of payoff while more pressing and promising issues abounded, particularly when a more active ACDA role ipso facto meant conflict with the State Department. Although the number of ACDA analysts working on arms transfers increased from just a few in 1969 to eight or ten by 1977, they "work as if the Director doesn't exist," as an analyst said in 1976. Given the dismal outlook for an arms control agreement, except for limited regional naval limitations, ACDA's role—particularly as State sees it—is to urge unilateral U.S. export restraints. When this perception is added to the normal jurisdictional protectionism, the reasons for the ferocity of State's resistance to ACDA become evident.

Congressional concern about U.S. arms sales policy and ACDA's exclusion therefrom, discussed in Chapter 13, is almost solely responsible for whatever role ACDA does enjoy. Especially important were the Foreign Relations Authorization Act (1975) and the International Security Assistance and Arms Export Control Act of 1976, which gave ACDA considerable legal authority. DOD and State, both of which testified against giving ACDA an enhanced voice, resisted the law's implementation. ACDA began, haltingly, to benefit from this legislation only after a protracted struggle.

"Prior to 1975," the head of ACDA's Arms Transfer division testified, "ACDA's involvement in the arms transfer decision-making process was generally limited to the review of selected commercial export licenses and occasional participation in policy studies."[36] Although ACDA's role in the process was formalized when Nixon issued Executive Order 11501 in 1969 directing the Secretaries of State and Defense to consult with ACDA's Director concerning foreign military sales, this had little practical effect. The FSO who headed the Arms Transfer Division for much of the first Nixon administration belittled this directive's impact. He seemed resigned to playing a tertiary role. ACDA did sit on the interagency Security Assistance Program Review Committee, which was established in 1971 to help State in the preparation of annual security assistance programs, but this was no substitute for daily involvement in the substance of policy. ACDA was regularly excluded from fairly routine decisions let alone such politically sensitive transactions as Nixon's promise in 1972 to sell the F-14 to the Shah of Iran. Most of the bureaucracy was excluded from this latter deal, thereby exempting Iran from the usual decision-making process. Philip Farley testified that during the Nixon administration ACDA lacked "any significant role" in Persian Gulf arms sales—"there wasn't a bureaucratic process which involved us . . . we did not get into the act."[37]

By 1975, as legislation was emerging to bolster ACDA's role, State was suddenly more forthcoming. That spring it established a special board with ACDA membership. Later, however, when the legislation appeared to be in trouble, State abolished the board. Still, slight improvement was recorded in 1975. ACDA acquired membership on DOD's Defense Security Assistance Council; it had a modest part in some interagency NSC studies; and it was more regularly consulted by State regarding commercial export licenses. During the first six months of 1975 ACDA commented on 330 specific arms sales requests from foreign governments; prior to 1975 the Agency had rarely commented on more than three hundred in an entire year.[38] But two months after the Foreign Relations Authorization Act was signed into law in November, a senior ACDA official said that it was "being blatantly violated by State, especially the regional bureaus. They simply will not cut ACDA in on essential information." At the core of the problem was the inaccessibility of crucial data, a subject addressed in the next chapter.

In the spring of 1976, as yet another piece of legislation upgrading ACDA's role was in the offing, the Agency experienced the first significant improvement in its hearing on conventional arms transfer decisions. Information flow increased somewhat, and ACDA officers attended relevant meetings of the regional Assistant Secretaries. Still, ACDA often was not consulted until it was too late to make a difference; it was left out of several important transactions; and it continued to be excluded from much significant cable traffic and other vital information. Later that year John Lehman predicted: "The current restructuring may turn out to be only a façade and may not be adequate."[39]

The restructuring Lehman referred to had occurred in February 1976, when ACDA and State negotiated a "treaty" that took the form of a memorandum issued by the Under Secretary of State for Security Assistance implementing the 1975 legislation. It directed full and timely State Department cooperation with ACDA in all significant arms transfers. But Lehman's skepticism was justified. Another memorandum had to be issued in June pointedly stating that "compliance with the spirit of the new legislation requires that ACDA be involved . . . at the earliest possible moment in the decision-making process. . . . I again urge all concerned to be mindful of ACDA's legitimate interests."[40]

But full compliance was still not forthcoming. Between October 1976 and late January 1977 the State Department's Inspector General of Foreign Assistance investigated the problem. At the request of House International Relations Committee Chairman Clement Zablocki (D–Wis.), this unusually revealing document was declassified. Predictably, it found ACDA to be an "outsider" suffering from "an aura of impotency" in the arms transfer area: "It has been viewed, sometimes correctly, as merely a 'nay sayer' and therefore, if it was not 'unwanted' by policymakers, it has at least been 'unused.'" The report strongly recommended a presidential policy statement "affirming the significant role of ACDA in security assistance and reflecting recent legislation, while stressing the President's intention to make maximum use of ACDA opinions." It found that:

> Although possessed of a large staff of highly qualified personnel, ACDA, as the agency within the executive branch charged with imparting its views on arms control, has no precise point for rendering its opinion on arms transfer matters. Although ACDA is given a formal opportunity to respond to some individual transaction requests, and although it is given an opportunity to participate in the SAPRC [Security Assistance Program Review Committee] meetings, there is no regular forum at which ACDA can present its positions on all those transactions that it deems important from an arms control standpoint. . . . [T]his deficiency is so basic that ACDA and State have, on occasion, appeared before a committee of Congress without knowing the nature of the other's testimony. We believe there is a decided need to provide ACDA with an opportunity to express its views—as an integral partner in the policymaking format—on both individual transactions or country programs and on overall arms transfer policy. . . .
>
> Although the legislative mandates and delegations of authority clearly explain what ACDA should do within this operational framework, . . . ACDA has not been treated as a vital element in the arms transfer policy process. . . .
>
> Despite progressively greater opportunity and authority for ACDA participation in the arms transfer processes . . . we found clear indications that ACDA is not always, in fact, (1) regularly consulted on arms transfer matters, (2) able to provide its opinions prior to final decisions being made, and (3) viewed as an integral party in the arms policy arena. . . . We do not believe this problem can be resolved through reorganization; instead it should be met by a clarification of the role that ACDA will play.[41]

These findings were elaborately detailed. For instance, concerning commercial sales, the Office of Munitions Control was found to be in direct violation of the February memorandum. As for foreign military cash sales, that memorandum's stipulations, said the report, were "not being met" by the Office of Security Assistance and Sales.[42]

In January, as the Inspector General was concluding his study, President Ford issued an executive order implementing the Arms Export Control Act of 1976, which, among other things, required the executive branch to prepare "arms control impact statements" for Congress to accompany major overseas arms sales. Ford directed ACDA and OSD to assist in their preparation and further directed State and Defense to consult with ACDA on arms transfers.[43]

When President Carter moved into the White House and declared his personal interest in U.S. arms sales policy, it appeared that State was finally affording ACDA a decent hearing. Warnke reported in 1977 that ACDA now annually reviewed 1,000-plus proposed transfers, a sharp increase over the prior year. Said Warnke, "[A]s a result of the amendments to the law adopted in 1975, we are now included in *all* arms transfer decisions, and we . . . are taken more seriously. . . . [O]ur views are now presented as an integral part of the formal and informal executive branch decisionmaking processes."[44]

This came only after presidential and senior State Department intervention plus persistent congressional prodding with the implicit threat of even more legislation. While marked improvement did occur in 1977–1978, it should not be assumed that the problem will vanish.[45] Arms sales policy remains, and is still considered to be, uniquely State's. Whether the "outsider" will improve or even retain its present role in future years is uncertain. At a minimum, continued executive–legislative monitoring will be required.

OTHER ARMS CONTROL ACTIVITIES

In 1969 Melvin Laird, for whatever reason, took an interest in limiting chemical and biological weapons. He supported the issuance of NSSM-59 that year, which examined U.S. policy options on the subject. As part of this interagency process, Laird ordered his own ISA to prepare a review independently of a parallel JCS study. While the JCS opposed limitations, the final ISA report was highly critical of the battlefield utility of biological weapons. Laird supported the ISA position.

NSSM-59 was handled in precisely the way the Nixon NSC system was originally designed to function. Parts of the study were parceled out to relevant agencies. It was coordinated by a lower-level NSC working group. It was shepherded along by NSC staffers, who were present at working group sessions. The group's report was considered by the Kissinger-chaired NSC Review Group in October 1969. On November 18 the full NSC (including ACDA) met and recommended, with only General Earle Wheeler dissenting, that the United States move to eliminate existing stockpiles of biological weapons and ban military research and development in that area. President Nixon elected this option and issued a NSDM to this effect on November 25. The United States, the Soviet Union, and other nations signed the Biological Warfare Convention in 1972. The formal NSSM process, with its requirement that the President be given options, meant that ACDA and others had a full hearing. This was quite a change from the Johnson administration, where the military was able to bottle up this issue. With NSSM-59, ACDA and others were *expected* to express their views. These views were then reflected in the options presented for presidential decision.[46]

A comprehensive nuclear test ban was never a live issue during this period. An NSSM issued on the subject in the first Nixon administration was mostly a technical instead of a policy review. Nixon decided not to depart from existing policy, and Ford gave ACDA no reason to expect a better reception.

However, as early as the Johnson administration ACDA had suggested approaching the Soviet Union about negotiating a ceiling or "threshold" for the permissible yields of underground nuclear explosions. The Agency was rebuffed by senior officials. During the first Nixon administration some ACDA consideration was again given to a threshold test ban as well as to the idea of having "diminishing quotas" of tests. But a threshold test ban was seriously considered only by early 1974, after Moscow indicated its interest. Shortly thereafter an American technical team, with ACDA analysts, went to Moscow, where discussions progressed so rapidly that it was asked to stay on. ACDA's analyses were used by Kissinger to counter AEC–Pentagon opposition. ACDA's Robert Buchheim chaired the interagency coordinating committee for the Threshold Test Ban Treaty (1974) and the follow-on Peaceful Nuclear Explosion Treaty (1976).

Most ACDA people would have preferred a comprehensive test ban but supported the threshold concept as the only politically and bureaucratically feasible alternative. One ACDA officer—after listing his reservations about the high 150-kiloton threshold, difficulties of verification, and dangers of permitting peaceful nuclear explosions—said, "Still, the bureaucracy, especially Defense, has to be *led* to arms control step-by-step. This is better than no agreement and is a possible step toward a

comprehensive ban.'' Iklé had backed the threshold approach, but his
support apparently cooled after Kissinger negotiated such a high threshold
without consulting him. Again ACDA was excluded from high-level
deliberations. As an NSC staffer stated, ''Iklé had no choice but to accept
this [150-kiloton] level.'' But the Pentagon and the AEC were even less
pleased than ACDA with an outcome which they viewed as jeopardizing
nuclear weapons development and modernization.[47]

In other arms control-related areas ACDA's involvement ranged from
limited (terrorism, strategic doctrine) to substantial. ACDA generally had
an adequate hearing concerning possible arms control measures for the
Indian Ocean region, though it was a matter that elicited little interest at
senior levels, and ACDA had not been informed of NSC deliberations
during the Indo-Pakistan war of 1971. Prompted by congressional interest, a major NSC study on possible naval limitations agreements in this
region was concluded in the spring of 1976, but the consensus view,
shared by Iklé, was that the timing was inappropriate considering recent
Soviet incursions into Africa. Later that year Congress passed the International Security Assistance and Arms Export Control Act, which requested
the President to begin negotiations with the Soviet Union on limiting
forces in the Indian Ocean area; these negotiations were initiated in 1977
by President Carter.

At the July 1974 Moscow summit meeting Nixon and Leonid
Brezhnev announced that bilateral talks would be convened on the limitation of environmental modification techniques for military purposes. Although ACDA had participated in a 1971 interagency study on the military implications of weather modification, prior to the summit conference
the Agency had been largely excluded from this area. Subsequently,
ACDA became a full participant, and Agency representatives took a
leading role in the 1974–1975 technical discussions with the Soviets and
in the 1976 multilateral negotiations at the CCD in Geneva. The entire
process within the U.S. government was generally handled at a low level.
Many doubted that the environment could be effectively utilized for military purposes, hence an environmental modification ban was not threatening to the Pentagon. Working-level ACDA analysts, with some allies in
State, made a strong analytical case for a comprehensive ban on all
environmental warfare applications. But the Pentagon opposed a comprehensive ban, and ACDA's leadership was either unwilling or unable to
circumvent DOD resistance. An ACDA analyst remarked, ''Iklé was not
about to 'go to the mat' on this one. A compromise was reached partly to
bring peace with DOD, partly because some ACDA officials were pessimistic that even the few allowable areas of activity would ever amount

to much in practice.'' So the agreement signed in May 1977 forbade (Article I) only the hostile use of those environmental modification techniques that have "widespread, long lasting or severe effects."

Weapons Acquisition

Few things more fundamentally affect arms control than the U.S. weapons acquisition process, yet ACDA has always been either wholly or substantially excluded from that process. The military services jealously guard their sovereignty over this most critical budgetary area and fend off not only arms controllers but other civilians as well. ACDA's exclusion is reflective of a much larger problem: Even very senior officials and Congress have grave difficulty controlling, or even understanding, the weapons acquisition process.[48] The substantial autonomy of this process from the rest of government stands in sharp contrast to arms control proposals from ACDA (or anyone else), which, as a senior ACDA official remarked, "are cleared to death." Until key weapons decisions are given similarly rigorous political scrutiny, many American arms control efforts will be seriously deficient.

One of ACDA's most persistent problems, as will be seen in Chapters 7 and 14, has been obtaining essential data about U.S. defense programs. During the McNamara years ACDA had no impact on the defense budgetary process. It did not even receive a copy of the Draft Presidential Memoranda, let alone comment on these major defense planning documents. When the Agency learned of a new weapons development bearing upon arms control, it was usually, as Adrian Fisher said, "by the grapevine."[49] By the time of the Nixon administration the existence of SALT, MBFR, and chemical–biological weapons negotiations meant that some defense program decisions invariably intersected with these ongoing arms control activities, and the two had to be taken together. But there was no systematic arrangement for consistently integrating arms control and weapons program decisions. ACDA has never had any say in weapons Program Decision Memoranda; legislation passed in 1975, as we shall see, failed (certainly until 1977) to secure ACDA a voice; the NSC's Defense Program Review Committee (DPRC), established by Kissinger to relate the defense budget more systematically to larger foreign and domestic policy considerations, was stymied by Laird; and the Verification Panel, while it did afford ACDA a previously unknown opportunity to comment upon some SALT-related systems, usually met far too late in the process to be decisive, besides which much of its discussion focused on tactical negotiating problems rather than long-term ramifcations of key weapons systems, and crucial decisions were made elsewhere.[50]

Although ACDA had examined the arms control implications of the ABM at least as early as 1964, it never participated in the senior-level discussions that preceded McNamara's and Johnson's deployment decisions. The study that led to Nixon's March 1969 decision to request funding for the Safeguard ABM was done by OSD and the White House before the Verification Panel was formed. ACDA saw some of the staff papers, but it had no significant role in the study. However the panel's establishment did give ACDA a chance, for the first time, to have a slight say in some weapons-related issues.[51]

When it was belatedly discovered in 1968–1969 that MIRV deployment had profound arms control implications, it was probably too late to halt the program. ACDA apparently first learned of MIRV in 1964, but the Agency shared McNamara's view that, on balance, MIRV strengthened arms control in that it protected against possible Soviet ABM deployment and provided McNamara with a rationale for not deploying several expensive strategic systems. In 1968, when internal studies highlighted MIRV's threat to SALT, ACDA broke from the otherwise unanimous executive branch MIRV coalition. But even on the eve of MIRV flight tests that year ACDA was more concerned about banning the ABM and decided not to press for a flight test moratorium. Though ACDA's stand against MIRV became more visible in 1969, as did the dangers of its deployment, the time for reversing the momentum soon passed. In 1974 Kissinger lamented, "I would say in retrospect that I wish I had thought through the implications of a MIRVed world more thoughtfully in 1969 and 1970 than I did."[52]

ACDA's role in some other major arms-control-related weapons decisions was even worse. For example, it had no voice in the decision to deploy the Trident submarine; earlier, even key OSD civilian officers had been largely excluded from decisions affecting its design.[53] The Agency was entirely excluded from a say in the development of cruise missiles, and the Army did not consult ACDA before its 1973 decision to produce binary weapons (though Iklé subsequently persuaded Congress to delete funds for their production).[54]

The DPRC, as originally designed, was to be a Kissinger-dominated senior NSC forum for structuring overall defense posture and reviewing major DOD fiscal policies and programs in light of their domestic and international implications. Its membership included the usual national security actors plus the Office of Management and Budget and the Council of Economic Advisers. ACDA was not an official member, but Smith or Farley could usually attend when they considered it necessary, and an ACDA officer regularly attended meetings of the DPRC's working group.

Despite its lofty purpose the committee never functioned as intended. The very notion underlying the DPRC's creation was that the size and nature of the defense budget affect everything from the health of the American economy to diplomatic relations and, therefore, must not be the narrow and exclusive preserve of the Pentagon. Laird successfully challenged this rationale and retained DOD's dominion over "its" budget. Laird went to Nixon and made his opposition to outside interference unmistakably clear. Until Kissinger retreated, Laird refused to cooperate with the DPRC. The NSC staff, working through this committee, was denied requested budgetary data, and DOD even refused to do certain studies assigned by the NSC staff to the DPRC. By late 1970 and early 1971 Laird had prevailed. He could announce to the Senate Armed Services Committee: "The National Security Council does not get into weapons systems and if they ever start getting into weapons systems, that is the time I leave as Secretary of Defense."[55]

After 1971 the DPRC met infrequently and fell into disuse. In its short life the committee did examine the defense budget, as well as other matters, but its examination came too late in the process. The DPRC became in effect a platform for the services to plead for additional funds.[56] The DPRC was officially abolished in 1975. It was replaced in January 1976 by the Defense Review Panel, chaired by Defense Secretary Rumsfeld. The new group met sporadically. In the words of a senior ACDA official, with "the fox watching the chickens" it could hardly play a useful role in defense budgetary reviews.

The DPRC passed into oblivion, but ACDA did gain something of potentially significant value. Partly to support its activities on the committee's working group, ACDA hired its first cost analyst with defense budgetary experience in the fall of 1972. This expertise was later augmented. The Agency could now analyze the cost-effectiveness of those weapons programs which had possible arms control implications. Such analyses could be used by ACDA to strengthen the case for restraint. After the passage of the 1975 legislation requiring "arms control impact statements" to accompany certain requests for appropriations and authorizations for key weapons programs, ACDA sharply increased its analytical capability for reviewing weapons systems. But the problems encountered were substantial. They are more fully discussed in Chapter 14.

7 Access to Information

No BUREAUCRATIC ACTOR can function effectively without adequate access to information germane to its functions. Reasonable men, of course, differ in their conception and definition of "adequate" and "germane"; often at the core of the difference is a struggle to maintain or enlarge one's own jurisdiction and freedom of action while denying entrance to a competitor. Information is the grist of the policy process and can be utilized to influence outcomes. Problems arise and hard bargaining frequently results when a department withholds, partially withholds, or delays submission of information deemed vital by another bureaucratic actor.

ACDA's concerns in this regard are the same as those of other governmental units, but there seems to be a difference of degree. ACDA is small, functions largely in a staff capacity, does not collect the masses of raw data gathered by the senior departmental actors, and is not a member of the intelligence community. Far more than senior actors, ACDA depends upon the cooperation of others to gain access to information.

Since informational concerns permeate the entire policy process, they are discussed in virtually every chapter. The purpose of this chapter is twofold: It sketches an overview of ACDA's experience by summarizing several interrelated factors that have affected the flow of information to the Agency, and it examines ACDA's relationship with the intelligence community.

Factors Affecting Access

Neophytes. ACDA's informational problems were greatest during its first four or five years of existence, when both the Agency and arms control were untested commodities. Resistance from others, particularly

DOD and the AEC, was considerable in some areas, and ACDA had to learn how to operate in uncharted waters. Also, while Adrian Fisher and some others were exceptions, there may have been a certain "siege mentality" that contributed to a reluctance to reach out actively for data. One former ACDA analyst recalled, "At first we didn't actively seek out others in the bureaucracy to really ferret out information. This was probably a function of the newness of the game."

With time the game became familiar. Of course, new people are always coming aboard, and each individual, especially if he lacks government experience, must learn the rules of the game in order to maximize his own access to information held by other agencies. And like all actors, ACDA must decide, when considering whether or not to fight for a particular body of data, if the bureaucratic benefits of making the attempt outweigh the costs.

System. When the policymaking system was structured so as to invite or even require the input of actors like ACDA, information flow increased. The Johnson foreign policy system did not encourage a diversity of inputs, whereas, at least below the highest levels, the early Nixon NSC system did. Thus, for example, under Johnson DOD monopolized information relating to U.S. chemical and biological weapons programs. This practice ended when NSSM-59 was issued in 1969. Members of interdepartmental committees in the Nixon NSC dealing with White House studies had access to data held by other departments. When problems arose the NSC staff would generally pry the information loose.[1]

Congress, too, can be an important factor. The scheduling of a hearing, the hearing itself, a specific query from an individual legislator or congressional staffer, prospective legislation, or the actual passage of legislation can all affect information flow to the Agency. But there are limitations on Congress's leverage. State did not initially comply with the 1975 legislation that required information sharing with ACDA concerning conventional arms transfers, and, certainly through the Ford administration, Defense refused to give ACDA complete and timely access to data bearing upon the U.S. weapons acquisition process, despite the letter and spirit of the 1975 legislation mandating such cooperation. To some extent (depending on many factors), at least with Defense, there sometimes might be a very rough correlation between the extent to which the rules governing information flow are formalized by law and DOD's willingness to free information that it normally holds closely. That is, a legal requirement to forward sensitive data to ACDA may transform what would otherwise be only a potential threat to DOD into a real one, thereby inducing even less cooperation. This is particularly so when, for instance, the law also obligates ACDA to furnish Congress with information about weapons programs that the Agency has received from Defense (see Chapter 14).

Mission and Budget. Noncompliance or perceived noncompliance with the law is serious business, which entails considerable risk. Generally the stakes must be high for a department to elect this course of action, particularly without the tacit support or acquiescence of the President and other senior policymakers. The stakes will seldom be considered so crucial unless the law is thought to threaten a department's essential mission and/or budget; the possibility of punitive sanctions or successful enforcement procedures must also be carefully weighed. State and Defense clearly viewed the 1975 legislation as opening the door to possible ACDA encroachment into their respective preserves.

Law or no law, a department will be more hesitant to release data if it fears this could jeopardize its missions or budget. Additionally, there is frequently a reluctance to share information about planned expenditures and actions.[2] Hence the AEC/ERDA, with special responsibility for testing nuclear explosive devices and (especially before 1975) for U.S. nuclear exports, was always reluctant to release information that might be used by ACDA to challenge these missions. ACDA tried a variety of internal maneuvers, including contacts between its own senior military officers and their military counterparts on assignment to ERDA, but the end result was often continued frustration. ERDA as well as DOD was subject to the 1975 legislation requiring information sharing with ACDA on certain weapons developments and, as in the case of DOD, ERDA's compliance was incomplete. In 1977 an ACDA officer with prime responsibility for such matters said, "It's not just PNE's [peaceful nuclear explosions], it's information across-the-board. They [ERDA] will rarely say 'no,' but will give us bits and pieces and often too late to be of much use."[3]

The State Department has generally been forthcoming. Indeed, State has relied heavily on ACDA for technical expertise and analysis on arms control issues. The chief exceptions concern information that ACDA could conceivably use in a way that might strain diplomatic relations with a particular country or region. With full and timely notice of a proposed arms sale, for example, the Agency would be in a position, should conditions warrant, to advise against it. State's normal disposition is to support arms sale requests and avoid ruffling diplomatic feathers.

Therefore, although ACDA's overall access to information about conventional arms transfers improved by 1977, the State Department's Inspector General could still report early that year, "Bluntly put, ACDA does not receive all the information it requires to make valid judgments and . . . there is no presently viable system to provide ACDA with communications'' essential for making sound assessments of prospective arms transfers. The report stated that, of the 1,718 applications for arms export licenses received by the Office of Munitions Control in the Bureau of Politico-Military Affairs in July 1976, ACDA received only 31; in November 1976 only 55 of 2,218 applications to that office were passed to ACDA. In 1978 Deputy Director Spurgeon Keeny testified: "The one area where there may sometimes be a problem [gaining access to information] is the conventional arms transfer area and possibly technology transfer."[4]

For arms control to be feasible and durable, those charged with analyzing and formulating arms control proposals must have access to U.S. military plans and capabilities, as that information often bears directly upon U.S. arms control policy and negotiations. Hence the withholding of such data by the Pentagon is particularly consequential. While DOD has generally been cooperative concerning present, active arms control negotiations, it often balks at releasing certain data relevant to possible future negotiations and has been especially resistant concerning sensitive defense budgetary matters. Likewise, DOD has closely held information related to current battlefield developments, even though it bears directly upon arms control considerations. For instance, ACDA had no part in executive branch deliberations concerning the military application of weather modification techniques when they were actually being attempted in Southeast Asia.[5]

During ACDA's earliest years DOD would not even disclose such things as the number, purpose, and plans for future use of U.S. military bases.[6] This kind of information was eventually acquired, but ACDA has always encountered problems obtaining complete and timely information about U.S. weapons developments bearing upon arms control, particularly if that information does not relate (or the Pentagon can argue that it does not relate) to current negotiations. Important defense budgetary documents are regularly denied the Agency and other actors as well. For instance, in 1973 an ACDA analyst said he was shocked to discover that the Agency did not have a copy of DOD's Five Year Defense Plan. Before joining ACDA this analyst had had regular access to it. Laird reportedly denied Gerard Smith's request for the document, and the analyst, working through personal contacts, had to go in person to the Pentagon and read it there, as he was not permitted to take a copy out of the building.

Gaining access to data held by DOD concerning weapons programs will be among ACDA's most formidable yet important tasks. In 1975 Iklé frankly admitted that it was "really a problem."[7] Passage of legislation that year to alleviate the difficulty did not have the intended effect until the Carter administration, and even then significant problems remained. A measure of the immensity of the problem confronting ACDA and other interested actors is poignantly described by J. Ronald Fox, former Assistant Secretary of the Army in the Nixon administration. He relates numerous specific instances when even very senior civilian officials in Defense were given misleading or incomplete data—or no information at all—at critical junctures in the development of major weapons programs. For instance, Fox reports that in 1971 Deputy Secretary of Defense David Packard learned that the military had misled him concerning the current status of several major programs. Fox relates that a fellow service Assistant Secretary had remarked, "It was my experience that adequate, reliable information usually did not exist for decision-making on major issues." Fox further states that, "when a military Chief of Staff makes it known that he wants his service to undertake a weapons acquisition program, it is highly unlikely that unfavorable information about that program will ever reach the Secretary of Defense through official channels."[8]

Current Negotiations. When negotiations are actually under way, whether bilaterally with the Soviet Union as with SALT or the Threshold Test Ban or multilaterally as at the CCD, ACDA's access to information directly affecting these negotiations is generally adequate. Occasional disputes still occur, but they are usually manageable. When, for example, is a certain body of data "directly" relevant to the negotiations? The more serious problems arise when ACDA seeks to free sensitive information related to possible future talks, especially when the information sought relates to departmental missions or budgets.

"Technical" Versus "Policy" Information. When discussing adequacy of information flow from other actors during ongoing negotiations, senior ACDA officials during the Nixon and Ford administrations often distinguished between what they called "technical" and "policy" information. Regarding "technical" data (such as finished intelligence on Soviet strategic capabilities or specific information on present U.S. strategic capabilities), problems were minimal. But Kissinger's close-to-the-vest style and penchant for secrecy sometimes meant that ACDA and others were unaware of crucial "policy" decisions and developments. Exclusion from high-level policy matters was most troublesome in the SALT negotiations, but it also occurred in other areas. The usual bureaucratic players did not participate fully in decisions leading to the 1974 civilian nuclear agreements with Egypt and Israel or the massive 1972

arms transaction with Iran. Admiral Zumwalt states that the JCS learned of NSDM-256 (issued on June 11, 1974), which officially sanctioned a threshold test ban accord, only the day before its issuance and after the Russians had been informed of its contents.[9]

Since the opening of SALT negotiations in 1969 the flow of related technical data from the Pentagon and the intelligence community has generally been excellent. For several months following the May 1972 signing of the SALT I accords, the military services did deny ACDA vital information, including documents on the accuracy of U.S. missiles. But when Iklé became Director following the ACDA "purge," the problem virtually disappeared. When difficulties arose the NSC staff generally saw that the information was released. A Nixon administration NSC staffer said, "ACDA had no difficulty getting information from or through the NSC staff, except for very rare and extremely sensitive matters."

The Agency was blocked precisely on these sensitive policy matters, particularly in the Nixon administration. Smith was not told about some of Kissinger's backchannel negotiations with the Soviets or of some other closely held matters. Kissinger's private negotiations with Soviet officials in early 1971, which led to the May breakthrough in the talks, were unknown to Smith, even though his Russian counterpart across the negotiating table was aware of them. Also that spring, before informing his own bureaucracy, Kissinger told Moscow that a SALT I agreement could be concluded with or without the inclusion of SLBMs. When he later posed this issue to members of the Verification Panel they unanimously and vigorously insisted on including SLBMs.[10] Gerard Smith and ranking military officers alike were concerned that Kissinger's secretive *modus operandi* and preference for exclusive control of policy information ran a high risk of bringing about a less than satisfactory SALT agreement. As America's chief formal SALT negotiator, Smith was also personally offended when Kissinger withheld confidential information from him. This contributed importantly to his decision to resign in 1972.

Personal Considerations. To a considerable degree the ease with which informational access to another department is gained varies with the individual. An analyst or officer who has been with his agency for several years, knows his bureaucratic fellows, enjoys harmonious personal relations with them, and, perhaps, shares some of their values will have better luck than one who is new, inexperienced in bureaucratic mores, and personally abrasive. Abrasiveness may be a useful trait, but not for a recently arrived young academic attempting to pry protected information from the Navy.

One's background, style, and rank may be important. A function performed by those active-duty FSOs and military officers assigned to ACDA is to facilitate information flow from State and Defense. ACDA's military officers, for instance, have acquaintances in their respective services and are more likely to have information confided to them than a known or suspected arms controller. How information is sought (tactics) is also important. One ACDA analyst, a retired military officer, reported that he encountered few problems with the Pentagon but added that "some young civilian in the Science and Technology Bureau might be real brash and not get what he wants. Just do it the right way." And the more senior one's rank, the greater the likelihood that he will receive requested information.

Intelligence Community

The CIA's cooperation with ACDA has usually been satisfactory. Throughout most of ACDA's first seventeen years at least one of its higher-ranking officials had previously held a responsible position in the CIA. Moreover, the two agencies were often allied on arms control issues, frequently against Defense and its intelligence units.

Prior to 1966 relations with the Defense Intelligence Agency were stormy. That year Lieutenant General John Davis, U.S. Army, with a long career in intelligence, became the head of ACDA's WEC Bureau. General Davis had the confidence of the Pentagon, and the former difficulties soon diminished to manageable proportions.

ACDA has an intelligence adviser with a one- or two-man staff. He serves as liaison to the intelligence community and may consult with the Director on such matters as conflicting intelligence estimates. Until 1974 the intelligence adviser's formal contact with the community was through State's Intelligence and Research Bureau, though ACDA often dealt directly with individual community members. After severing this State Department tie, ACDA went directly to the CIA, through the Intelligence Community Staff, and to the Defense Intelligence Agency. One ACDA officer reported that while the relationship with the Intelligence and Research Bureau had been satisfactory, there was an improvement when ACDA managed its own access to intelligence, because "the INR people would occasionally squirrel things away."

The intelligence adviser has been selected with an eye toward his personal contacts in the defense intelligence area. Warnke in 1977 named his senior military officer as ACDA's liaison with the intelligence community. For all intelligence produced by DOD, ACDA went through the Defense Intelligence Agency, though that Agency permitted ACDA to use DOD intelligence products only for internal ACDA purposes. When ACDA wanted to employ this information in interagency memoranda, it had first to obtain the Defense Intelligence Agency's approval. This was a bothersome requirement but did not appear to be unduly restrictive in practice.

By the late 1960s, and certainly by the 1970s, there was wide agreement that ACDA had a good working relationship with the intelligence community. Intelligence, that is, information about *foreign* intentions and capabilities, was seldom refused when ACDA had a need to know. A noteworthy exception to this general rule was, however, cited by an ACDA officer with central responsibility for SALT verification:

> By far the biggest problem ACDA had under Iklé concerning SALT verification was getting involved at all in the actual verification process [within the intelligence community]. Iklé launched a gigantic onslaught to get us involved. He saw Colby, Bush, Kissinger, and Scowcroft but was, at best, only modestly successful. Under Iklé, ACDA *was* somewhat involved in such "intelligence" questions as Soviet SALT compliance [through the Standing Consultative Commission, for example], but only over everyone's dead body. The intelligence community . . . believes *it* is responsible for verification . . . But the Arms Control and Disarmament Act gives us authority here too. . . .
>
> There is a special SALT monitoring group under DCI [Director for Central Intelligence]. Until the spring of 1977 four of the five departments concerned with SALT were represented on this group: DOD and JCS (through their intelligence units), State (with INR), and CIA. ACDA was not on this group despite Iklé's protests. CIA's standard response was that ACDA is a "policy agency," not an "intelligence agency" and hence has no right to be on this intelligence group. But isn't State a "policy agency"? . . . This group was responsible for the production of the basic SALT verification report which was about two inches thick. It was this report which Iklé was *never* able to gain access to.
>
> Actually this was far less an information problem than . . . a problem of not being able to be involved in the verification *process*. . . . I suppose if I really wanted to see that report I could have had a buddy [in DOD] show it to me. But it really wasn't all that important—I know what it's going to say anyway. But I wanted it so I could "critique" it. . . .
>
> When Warnke went to Moscow with Vance in the spring [1977],

neither Warnke nor anyone else in ACDA had seen this . . . report. Indeed, at an NSC meeting charts were shown concerning Soviet capabilities and ACDA even then didn't have the supporting evidence which could've only been had from this report.

Then, as PRM 11 [Presidential Review Memorandum concerning the intelligence community] was issued, ACDA wrote a letter to a top CIA officer pointing out that Warnke had not had this information. Anyway, by the early summer all five of the SALT agencies are *now* fully represented on this SALT monitoring group and ACDA now *does* get access to this report. . . .[11] Indeed, we get all finished intelligence. The unfinished stuff is often a problem, but the intelligence community has a right to use discretion here.

⑧ The ACDA – State Department Relationship

ASPECTS OF ACDA'S ASSOCIATION with the State Department are addressed throughout this book. Their legal relationship under the ACD Act was examined in Chapter 2. Here we look at two important features of the relationship: possible alternatives to ACDA's present semi-independent status and personal dealings between the Director and the Secretary of State.

The degree of ACDA's "independence" has varied considerably depending on the Secretary of State's inclination and ability to insist that the Director act under his direction. Secretary Kissinger sought to keep ACDA under tight control, whereas William Rogers gave ACDA extensive autonomy. Neither approach seems wholly desirable. Excessive control might stifle the distinct voice that ACDA must have to execute its mission faithfully. But too much distance between Director and the Secretary jeopardizes coordination.

Both ACDA's Director and the Chairman of the JCS have a legal right to go to the President, but, since McNamara, the Chiefs know that they work under the Secretary of Defense and consult him before seeing the President. Similarly, ACDA's Director usually coordinates his actions closely with the Secretary of State. However, under Secretary Rogers this was not always the case. Gerard Smith was instructed by the White House not to divulge certain important SALT matters to Rogers. This not only placed Smith in an awkward situation but deprived the Secretary of State of information bearing upon one of the most important international negotiations since World War II.

The Director and the Secretary

William Foster and Adrian Fisher had good working relationships with Secretary Rusk. Rusk supported ACDA on the principal arms control agreement of the 1960s—the Non-Proliferation Treaty—despite opposition from his own European Bureau. Later Rusk testified:

> Mr. Foster would normally sit in on my morning staff meetings, even the staff meetings of the half dozen senior officers as well as the larger staff meetings where there would be 30 or 35 officers present. He or his deputy would almost always be at those meetings so that they could be fully abreast of all the gossip that was going on at the top of the Department. . . . Mr. Foster always found my door open. There was never any problem about his seeing me, or if he wanted me to see the President.[1]

Gerard Smith's personal relationship with Secretary Rogers was "exceedingly close."[2] But Rogers was not a strong Secretary of State, which, in addition to other factors, probably contributed to the unusual independence ACDA experienced during the first Nixon administration. It also facilitated Kissinger's dominance of foreign policy. Said one senior official: "It was the weak personality of Rogers which permitted Henry to dominate. If there had been a more normal relationship between the President's Assistant for National Security and the Secretary of State, Kissinger would never have acquired his monopoly position."

Difficulties did arise after September 1973, when Kissinger became Secretary of State. At the Senate hearings on his nomination as Secretary, Senator Edmund Muskie (D–Me.), concerned that ACDA had been "emasculated" in 1973, queried him about the Agency's future. Kissinger, once a consultant to the Agency in 1962–1963, replied that ACDA would be able to present its views "at the highest level. . . . [T]hey will have my full support and they will be actively engaged in the formulation of our position."[3] But although Iklé—whose appointment to the ACDA directorship was personally endorsed by Kissinger—could generally see the Secretary of State when necessary, their relationship was not always congenial.

When Kissinger moved to State his key NSC aides accompanied him. So did the policy "action." State, or more accurately, chosen State Department officers and subunits, enjoyed new life. That was certainly so in the arms control field. SALT continued to be controlled by Kissinger until late 1975. State became far more active in the nuclear proliferation area. The Policy Planning Staff headed by Winston Lord, which at the time had three former ACDA officers, emerged from dormancy to become deeply involved in operations. Helmut Sonnenfeldt and his staff had a crucial role in SALT and MBFR. And the Politico-Military Affairs Bureau's arms control offices increased in size and importance.

Kissinger's style remained constant. He expected others, certainly ACDA, to be responsive to him, especially as he continued to be the President's Assistant for National Security Affairs until the fall of 1975. Shortly after Kissinger became Secretary, a senior ACDA official expressed concern for the Agency's independence saying, only a bit facetiously: "Under Kissinger, ACDA *is* the State Department." Another high-level ACDA officer remarked in the spring of 1974:

> Henry runs a very tight shop and likes to control things—including ACDA. Henry sees ACDA as having two roles: (a) serving State and his staff, which means producing good papers, and, (b) he uses ACDA when he wants added support in bureaucratic politics to back up his position. ACDA *should* serve Henry. In fact, it *must* do so if it is going to have *any* influence at all. This means it can't be a raving and wholly independent advocate.

Kissinger's close control probably contributed to some early tension with Iklé. Friction was clearly evident when, by 1975, Iklé often sided not with Kissinger but with the Pentagon, which now successfully challenged Kissinger on SALT. Some of Iklé's public statements and a clash of personalities further exacerbated the relationship until it became noticeably strained.

Relations between Paul Warnke and Secretary of State Cyrus Vance in the early Carter administration were close and cordial. They maintained open lines of communication with each other, and coordination was not a problem.

Quasi-Independent Status

ACDA's legal mandate is broad but must be exercised within the penumbra of the Secretary of State. ACDA is neither a bureau of State nor entirely independent. The working relationship is such that ACDA does not act mechanically under specific instructions from State. Rather, there is an effort, formally and informally, to coordinate positions.[4] ACDA, then, has a quasi-independent status vis-à-vis State.

Most of the Agency is, however, physically situated in the State Department building. While physical proximity may incline some State

Department officers to see ACDA as just another one of their bureaus, most Agency people consider its location advantageous. It facilitates day-to-day contact as well as access to cable traffic and secure communications. Since the early 1970s a growing number of ACDA employees have been housed on the Virginia side of the Potomac in Rosslyn because of insufficient space at State. This caused considerable inconvenience. One Rosslyn analyst reported that his job efficiency decreased 50 percent, partly because he could no longer go down the hall to speak with others in his functional area. Some Rosslyn analysts during the troubled 1973–1976 period felt they had been sent to that "bureaucratic Siberia" as political punishment for being too liberal. ACDA's leadership denied this, though several natural scientists widely considered strong arms control advocates were transferred to Rosslyn at the time. When Warnke assumed office he acknowledged the complaints and announced that in the future, instead of being functionally divided, entire units would go to Rosslyn. This was expected to mitigate the problem.

The overwhelming majority of ACDA's civilian professionals are content with the Agency's quasi-autonomous status. Alternatives to the existing organizational arrangement are, of course, conceivable. Merging ACDA with DOD has never been seriously considered,[5] but one or two employees expressed a desire for an entirely independent agency. A somewhat larger number—and the Senate Foreign Relations Committee in 1961—urged full integration with State.

COMPLETE INDEPENDENCE?

One of the few ACDA officers advocating complete separation from State asserted that without independence ACDA can only be a staff to others, a "service outfit" condemned to secondary status. He said (in 1975), "[W]e're subservient to State; instead, we should have a strong Director with a direct line to the President." He further argued that Congress's more favorable orientation toward arms control and ACDA would ease the transition and bolster a newly independent agency. His case is not persuasive on three accounts:

1. In one sense the entire executive branch is the President's staff. ACDA serves in a staff capacity for the President as well as for the Secretary of State and the NSC. There is no assurance that autonomy will enlarge ACDA's presidential advisory role. The image problem will not disappear; indeed, it would probably be aggravated by greater apartness from the rest of the national security bureaucracy. The Director should

have a line to the White House, but this depends on the President's disposition, not organizational location.

2. This official's preference for divorce came when Kissinger was Secretary of State. Kissinger held, or attempted to hold, ACDA (and everyone else) in tighter rein than any other Secretary, and even then ACDA assumed a distinctly noncomplaint stance, particularly on SALT. Both political wisdom and the law demand that arms control be an integral part of foreign policy, and it seems appropriate that this be reflected in organizational relationships. When ACDA had unusual autonomy, under Smith, the Secretary of State was sometimes uninformed of crucial developments. Such blatant noncoordination is clearly unhealthy. Also, the physical proximity to State is useful to both ACDA and State.

3. The congressional mood has changed, but has it changed sufficiently to sanction a separate agency, especially when it is unlikely to benefit ACDA? Neither the President nor the Secretaries of State or Defense are likely in the foreseeable future to endorse such a move.

MERGER WITH STATE?

There is some support for merging ACDA with State.[6] Somewhat surprisingly, one of ACDA's most senior officials, but only one, favored merger:

> There's nothing sacred about having an independent ACDA; indeed, the arms control perspective could be just as effective if it was located in State if we had a Secretary of State and a President who were interested in arms control.... A separate ACDA invites intense animosity, more so than if it were a part of an established, "respectable" department.... No other nation, including the Soviet Union, has a separate arms control unit. Their [the Soviet] system works well for them.

Others add that integration would improve coordination and address the situation wherein ACDA, owing to its inherently weak bureaucratic position, has little impact in some areas vitally affecting arms control. I. M. Destler remarks that integrating ACDA with State's Politico-Military Affairs Bureau "might increase, at least potentially, the contribution of ACDA experts to the broad policy issues of weapons system development and general U.S.-Soviet relations, both critical to arms control prospects but both tending to fall outside ACDA's effective influence."[7]

Merger would improve coordination and alleviate the image problem. It would, however, almost certainly dilute the arms control perspective within government and eliminate the several advantages of quasi-independent status. Integration should be rejected by those seeking to augment internal pressure for arms control for these reasons:

1. If the President is not interested in arms control, movement is unlikely regardless of ACDA's location. Should the President be interested while the Secretary of State is reserved or neutral, arms control specialists would not want to be buried in State. But the main argument against merger is that it would, on balance, diminish the priority accorded arms control even if the Secretary *was* supportive. Any Secretary of State must deal daily with many diverse issues; he could not and should not focus too heavily on arms control. The Director, however, does precisely this. Regardless of the Secretary's receptiveness to arms control, the Director can go, and often has gone, elsewhere for allies.

2. There is no evidence that State has been or would be more successful than anyone else in loosening DOD's grip on the weapons acquisition process. At least ACDA, aided by legislation in 1975, began to show an active interest in influencing U.S. weapons development. State has not demonstrated a comparable interest.

3. Even aside from the relative paucity of reliable information about the Soviet foreign policy system, what standard should be used to determine how "well" it operates? One might as easily argue that it appears to exhibit decidedly weak internal forces for arms restraint, which augurs poorly for the Soviet Union's long-term security and economic prosperity as well as for world peace.

Complementing this rebuttal are eight interrelated reasons why a semi-independent ACDA is worth preserving (again, assuming the objective is to strengthen arms control):

1. Two ACDA Directors used the word "catalyst" in defending ACDA's present status. By this, Fred Iklé meant that ACDA keeps "sound arms control ideas moving" and nudges "other agencies to seize opportunities when they arise." For example, Iklé said that ACDA took the initiative in strengthening the "firebreak" (the distinction in war between the use of even the largest conventional weapon and the smallest nuclear weapon) by obtaining an official policy pronouncement that the U.S. would not deploy so-called mininukes (very small-yield nuclear weapons).[8] In the 1960s it was ACDA that first raised the possibility, within government, of having a Non-Proliferation Treaty. ACDA did most of the analytical work for the treaty and was its most ardent proponent. It is possible, especially considering the resistance from State's influential European Bureau, that without ACDA either the treaty would never have materialized or would have come too late to be useful.

2. Iklé also painted ACDA as a "bureaucratically independent conscience." He cited two illustrations. ACDA studies of peaceful nuclear explosive devices demonstrated their extremely limited economic benefits. "Some bureaucrats," said Iklé, "wanted to suppress the findings." Second, Iklé revealed that he resisted "another cover-up attempt" of an ACDA study that indicated that a large-scale nuclear attack could gravely affect the earth's ozone layer with potentially disastrous results for the world's population.[9] ACDA brings continuity to U.S. arms control efforts, and its independent research capability permits it to raise questions that might otherwise be slighted.

3. Integration of ACDA with the State Department would mean one less arms control supporter at NSC meetings and interagency committees. The numerical strength of bureaucratic arms control alliances would diminish.

4. ACDA's distance from State, "the establishment," has probably been a factor in attracting some bright young academics to the Agency. ACDA has one of the highest percentages of Ph.D.s of all government agencies. Though this consideration should not be given undue weight, there is a perception (almost universal among those who have systematically studied it) that the Foreign Service is stodgy and museum-like; that while new ideas are rare in human affairs, they are rarer still in government, and unknown at Foggy Bottom. ACDA's intellectual assets have paid rich dividends. An ACDA scientist stated, "I am unaware of any *conceptual* arms control ideas or *conceptual* arms control initiatives which did not, within government, originate with ACDA." He added, "During the Nixon–Ford era, ACDA did 50–95 percent of the analysis and paper writing on arms control, depending on the issue. The basic role of other agencies, then, was to criticize these papers." A State Department official who had been with the Agency in the 1960s observed:

> One gains a different perspective in ACDA. For example, until the late 1960's the Office of Systems Analysis [in OSD] never really examined U.S./Soviet interaction as it bore on arms control from the *Soviet* perspective. But ACDA *was* doing this and finally was able to plug in this kind of input. That is, there is an intellectual and perceptual argument—as well as the bureaucratic one—for an independent ACDA.

5. Merger would not necessarily ensure the same quality of scientific and technical support that ACDA currently provides State and the NSC. Traditionally, scientists have not fared well in the Foreign Service. A scientific career has been well outside the usual route for career advancement. State has few top scientists. Among those it does have in the arms control area are former ACDA scientists who transferred there either

following the 1973 "purge" of the Agency or because they were offered unusually attractive positions.

6. The institutionalization of arms control in the form of an identifiable and separate organizational entity may, to an extent, be useful in itself. A senior ACDA official with intimate knowledge of all the treaties he referred to said, "There are times when just by being there ACDA—or the CCD [Conference of the Committee on Disarmament] for that matter—creates certain notions that it should be used, though often on less crucial issues. The Seabed Treaty is an excellent example of this, to some extent the Threshold Test Ban Treaty, and—to a lesser extent—the Biological Warfare Convention. The Seabed Treaty and the Biological Warfare Convention also gave the CCD something to do."

7. Elimination of ACDA's independence would be interpreted at home and abroad as a sign of America's retreat from a commitment to arms control. Indeed, Destler cites this as his reason for ultimately advising against merger.[10]

8. Finally, merger with State would meet decisive resistance from Congress. Much of the impetus behind the important changes in ACDA's legal charter in 1975 was the desire to *increase* ACDA's freedom of action vis-à-vis State and Defense. Senator Humphrey articulated this sentiment: "I want its [ACDA's] autonomy to be something more than just symbolic."[11] Hence Congress gave ACDA responsibility for drafting arms control impact statements, the Agency acquired official advisory status on the NSC, and it was charged with playing a greater role in conventional arms transfers. State initially opposed all of these legislative changes.

⑨ Negotiations, Research, and Public Information

ACDA'S OVERRIDING FUNCTION is to see that an arms control perspective is adequately represented in the policy process and that, when advisable and feasible, arms control considerations are integrated into American foreign policy and national security decisions. Distinct from, though variously related to, this primary role in decision-making are three additional functions: negotiating arms control agreements, conducting in-house and sponsored research, and engaging in public affairs activities.

Negotiations

Because of its negotiating responsibilities ACDA has a significant role in the implementation of U.S. arms control policy. Section 2(b) of the ACD Act permits, but does not require, ACDA to prepare and manage U.S. arms control and disarmament negotiations. This is a shared authority, as ACDA acts under the direction of the President and Secretary of State. In practice, ACDA's role in most formal negotiations is substantial.

This seeming territorial infringement on State's natural terrain (negotiations) engenders surprisingly little resentment, partly because ACDA negotiators are often themselves FSOs on assignment to the Agency, and when they are not FSOs, State is always represented on the delegation. Most resistance comes from DOD and the military services. They object to giving arms controllers—always suspected of weakness and naiveté—a leading role in negotiations that, like SALT, could jeopardize their budgets and missions.

SALT: ONE OR TWO HATS?

Gerard Smith and Paul Warnke had two official "hats," SALT Ambassador and Director. Iklé wore only one. Which is preferable? The question transcends SALT and can be rephrased: What are the advantages and disadvantages for ACDA in its Director's heading any important, time-consuming negotiation?

The main argument against a two-hatted Director is that negotiations take him away from Washington and the real policy action. Policymakers should make policy. Whether or not ACDA's Director is SALT Ambassador, the Agency is always represented on the delegation. In addition, it chairs the SALT backstopping committee. Hence it has a hand in policy implementation even when the Director is not SALT Ambassador. Heading the delegation and absence from Washington can hurt in at least four ways:

1. Even an able Deputy cannot exert maximum bureaucratic leverage in interagency councils. Nor can the Deputy have as easy access to senior policymakers. A Nixon NSC staffer has said, "Though Farley was good, there were many occasions when it would've been very helpful to have had Smith in Washington." Although Warnke, in his first few months as Director, attended "most" of the private conversations between Secretary of State Cyrus Vance and Soviet Ambassador Anatoly Dobrynin,[1] his prolonged absences from Washington reportedly had a negative effect on ACDA.

2. A Director who spends much of his time overseas negotiating a SALT accord may be unable to devote adequate attention to other pressing issues. Smith virtually ignored the equally urgent problem of nuclear proliferation.

3. The SALT Ambassador speaks for the entire government, but he leads a delegation whose members reflect various departmental interests and viewpoints. He must, particularly if he is an arms controller, both faithfully represent the government and preside impartially over a diverse delegation. An ACDA officer who worked closely with Smith remarked, "He felt he should be a mediator [on the delegation]. He was simply first among equals. ACDA gained no real advantage from Smith heading the delegation. . . . There is an advantage to *not* being neutral."

4. An ACDA Director as SALT Ambassador invites suspicion from the Pentagon and congressional conservatives. Neither ACDA nor the President relishes this prospect. Suspicion can be avoided if the State Department leads the delegation.

Those who favor having the Director as SALT Ambassador stress two points. First it does matter, in policy terms, who heads the delegation. Despite Kissinger's penchant for backchannel negotiations, Smith was convinced that his access to sensitive information and policy developments would have been far less if he were not SALT Ambassador. Furthermore, whereas the controversial Interim Agreement was basically negotiated by Kissinger, not the delegation, the ABM Treaty was largely the delegation's product. Indeed, Article I of that Treaty was drafted by the delegation without *any* guidance from Washington.[2] Also, when important decisions are being considered, the Director can return to Washington. Then, because he is SALT Ambassador, he has greater weight in policy circles. This point was made by Admiral Moorer in testimony opposing Warnke's nomination as SALT Ambassador. Moorer, who was in government during Iklé's first year in office, asserted that the President had far more contact with Ambassador U. Alexis Johnson than with the Director. He added that at NSC meetings "the chief negotiator will speak 10 times as often as the chief of ACDA."[3]

Second, Warnke's critics were not the only ones convinced that it makes a difference who heads a delegation. So were many liberal and moderate congressmen. In keeping with the letter and spirit of the ACD Act, ACDA has had an important negotiating function. It is fitting for the Arms Control Agency to head arms control talks. When the Director did not lead the SALT delegation, after the purge, ACDA was being symbolically and actually downgraded. Arms control is reputable. It is "out of the closet." ACDA's stature in negotiations should reflect that fact.

Clearly there are costs and benefits whether the Director wears one hat or two. In 1975 Adrian Fisher proposed the creation of a new ACDA officer, a "most-of-the-time negotiator" with sufficient rank to conduct important negotiations but "not such a big wheel that there is embarrassment when the Director comes . . . and takes over the chair."[4] This would free the Director to spend time in Washington, except when his presence was demanded at the negotiations. In 1977 Congress authorized such a position with a rank equal to Deputy Director—the Special Representative for Arms Control and Disarmament Negotiations. It was expected that the Special Representative's main function would be to serve as alternate chairman of the SALT delegation, although the Director could assign him to other arms control negotiations.[5] The legislation does not completely resolve the one- or two-hat controversy, but it does help keep the Director in Washington—which is vital—while permitting him to retain formal leadership of the delegation.

OTHER NEGOTIATIONS

The Agency has usually played a significant role in formal "frontchannel" arms control negotiations. Occasionally, however, it has been entirely excluded. The 1963 "Hot Line" accord with the Soviet Union was negotiated by Ambassador Charles Stelle and two specialists from DOD. U.N. Ambassador Arthur Goldberg conducted the talks leading to the Outer Space Treaty in 1967, supported by ACDA's Sidney Graybeal and others. Discussions resulting in a 1972 Soviet-American agreements concerning incidents at sea between their two navies was handled by the Under Secretary of the Navy.

In 1961 the superpowers established the Eighteen Nation Disarmament Committee (ENDC) in Geneva, which was endorsed by the U.N. General Assembly. The Committee, co-chaired by the United States and the Soviet Union, reported to the General Assembly and the U.N. Disarmament Commission. In 1969 the committee's name was changed to the Conference of the Committee on Disarmament (CCD), and its membership was enlarged. By 1977 it had thirty-one members. Following the U.N. General Assembly's 1978 Special Session on Disarmament it was agreed that the CCD would again expand its membership and that the joint superpower chairmanship would be replaced by a system whereby the chairmanship rotated among all the member states. The CCD discusses the whole gamut of arms control and disarmament issues and, often after prior bilateral discussions and agreement between Washington and Moscow, is a forum for multilateral negotiations. The Non-Proliferation Treaty, Biological Warfare Convention, Seabed Treaty, and Environmental Modification Ban were all negotiated at the CCD.

ACDA normally has the leading role on the U.S. CCD delegation, and an ACDA officer has been the U.S. arms control spokesman on the U.N.'s First Committee (Political and Security) since 1961. The American Ambassador to the CCD is almost always from ACDA, and the U.S. delegation is partially staffed by the Agency. ACDA is active in the bilateral talks with the Soviets that often precede or parallel an item's consideration by the full CCD. ACDA led the U.S. delegation to the CCD negotiations on the Non-Proliferation Treaty. The Agency has since maintained its position as chief U.S. CCD negotiator.

On some other matters or in other forums, ACDA has had an important, though not necessarily leading, negotiating role. ACDA was intimately involved in talks preceding the Partial Test Ban Treaty. In January 1963 Foster met with Soviet representatives in New York and

Washington; he then presented the U.S. position to the ENDC that spring. However, the final negotiations in Moscow in July were conducted by Kennedy's special representative, Averell Harriman. Harriman was accompanied by, among others, Adrian Fisher and other ACDA officers.

The U.S. Ambassador to the MBFR talks, which began in 1973 in Vienna, came from the State Department. But ACDA chaired the MBFR backstopping committee (until 1977) and provided a principal member, several advisers, and staff personnel to the delegation. Also, the Washington office of the Ambassador was physically located in ACDA, which facilitated personal contact and coordination. Few ACDA officers objected strongly to State's heading the delegation. Most doubted the negotiations would be fruitful; if they did prove productive, fundamental foreign policy issues—beyond arms control—would then be at stake.

ACDA specialists were actively involved in the bilateral technical discussions with Moscow that preceded the 1974 signing of the Threshold Test Ban and the Peaceful Nuclear Explosion Treaty in 1976. However, the Threshold Test Ban was concluded by Nixon and Kissinger at the Moscow summit. Iklé was not in Moscow, but he was contacted twice during the negotiations and made some input. Iklé was disturbed by the high 150-kiloton threshold, which was negotiated by Kissinger and not ACDA.

ACDA has been active in a variety of other areas. For instance, in the nuclear proliferation field ACDA led the U.S. delegation to the 1975 Non-Proliferation Treaty Review Conference; it supported the meetings of nuclear supplier countries; and it was deeply involved in the activities and meetings of the International Atomic Energy Agency. In the spring of 1977 the United States and the Soviet Union agreed to establish eight joint working groups to deal with a number of arms control issues. That year bilateral talks were held on a comprehensive nuclear test ban, the Indian Ocean, chemical and radiological weapons, and conventional arms transfers. ACDA participated fully in all of these negotiations.

The wishes of the President will and should determine the leadership and conduct of international negotiations. Individual ACDA Directors will also have different preferences for allotting their time. Still, sound arms control policy as well as ACDA's interests will generally require: (1) ACDA's Director must spend most of his time in Washington. (2) He should, however, be free to visit the delegation. If ACDA heads the delegation, the Director would assume leadership when present. (3) ACDA should play an important part in all arms control negotiations. (4) If the delegation head is not to be an ACDA officer, the President should at least consult the Director about the appointment. The chief negotiator should report to both the Director and the Secretary of State. (5) ACDA should backstop all arms control negotiations.

At times the President may, with good reason, choose to work through more direct and personal channels of negotiation, bypassing ACDA. This would be of concern, however, if he were motivated to do this because of lack of confidence in ACDA. It would also be troubling if the President or Secretary of State kept particularly sensitive information about backchannel negotiations from the Director, especially if information was withheld because of lack of confidence in the Director or because of doubts about the loyalty of supposed arms controllers.

Research

High-quality analysis is always an asset for a bureaucratic actor. For ACDA, it is indispensable. ACDA does not have the institutional size or leverage of other agencies. It is competitive largely because it produces an analytical product deemed useful by senior officials. Rigorous analyses and sound ideas will not, of course, always prevail. The notion that knowledge somehow ultimately wins out is ludicrous.[6] But without a solid analytical base ACDA is effectively disarmed.

ACDA's research activities are of two types—in-house and contracted. The Agency has formidable in-house, cross-disciplinary defense expertise. It combines technical, scientific, economic, and foreign affairs specialists with one of the largest defense systems analysis operations outside the Pentagon. This capability affords ACDA a measure of independence vis-à-vis State and Defense and, to the extent it is used by policymakers, a degree of influence. By the mid-1970s State began to augment its generally weak technical expertise in arms control. In the civilian nuclear area its capability is impressive. But in most arms control areas State still lacks a comparable array of analytical talent.[7]

Research is also done for the Agency by outside contractors and, to some extent, by other government agencies. Table 1 lists annual expenditures for contracted research and field testing.

In 1961 many felt that ACDA's main function was to conduct and promote research, particularly external contracted research. The ACD Act not only authorizes the Agency to conduct, support, and coordinate research (section 2[a]), but states that the "Director shall, to the maximum extent possible, make full use of available facilities, Govern-

TABLE 1. U.S. Arms Control and Disarmament Agency Research and Field Testing Obligations by Fiscal Year

FY	RESEARCH	FIELD TESTING	TOTAL
1962	$ 600,000	$ ---	$ 600,000
1963	2,756,000	804,000	3,560,000
1964	3,172,000	862,000	4,034,000
1965	4,508,000	891,000	5,399,000
1966	4,619,000	1,190,000	5,809,000
1967	3,515,000	1,250,000	4,765,000
1968	3,666,000	834,000	4,500,000
1969	2,489,000	1,113,000	3,602,000
1970	1,826,000	684,000	2,510,000
1971	1,160,000	548,000	1,708,000
1972	1,416,000	483,000	1,899,000
1973	1,697,000	278,000	1,975,000
1974	1,100,000	---	1,100,000
1975	1,500,000	---	1,500,000
1976	1,700,000	---	1,700,000
1977	2,238,000	---	2,238,000
1978*	4,700,000	---	4,700,000

*Budget estimate
SOURCE: U.S. Arms Control and Disarmament Agency

ment and private'' (section 31), to carry out research on virtually anything related to arms control or disarmament. With this mandate, William Foster initiated a broad-based external research program. The field was relatively unexplored. It was thought that basic research was needed in disciplines as varied as psychology and physics. Consequently, by the mid-1960s about 50 percent of ACDA's budget went for contracted research and field testing, the latter related to the supposed need for on-site verification capabilities.

By the late 1960s and through the mid-1970s, external research was sharply curtailed. The reduction came principally in the field testing program, which was phased out, and in social science research. Many of the early contracted studies were ill-focused, unrelated to present or future policy concerns, and wasteful. Publicly, Agency spokesmen discreetly stated that this research, particularly in the social sciences, had amassed a substantial and sufficient "basic fund of knowledge." No more was needed. Smith and Farley were highly critical of the contracted research programs. Smith thought that most projects, at least in the social sciences, could be handled internally; all ACDA required were a few bright people with good ideas. By FY 1973 general social science studies constituted only about 10 percent of the research contracts, while 90 percent related directly to ongoing negotiations or existing treaties. Half of all external research expenditures either supported SALT or examined nonproliferation safeguards.[8]

With the 1973 purge ACDA's research budget reached its lowest point—$1.1 million for FY 1974. Social science research was almost eliminated, and some necessary technical work in the SALT and nonproliferation areas could not be funded.[9] Under Iklé, the research budget gradually increased. By FY 1977 more than 50 percent of the total program went to nonproliferation safeguards. Most contracts were for highly specific technical studies, many of them related either to verification or operations analysis research. Like Smith, Iklé (himself a social scientist) was skeptical about the utility of general social science studies. What little social science research remained pertained to a few closely defined problems. In Warnke's first year (FY 1978) ACDA requested $2.5 million for external research. However, Congress doubled that amount, earmarking most of the increase for seismic research in support of a comprehensive test ban and for nonproliferation-related research.[10]

A thorough evaluation of the external research program would require scrutiny of scores of individual studies. Some are classified. Many demand expertise in one or more of several disciplines. Such an examination is beyond the scope of this book or the ability of a single individual. My analysis is therefore only a general assessment of the overall program based partly on the judgments of ACDA officers familiar with it. But more detailed attention is given to the contracted social science research. There are four reasons for emphasizing the smallest segment of the external research effort: (1) In-house research, with some exceptions, is virtually indistinguishable from almost everything ACDA does. Hence it cannot be easily isolated for separate treatment. (2) Contracted technical and scientific research, while not without its problems and lemons, has been consistently supported by all ACDA Directors and Congress. It has contributed substantially to several arms control agreements as well as to important new developments, especially regarding verification. (3) The author's professional background is in the social sciences—international relations, political science, and law. Several ACDA social science studies have been read in their entirety. (4) The social science contracts are controversial. Most ACDA officers and analysts are fiercely critical of the utility and, often, the quality of much of this research. However, by the mid-1970s there was mounting pressure from congressional liberals and some academics to increase expenditures for such studies. The rationale for doing this, therefore, deserves careful consideration.

IN-HOUSE RESEARCH

The Agency has not been able to formulate a workable definition of in-house research. Some internal research resembles external research in its depth and scope. But most internal efforts are more near-time-oriented: preparing position papers for negotiations, contributing to interagency studies, and drafting responses to queries from senior policymakers or ACDA's own leadership. It is difficult to separate most internal research from other staff work. "For example," said Iklé, "you get a question from Geneva as to some technical issue in SALT and you may have to spend 2 days to answer that question.... Is this research, or is it policymaking, or attending to negotiations?"[11] Nor is it easy to determine the exact size of the internal research effort, since most employees daily perform several interrelated tasks only some of which could be labeled research.

One group that does perform in a more or less identifiable research mode is the Operations Analysis unit. Established in the mid-1960s, Operations Analysis usually had, by the 1970s, about fifteen analysts, many of whom were military officers on assignment to the Agency.[12] It does quantitative analyses of arms control and defense issues. In the arms control area it conducts more studies than comparable systems analytical units in OSD and the military services. Its studies, which often try to anticipate future concerns of policymakers, have covered a wide spectrum of issues, including nuclear war simulations based upon hypothetical SALT-imposed strategic weapons limitations, the development and re- finement of mathematical models bearing upon MBFR and a comprehen- sive nuclear test ban, and the survivability of U.S. ICBMs. Its studies have been sought and used by the NSC staff and even the Pentagon. On some SALT I requests from the NSC staff, Operations Analysis did 75 percent of the research.

There are few important arms control issues where ACDA has not done a heavy share of the analytical spadework. Without this capability there would not be an effective analytical counterweight to DOD. How extensively and in what capacity this instrument is employed by policy- makers vary with the issue and the preferences of senior actors. Until the late 1970s ACDA was not regularly used to examine critically the arms control implications of developing or deploying certain weapons systems, despite their clear bearing upon future arms control prospects. By the early 1970s, however, ACDA was asked to examine several key defense questions, such as the Minuteman missile's vulnerability to Soviet MIRVs and its implications for U.S. deterrent posture. ACDA's findings often differed sharply from DOD's; they provided policymakers with a far more balanced spectrum of views than they otherwise would have received.

ACDA's analytical capability provides a more balanced perspective in other areas as well. In MBFR, where the State Department is preoccupied with NATO, ACDA's team of defense, foreign affairs, and systems analytical experts are accustomed to looking at the interaction of opposing forces rather than just their separate capabilities. ACDA, not State or Defense, developed alternative approaches to MBFR verification and limitations. Kissinger and the NSC staff, during the SALT I process, deliberately employed ACDA to counter what an NSC staffer called "the super threat tone" of DOD. Even under Iklé in the SALT II process the NSC staff benefited from the work of lower-level ACDA analysts who often differed with the Agency's leadership. Assuming a quality product, effective advocacy, and receptive senior officials, ACDA can keep State and Defense analytically honest.

In some instances ACDA's internal efforts, often buttressed by contracted technical research, have been especially critical. To a considerable degree, they laid the foundation for advances in several verification techniques, a nuclear test ban, much of the American nonproliferation effort, limitations on biological and environmental warfare, and many other notable achievements. Quality in-house research is ACDA's requisite commodity.

CONTRACTED TECHNICAL RESEARCH AND FIELD TESTING

There are numerous instances when a contract for technical or scientific research assisted the Agency. In 1964, for instance, data from a study by the Aerospace Corporation projecting improved MIRV accuracy eventually contributed to ACDA's concern that MIRV could threaten stable deterrence and complicate arms limitation negotiations. Before the mid-1960s little thought was given to restrictions on biological and chemical warfare. By late 1967 ACDA had completed three external research projects in this area, which complemented its internal efforts and provided useful insights into areas for possible arms control agreements. By the

1970s most external research was technical or scientific, and ACDA began to use some contractors to facilitate quick responses to finite problems.[13]

One of the most successful long-term programs has been the development of nuclear safeguard techniques and equipment. It was first instituted in 1966, and by the 1971–1978 period between 30 and 50 or more percent of total annual contracted research expenditures supported this program. In 1977 Congress even gave ACDA more funds than it had requested for this program. Senator Charles Percy (R–Ill.) expressed the prevailing congressional mood when he assured Warnke that ACDA would be "fully funded" in this area for "all that you can appropriately and adequately spend."[14] Much of the program supported the monitoring function of the International Atomic Energy Agency regarding the peaceful use of nuclear energy at a time when that organization was understaffed and inadequately funded. ACDA-sponsored research developed: advanced techniques for verifying reactor plutonium production, tamper-resistant unattended safeguards surveillance instrumentation, safeguards seals, and portable measuring instruments so an inspector could determine amounts of uranium and plutonium without destroying the container in which the fuel was sealed.[15]

Unlike nuclear safeguards research, the field testing program had mixed results. Its origin dates from October 1961, when Foster established and chaired an interagency group whose task was to define and evaluate arms control inspection and verification needs. The group's report stressed the necessity of field testing to determine the capabilities and limitations of various inspection systems and techniques. In March 1962 Foster asked President Kennedy to approve a $35 million field test program for determining the capabilities of various ground and airborne inspection systems. This proposal was rejected but, after some refinement, a joint ACDA–DOD field test program—Project Cloud Gap—was approved in September 1962. Although field testing began in 1963 under the joint direction and staffing of ACDA and DOD, the cooperative arrangement was not formalized by a signed, written working agreement until May 1965.

Cloud Gap's mission was "to field test and refine arms control concepts, techniques, equipment, and systems for inspection and verification developed by ACDA or DOD."[16] Primary attention was given to on-site inspection, which at the time was thought to be critical if arms control schemes were to progress. Field tests were run in several areas. Some involved more than two hundred military personnel. But Cloud Gap was plagued by numerous problems, and in 1967 Congress denied DOD funds for continuing the project. ACDA then assumed full responsibility for field testing. However, internal ACDA skepticism about the utility of field testing, along with congressional criticism, led to sharp reductions in the program after 1969 and its complete elimination by 1973. After 1967 field testing was coordinated by the Field Operations Division of the Weapons Evaluation and Control Bureau until that Division too was abolished in 1972. Before its demise, however, it did some useful work in seismic detection methods and nonproliferation safeguards.

The few defenders of Cloud Gap argued that it helped the Agency's image to spend large amounts for inspection and verification, that much useful information was obtained, and that four inspection systems were developed that, if necessary, could have been deployed. The critics replied with several telling arguments:

1. Cloud Gap was misdirected in focusing so heavily upon on-site inspection. While this was understandable in 1962, its justification was soon undermined by a technological revolution in national technical means of verification, especially photoreconnaissance. Perhaps, because of new agreements and the limitations of national technical means of verification, on-site inspection will again demand serious attention. However, we can prepare for virtually all probable on-site inspection needs in a more cost-effective and a better-targeted manner than was the case under Cloud Gap.

2. Two ACDA officials described Cloud Gap in identical words: "a dual-headed monster." DOD was asked to perform an inherently alien task—to perfect techniques for limiting armaments. It responded predictably. There were constant coordination problems in this "joint" endeavor where Defense controlled most of the equipment and personnel. The ACDA–DOD steering committee never succeeded in giving the program coherent direction, and the top DOD officer for Cloud Gap was changed repeatedly. Also, because of ACDA's strained relations with the defense intelligence community before 1966, vital intelligence data on verification were withheld.

3. Finally, the four inspection systems that allegedly were deployable were, with one arguable exception (identification of underground nuclear tests), insufficiently refined. Seismic methods were being developed and improved within the government wholly apart from Project Cloud Gap. ACDA field testing might still be necessary—though the facilities of other agencies should be adequate for this purpose—and it is important for the public and Congress to be aware of ACDA's concern about verification. But the Agency's image cannot be enhanced by programs like Cloud Gap, which, one ACDA officer lamented, "no one could control."

CONTRACTED SOCIAL SCIENCE RESEARCH

THE RISE AND FALL

At first, ACDA promoted social science research on virtually anything researchable. There were contracted studies, for example, concerning social psychology's possible insights, U.N. peacekeeping, and general regional concerns. Besides the officially stated main purpose of exploring what outside social scientists might contribute to arms control policy, ACDA's entire external research program during the 1960s—not just social science—had three additional objectives. First, Foster encouraged a large program, according to a ranking associate, in order to "convey the message that ACDA has arrived." This official added: "There was a tacit understanding at higher levels—don't criticize contracted research in front of Foster or you'd lose." Second, sponsored research was to serve a public educational function.[17] Many of the nation's noted scholars were either ACDA contractors or consultants. The program stimulated interest in the subject and, since several studies were later published commercially, reached a fairly wide audience. Some officials also viewed this as a way around the ACD Act's inhibiting prohibition (section 49[d]) forbidding ACDA from disseminating "propaganda." The circumvention of section 49(d), according to one official, "was a very conscious thing which, obviously, was kept exclusively within the Agency—we didn't want Congress to know this." A third and related objective was to nurture a potential ACDA political constituency in academia and elsewhere. Some deny that this was an intended function of social science research, but others are quite firm about this, citing specific instances when it was discussed.

Few, if any, of the contracted social science studies in the 1960s (or subsequently) directly and unambiguously assisted the Agency in policy matters. This disturbed many, eventually including a vast majority of ACDA people. There was uneasiness about the propriety of subsidizing academia when there was no clear policy payoff. This feeling was heightened by some shockingly low-quality studies, one costing more than $500,000, which contract officers, often scholars themselves, recalled vividly years later. ACDA sometimes contributed to the problem by vague contract definitions, loose monitoring, and a rush to spend appropriated funds before the end of the fiscal year.

As difficulties in the program increased, ACDA decided in 1964 to create a Social Science Advisory Board composed of distinguished scholars from several disciplines. The board was intended, according to an ACDA official, "to lend legitimacy to the social science research program and help ward off Congress's attacks.'' It met two or three times annually until its abolition in 1973. The board offered suggestions in selecting contractors and grantees and served as a link between ACDA and universities; its members collectively and individually advised the Agency. Many of its members found this tie to government personally beneficial. But criticism continued, leading eventually to the virtual elimination of external social science research.[18]

A venture strongly endorsed by the Board was ACDA's Ph.D. dissertation support program instituted in 1968. Its purpose was to encourage research and general interest in arms control. It was open to students in any of the social or behavioral sciences, and its broad scope permitted vast diversity in subject matter. The program was funded by ACDA but jointly administered by the National Academy of Sciences, which set up a committee of scholars—ranging from anthropologists and historians to sociologists and psychologists—to assist in its implementation. More than forty dissertations were funded before the program was terminated by Farley after in-house and congressional criticism. Even the ACDA behavioral scientist who coordinated and heartily endorsed the program acknowledged its several problems, particularly its encouragement of research on matters having little or nothing to do with policy or even arms control. Topics included ''killing the rat,'' ''socialization of children,'' and ''a study of the Cosa Nostra.'' In early 1978, within weeks of Senator Humphrey's death, the Agency reinstituted a dissertation support program. The interdisciplinary Hubert H. Humphrey Doctoral Fellowship in Arms Control and Disarmament, unlike the prior program, expressly emphasized research with direct technical or policy implications.

Many of the social science contracts and some of the earlier dissertations were both well done and generally related to arms control. They at least advanced the public educational objective of the overall program. Several examples of exemplary scholarship might be given, but among the most frequently praised are the MIT studies on conventional arms transfers and local conflicts.[19] They had no immediate programmatic application, but they did stimulate some new ways of approaching and thinking about specific problems. Also useful were many of the more than thirty economic impact studies done between 1963 and 1973, which explored the likely results for the U.S. economy of possible arms control and disarmament agreements. They examined the probable impact of such agreements on key industries as well as their effect upon certain regions, communities, military bases, and industrial workers. Their collective conclusion, which was neither particularly surprising nor original, was that there is nothing unique about the challenge to the economy posed by reduced military expenditures; while there would be transitional problems, federal assistance plus proper monetary and fiscal policies could sustain output and employment. But the economic impact studies were directed at a real problem, as many people believed that arms control and disarmament would damage the economy. They exposed the basic unreality of these fears.[20]

THE FUTURE?

Ironically, when Smith and Farley cut back the external social science research program in response to congressional and in-house criticism, the Senate Foreign Relations Committee changed its tune: "In the mid-sixties, the Committee began to be concerned that ACDA was emphasizing . . . irrelevant research—at the expense of negotiations . . . This situation has now changed to such a degree that the Committee's concern is the reverse.' ''[21]

By 1972 several liberal legislators began calling for more social science research. That year some members of the House Foreign Affairs Committee urged a reexamination of the possible contributions of the behavioral sciences. Farley then approved a contract with a group of social and behavioral scientists at Ohio State University for this purpose. The express objective of this contract was to determine how the behavioral sciences might help ACDA accomplish its mission. It was to be consumer-oriented and was viewed as a key test by the Agency.

The study, which involved interviews with ACDA personnel and inputs from several behavioral scientists from around the country, was an acute disappointment. When a first draft went to ACDA for review, copies were distributed to fifteen analysts. Comments about the quality of the product were all negative. The Ohio State group attempted to meet these criticisms, but the final report was still unsatisfactory. But no one in the Agency disputed that group's final conclusion that "*no substantive knowledge from the behavioral sciences appears of immediate and unambiguous relevance to ACDA problems.*" Indeed, the evidence that supports the general propositions of the behavioral sciences "appears to be only trivial verification of folk knowledge." And the contractors acknowledged, in a classic understatement, that they probably benefited more from the study than did ACDA.[22]

The CIA's experience seems to confirm the conclusion that there are severe limitations on the applicability of the behavioral sciences to problems confronting government foreign affairs agencies.[23] Morris Janowitz, a former member of the Social Science Advisory Board, agrees with the Ohio State group that much of the behavioral science research purportedly relating to arms control has been "trivial, naive." However, Janowitz says that, overall, academic social science research on arms control has been worthwhile in that, among other things, it has sensitized people to the problems and contributed to "general enlightenment."[24]

Behavioral science research, like all legitimate academic pursuits, has an important educational value for those outside government. But whether ACDA or other governmental units should sponsor such research and, if so, how and to what extent, is debatable. By 1977–1978 Congress was seriously considering, over State Department opposition, establishing a "National Academy of Peace and Conflict Resolution."[25] Among the many questions that must be addressed before such an institution would be justified are the following: Can the objectives sought be met by existing organizations like the National Science Foundation? What are the objectives? Does ACDA's experience with the behavioral sciences suggest there is any reasonable prospect that they will ever relate to specific policy concerns? If not, why spend taxpayers' money? Granted, there is broad educational value in systematically and conceptually studying international conflict and its resolution (often called peace research), but why aid programs that are firmly established in many national and foreign institutions of higher learning?

By the mid-1970s Congress began to strap ACDA with other unwanted and questionable social science research duties apart from the behavioral sciences. In 1975 Representative Bella Abzug (D–N.Y.) succeeded in amending the Foreign Relations Authorization Act for FY 1976 (section 142), requiring ACDA to study the impact of arms control measures mutually agreed to by the United States and the Soviet Union on their respective military expenditures.[26] Hence, ACDA had to charge its small staff with examining a subject that was plastic, yet obvious. "What could we do? We had no choice but to somehow comply," said the ACDA officer charged with implementing the legislation. So, many man-hours and four contracts later, ACDA submitted its thirteen-page, $320,000 report to Congress ($1 million had been authorized; the actual cost figure excludes staff time). Naturally, it concluded that "U.S. and Soviet military expenditures, even those expenditures on strategic forces . . . , have apparently been little affected by arms control agreements to date."[27] A young analyst at the Congressional Research Service could have provided a similarly revealing response in far less time without feeding an apparently endless stream of public largess.

Projects like this, which further neither a policy nor a public educational function, can and should be avoided. An understanding might be negotiated with the House International Relations Committee and the Senate Foreign Relations Committee by which external social science research would be judiciously expanded for perhaps a four-to-six-year trial period. The focus could be one that would have a constructive educational spinoff but would strike a middle path between those advocating large-scale expansion and those seeking elimination of the program.

The case for sizable public social science research expenditures for vaguely educational or constituency purposes probably had some substance when arms control was an unknown and unappreciated concept. Today, though, scores of colleges and universities offer courses or entire programs in arms control. Certainly in the social sciences, the field is reasonably well covered and researched at many institutions of higher learning (though in 1978 the House International Relations Committee, assuming the contrary point of view, strongly urged ACDA to increase its support for university training, education, and research in arms control and asked ACDA to examine existing American arms control study centers and submit recommendations concerning the advisability of bolstering them with public funds).[28] Nor is there, nor should there be, much support for the notion that, wholly apart from policy ramifications, research contracts should be let to fatten some hypothetical constituency.[29] Indeed, greater understanding of arms control, or any area of human endeavor, can lead to informed criticism as well as to informed support. Finally, the assertion sometimes heard—that, because DOD spends lavishly, so too should ACDA—is absurd.

Government policy analysts lack the adventuresome, sporting quality that often characterizes scholars. For government analysts, as distinct from intellectuals, ideas must have instrumental value.[30] This is a legitimate expectation. Yet the refrain often heard within ACDA, that research must clearly relate to current or future negotiations, runs a dual risk. It encourages Abzug-type amendments from legislators who think differently and may deprive the Agency of some potentially helpful research from those with freedom to think unconventional thoughts.

A future external social science research effort could be structured around the following guidelines:

Background Information. Several analysts pointed to particular contracts, like MIT's analysis of local conflicts or the Brookings Institution's examination of China and arms control, as providing useful background on a range of issues. One analyst, citing specific contracts, said, "everything here is ad hoc. Rand and others have time to think broadly about things relevant to arms control, and this is sometimes helpful to us."

Careful selection of contractors and subject matter might provide additional assistance in this regard and, perhaps, some insights that elude harried analysts caught up in pressing immediate concerns. Donald Brennan asserts that an ACDA contract with the Hudson Institute concerning future military uses of the seabed belatedly stimulated the kind of perspective that contributed to the Seabed Treaty, though it was doubtful, says Brennan, that ACDA officials were aware of the connection at the time.[31]

Challenging Assumptions. Some contractors could be explicitly directed to examine an issue so as to challenge prevailing government or Agency assumptions. Are new nuclear-weapons-free-zones as unlikely as is generally supposed? Is there greater promise in certain unilateral measures than is sometimes thought? Findings could be presented in writing and orally, perhaps in a structured advocacy context. Outside researchers would have full access to classified data and would interact regularly with officials. Properly managed, with the full support of the Director, a climate potentially harmful to internal cohesion and morale could be avoided. While dramatic reversals of assumptions are unlikely, the exercise might result in refinements or adjustments, or might simply confirm prevailing views.

Planning. There is very little long-range speculative thinking within ACDA or, for that matter, the foreign affairs bureaucracy. Yet this is, as two very successful past ACDA contractors point out, academia's natural forte.[32] Many ACDA officers have worried aloud that the future is not being examined, that SALT II is all-consuming and no one is thinking about SALT III or IV. Iklé was concerned enough to twice set up small planning units but they went the way of most government planning staffs. March and Simon's dictum again rang true: "Daily routine drives out planning."[33] ACDA analysts who were good enough to think about the future were too good not to be working on more pressing current problems. Irresistible forces lure the able to the "real action," the present. But arms control's final judgment awaits the future. There are opportunities and needs here that outside contractors could address.

Analyzing Analysis. One pressing requirement is for ACDA, perhaps in regular consultation with an advisory group, continuously and systematically to evaluate the quality and character of external research in light of the Agency's changing needs and the results of completed contracts. The composition of the advisory group should not be such that it would invariably advocate social science research. It should be chaired by ACDA and perhaps have a representative each from State, Defense, and the CIA as well as noted scholars. Research with demonstrated promise would be encouraged. Less successful research would be eliminated.

ACDA would then be prepared, armed with specific supporting evidence, either to request additional funding for social science research or to fend off unwanted and unnecessary congressional initiatives.

Public Information

Section 2(c) of the ACD Act makes "dissemination . . . of public information concerning arms control and disarmament" one of ACDA's four "primary functions." But public affairs has been a pedestrian activity with little impact on the press or public. Most public information from the executive branch concerning arms control has come from the White House and State Department, not ACDA. Except for Fred Iklé, Agency officials, in contrast to civilian and military spokesmen from DOD, have not spoken out strongly in public. Prior to 1976 ACDA generally spent less than $300,000 annually on public information and assigned only three professionals to the area. A few publications were prepared, and requests for speakers and course curricula were answered, but ACDA was not an important factor in nongovernmental arms control activities. Students of arms control and interested citizens did not view ACDA as their prolocutor or even their preferred interlocutor.

The public information program is a barometer that indicates ACDA's reading of public and congressional receptivity to arms control. The Agency was long concerned that public visibility was dangerous, and its early experience with Congress lent credence to this view. But by the 1970s some congressmen began criticizing ACDA's inactivity in public affairs. Whereas Congress once discouraged a public presence, it now increasingly demanded one.

LOW PROFILE, 1961–1973

ACDA soon learned that disseminating public information could be risky. Congressional actions, partly rooted in a suspicion of arms control and disarmament, effectively thwarted the program. When ACDA was six months old Representative Glenard Lipscomb (R–Cal.) berated it for spending $1,000 for travel expenses of officers who spoke before college and church audiences. Representative John Rooney (D–N.Y.), whose subcommittee controlled ACDA and State Department appropriations, later criticized an ACDA public affairs officer who spent $452 of the taxpayers' money to address several California groups. In 1963 Rooney's subcommittee and its Senate counterpart formally requested that out-of-town travel for public affairs purposes be undertaken only when the host organization defrayed expenses. ACDA strictly complied with this request.[34]

That year Congress also amended the ACD Act. Section 49(d) now prohibited ACDA from disseminating "propaganda." Faced with this blanket ambiguous injunction, which could be, and was, cited by hostile legislators, ACDA abandoned any idea of an active public information program. Conservatives were the chief accusers, though Senator Fulbright once joined them. One congressman thought ACDA's entire second annual report to Congress was propaganda. Representatives Lipscomb and Hosmer argued that several ACDA publications qualified as propaganda. Hosmer even requested a GAO inquiry when he found the red and yellow cover of one publication inflammatory. At a White House conference in 1965 a group chaired by Jerome Wiesner expressed concern about the dearth of government-sponsored public information about arms control. But by that time ACDA had learned its lesson.[35]

ACDA Directors were inhibited by section 49(d), but by 1970 congressional attitudes were changing. Liberals like Representatives Jonathan Bingham and John Culver (D-Ia.) called for increased public affairs expenditures and assured Gerard Smith of strong support. But the program languished. ACDA press releases fell from twenty-six in 1969 to five in 1971. The public affairs budget did not rise above $274,000.[36] A majority of Congress probably would have responded positively if Smith had sought repeal of section 49(d), but he was uninterested in public visibility. To some extent, this reflected Kissinger's tight SALT control as well as ACDA's concern about alienating OSD. But Smith was also personally opposed to greater public activity. Soon after the SALT I negotiations opened he held a "backgrounder" for the press, which went poorly. That set the tone for the rest of his directorship. In Smith's opinion, the best public relations were agreements and concrete accomplishments, and the chief SALT negotiator should not be a public advocate. He did not enjoy public speaking and doubted its impact on public opinion.

Even Smith's small public information program managed to irritate Defense Secretary Laird. He objected that the ACDA publication, *World Military Expenditures,* overstated and misrepresented the size and nature of U.S.–NATO defense budgets, thereby jeopardizing DOD's appropriations in Congress. ACDA defended the accuracy of its report, but Laird complained to the White House. ACDA was then pressured to cease publication after the 1971 edition. This brought complaints from some liberal congressmen and outside organizations.[37] Though Iklé worried about OSD's reaction, he decided to republish the report after 1974, because the gathering of data on world military spending was clearly related to ACDA's mission. It was also prudent to avoid angering key legislators. The format was changed—more statistics, less comparative analysis—apparently to minimize a possible negative reaction from OSD.

INCREASED VISIBILITY

Fred Iklé adopted a more public stance than his predecessors. He had a busy speaking schedule, enlarged the public information program, and spoke out frankly on important issues. His outspokenness was sometimes officially rebuked. He told the press in 1973, and later Congress, that the Army's planned production of binary weapons would vastly complicate international efforts to control chemical weapons. Shortly thereafter, apparently without consulting anyone, Iklé told a reporter that the United States should "move away from reliance on land-based missiles." Iklé was pointedly informed that this was not the administration's position. When asked by members of Congress about these two statements, Iklé expressed regret that internal advocacy had made the headlines. But he continued to address other issues, particularly nuclear proliferation. His open and candid remarks about nuclear proliferation focused attention on the subject. They also prompted some phone calls from Helmut Sonnenfeldt and, in at least one instance, a public reprimand from Kissinger.[38]

Congressional liberals continued to urge greater activity in public affairs. In 1975 Congress repealed the restrictive section 49(d). The next year ACDA increased the number of professionals in public affairs to six, and expenditures rose to $580,000. In 1977–1978 Congress, with the full support of Paul Warnke, raised public affairs funding to $800,000. ACDA added eight more professional employees in this area, and the Senate Foreign Relations Committee reported that it "strongly supports" expansion of ACDA's Office of Public Affairs. ACDA's General Counsel issued an opinion that employees could no longer accept reimbursement from host organizations for out-of-town travel expenses when attending a conference or delivering a speech, because the ACD Act did not contain a gift clause specifically authorizing this. In 1977 Congress added section 41(g) to the Act, permitting acceptance of payment for travel and subsistence expenses from private organizations for such activities.[39]

Some legislators pointed to the disparity in public affairs expenditures between ACDA and DOD. In FY 1977 DOD spent $25.6 million and employed 1,337 people for public affairs. DOD had almost as many marching bands (160) as there were full-time ACDA professionals.

It is, of course, questionable whether the size of DOD's program is an appropriate yardstick for ACDA. Experience also suggests that ACDA must remain sensitive, though not servile, to the concerns of other departments. Furthermore, Gerard Smith's skepticism about the utility of government-sponsored public information about arms control cannot be casually dismissed. Certainly there are universities and private organizations performing an educational and informational function in this area. And simply throwing public funds at ACDA will accomplish little.

Nonetheless, greater attention to this neglected area is long overdue. With careful planning, the money can be effectively utilized. ACDA no longer has to be invisible. Arms control is better understood and has shed many of its earlier pejorative overtones. By the late 1970s Congress insisted upon a stronger public information program. Public confidence in arms control and ACDA might be related to an understanding—or at least an awareness—of both. Many things could be done: *World Military Expenditures* could be improved and expanded; the valuable ACDA-directed bibliography on arms control and national security, eliminated in 1973, could be reissued; ACDA officers could attend conferences and symposia more often; films for high school audiences could be produced.[40] Arms control is vital to national and international security. ACDA should not be embarrassed about or deterred from so informing the American people.

10 General Advisory Committee on Arms Control and Disarmament

SECTION 26 of the ACD Act permits, but does not require, the President to appoint a fifteen-member General Advisory Committee on Arms Control and Disarmament (GAC). The GAC, whose members must be confirmed by the Senate, is charged with advising the President, Secretary of State, and Director about matters affecting arms control and disarmament.

The committee is composed of prestigious people from government, academia, and the general public. It was originally designed to provide an interface between a new ACDA and a skeptical Congress. The GAC was to symbolize arms control's legitimacy and public support while ensuring that arms controllers would not sell out the nation's security. It was also intended as a vehicle for John McCloy to continue to play a role in arms control policy. After the passage of the ACD Act McCloy simply changed his title from Kennedy's special assistant for arms control to chairman of the GAC. He chaired the committee, sometimes called the McCloy Committee, until his departure in 1973.

The GAC, however, has rarely been a significant factor in the policy process. This chapter examines the reasons and considers whether there is justification for its continued existence.

Early Years

The statute does not provide fixed terms for GAC members, so changes in membership come through death or resignation. During the

1962–1968 period, when the Committee met only three or four times a year, there was a fair degree of continuity in membership. Among those who served with McCloy were Robert Lovett, Herbert York, General Thomas White, General Alfred Gruenther, George Kistiakowsky, and Roger Blough.

The McCloy–Kennedy relationship gave the GAC adequate access to the President. It had some input on the Partial Test Ban negotiations and, because of presidential access and the committee's stature, ACDA took it seriously. Indeed, the Agency has always been responsive to its informational and staff needs. But Foster was somewhat ambivalent toward this body, which was both a potential competitor with and an overseer of ACDA.

In the 1960s the GAC occasionally inquired into ACDA's performance. When General Gruenther learned of a congressman's complaint that ACDA had not "done its homework" on the Non-Proliferation Treaty, he pursued the matter until satisfied that the complaint was unfounded. A more representative illustration of GAC review of ACDA operations was McCloy's response to a question about ACDA's contracted social science research: "we are certainly aware of the research projects [but] we don't get around to as close an analysis of the research as we should."[1] Even in the 1960s the GAC usually did not stress its oversight role.

Lyndon Johnson made no use of the committee. When Johnson first met with it he had not been carefully briefed. The President gave the impression he did not know who they were, and some members threatened to resign. Its activities were pro forma—briefings, some recommendations to the President, and photographs with the Chief Executive.[2] McCloy, a vigorous supporter of NATO and the Federal Republic of Germany, initially opposed the Non-Proliferation Treaty. The Agency's relationship with the committee was awkward until McCloy reluctantly came to accept the treaty.

Brief Activity and Decline

President Nixon reconstituted the GAC in 1969 with the appointment of fourteen new members and the reappointment of McCloy as chairman. McCloy informed Nixon that he would not accept the position unless the committee had a greater policy voice, he had a say in committee appointments, and more staff assistance was provided. McCloy also decided, to

ACDA's relief, that he would concentrate on presidential advice and not oversee the Agency or regularly advise its Director.

Nixon was responsive. He requested GAC advice on SALT and other arms control issues, telling the committee that its input would be valued. The committee was also authorized to hire a small independent staff.

Among those who served on the GAC from 1969 to 1972 were William Foster, Dean Rusk, Jack Ruina and James Killian of MIT, Harold Brown of the SALT delegation, and General Lauris Norstad. During this period the GAC convened three times as often as under the prior two administrations. It held forty-two full-day sessions (eighteen in 1970) and gave the President recommendations on SALT, MBFR, and other matters. It had considerable access to internal policy papers and received dozens of wide-ranging briefings from Kissinger and others. Sometimes McCloy presented his views to the NSC; the full GAC met with Nixon once or twice a year. The committee became an arms control advocate whose level of activity indicated a desire to become part of the inner circle of advisers. It opposed development of the Safeguard ABM, favored a zero ABM position, and urged a Soviet–American moratorium on MIRV testing in 1970.

But despite this activity, there is little evidence that it had any impact on policy. Often the GAC considered an issue only after it would have been difficult to change its course. Once, a NSDM had actually been signed by the President before the GAC got involved. McCloy was not consulted on some crucial matters and, despite Kissinger's promise of cooperation, key NSC staffers were instructed to withhold certain policy documents from the committee. By 1971–1972 the GAC's membership fell to eleven through resignations, McCloy's access to the President declined precipitously, and the committee could no longer anticipate periodic meetings with him. The relationship with the White House became frayed. Adding to this strain was Kissinger's close personal control of SALT as well as the committee's support for measures that went beyond what the administration was willing to accept. The rationale for an independent presidential advisory group was undermined by the realities of the Nixon foreign policy system.[3]

In early 1972 the administration sought to offset the GAC's pro-arms control bent by submitting the names of four new nominees to the Senate Foreign Relations Committee. They included General Earle Wheeler and former CIA Director John McCone. Senator Fulbright objected that they were too conservative, and his committee refused to act on the nominations. The GAC continued to function at less than full strength until after the November elections, when the committee, like the rest of the arms control bureaucracy, was "purged." McCloy resigned after trying repeatedly to see the President. Nixon did not reconstitute the committee; it did not meet at all from late 1972 to August 1974.[4]

Iklé wanted the GAC discontinued but did not press the matter after being advised that this could antagonize liberal congressmen.[5] President Ford did continue the committee, and it met four or five times annually during his administration. Its chairman was Harold Agnew, who headed one of the nation's largest defense laboratories, the Los Alamos Scientific Laboratory. In the past, Agnew had opposed a comprehensive nuclear test ban and supported the Safeguard ABM. Agnew consulted with Iklé on an individual basis, but the committee did not advise the Director on ACDA's operations. As before, there was little evidence that it affected policy in any significant way. Gerard Smith resigned from the committee; it lost its independent staff; and Agnew, not close to Ford, apparently met with him only once. The GAC did not meet during President Carter's first year, though Carter did reconstitute it in late 1977. Thomas Watson of IBM was named chairman, and it met several times in 1978.

Future

It is a close question whether the GAC should be retained. Even John McCloy, whose name was synonymous with the committee, expressed doubt about its utility.[6] Presidents often ignore the GAC, and it has outlived its function as ACDA's overseer. It labors under constraints common to presidential advisory groups: irregular sessions, inadequate staff, and busy members with full-time positions outside government. And, most critically, its effectiveness hinges directly on the President's interest in its activities and confidence in its members. As the GAC's experience in the Nixon administration illustrates, it is difficult to be effective without threatening senior policymakers. Nor can it offer greater expertise than is available within government.[7]

Section 26 of the ACD Act should probably not be abrogated, however. It should be left to the President to determine whether or not to utilize the committee. He may do so if three conditions are met:

1. The President must know and have confidence in the chairman. The McCloy-Kennedy tie contrasts sharply with the Agnew-Ford relationship.

2. The President and his foreign policy system must be open to diver-

sity. He must want an arms control advisory group that may sometimes offer different views from those of departmental actors.

3. The GAC must bring the President advice and perspectives that are not otherwise always available to him. A presidential advisory body should be able to do two things. It should offer a broad, coherent overview of an issue; an independent viewpoint that rises above the fragments of foreign policy and is presented by those who are distant from the committal posture which often accompanies fierce bureaucratic infighting. The GAC might also be a troubleshooter, bringing matters to the President's attention that might otherwise remain submerged because of bureaucratic resistance.

If these conditions are lacking the GAC will atrophy. If they are present the committee could be active and useful.

11 Personnel and Size

QUALITY ANALYSIS depends on quality people. Ability and dedication are essential for an agency whose effectiveness is substantially determined by its analytical product. It becomes even more critical for an organization that has usually had fewer than one hundred civilian professionals (excluding clericals) to accomplish a broad mission. There is no room for deadwood.

An unusually high percentage of ACDA's professionals are on temporary loan from the Departments of State and Defense (Tables 2 and 3). Since FY 1962 active duty military officers and FSOs, together, have rarely constituted less than one-third of the Agency's total professional employees. In some years the number of these reimbursable employees has been even higher. This has caused some problems. But while the difficulties must be appreciated, on balance ACDA has profited from this system. So, too, have State and Defense.

Civilian Professionals

Civilian analysts hired by ACDA usually have advanced degrees, often Ph.D.s, plus considerable background in arms control and national security policy. Most come from other government departments or universities. Because ACDA requires highly trained, specialized analysts—particularly in the natural sciences, the vital core of the Agency—and because supervisory personnel must deal with very senior counterparts in other agencies, ACDA needs an extraordinary percentage of high-level, relatively high-paying civil service slots. In late 1977, for instance, ACDA had twenty-five civilians in supergrade positions (GS 16–18).

TABLE 2.   United States Arms Control and Disarmament Agency: Number of Authorized Personnel

FISCAL YEAR	PERMANENT (INCLUDES CLERICAL)	MILITARY	REIMBURSABLE FOREIGN SERVICE	TOTAL MILITARY AND FOREIGN SERVICE	GRAND TOTAL
1962	89	1	36	37	126
1963	166	18	36	54	220
1964	166	18	36	54	220
1965	164	18	32	50	214
1966	184	18	36	54	238
1967	184	18	36	54	238
1968	184	43	36	79	263
1969	189	43	36	79	268
1970	180	33	36	69	249
1971	180	29	40	69	249
1972	180	29	40	69	249
1973	174	25	45	70	244
1974	162	15	27	42	204
1975	168	21	27	48	216
1976	179	24	27	51	230
1977	180	24	27	51	231
*1978	185	24	27	51	236
*1979	199	18	34	52	251

*Budget Estimate
SOURCE: U.S. Arms Control and Disarmament Agency

This represented more than 25 percent of all ACDA civilian professionals. Forty-four employees were in the GS 13–15 ranks. So about 70 percent had a senior civil service grade, perhaps unique in the federal government.

This offered an appealing target to the Civil Service Commission. In 1974, for the first time in ACDA's history, the commission began an almost two-year audit of the Agency's personnel. Of the fifty-five professional and clerical civil service slots randomly selected (supergrades were not reviewed), the commission determined that twenty-eight should be lowered in grade. ACDA saved some from grade reduction, but most were reduced, some by four grades, and ten professionals actually left the Agency.

The commission's scathing report charged that ACDA's managers "failed to carry out their personnel management responsibilities"; the number of GS 13–15 employees "shows the effects of large-scale inatten-

TABLE 3.   United States Arms Control and Disarmament Agency: Actual On-board Personnel

FISCAL YEAR	PERMANENT (INCLUDES CLERICAL)	REIMBURSABLE TOTAL	GRAND TOTAL
1962	86	33	119
1963	147	44	191
1964	156	42	198
1965	157	35	192
1966	159	41	200
1967	155	44	199
1968	175	68	243
1969	156	70	226
1970	166	65	231
1971	166	61	227
1972	168	52	220
1973	141	32	173
1974	155	35	190
1975	167	42	209
1976	170	41	211
1977	169	50	219

SOURCE: U.S. Arms Control and Disarmament Agency

tion and is the most serious personnel problem in ACDA.''[1] The commission suggested substituting lower-level ''technicians'' for several of these officers. ACDA replied that the report and the commission's action reflected unfamiliarity with ACDA or its functions; that grade reductions for GS 13–15 staff members and supergrades (which it was feared might be next) could necessitate hiring a large number of low-ranking people, which would actually increase costs and lower efficiency; and that the effect of the commission's action was to deter ACDA from elevating the meritorious above a GS 13 level, thereby exacerbating an already high personnel turnover rate, because many of these able people could (and did) go elsewhere at higher salaries.

Iklé and Lehman considered asking Congress for legislation exempting ACDA—like the CIA, ERDA, and several other governmental units—from restrictive Civil Service regulations. They hesitated, though, for fear liberal legislators would see this as an attempt by ''hardliners'' to fire those holding different views. In 1977 the author proposed such legislation in congressional testimony and, after ACDA assented, it was enacted into law. Section 41(b) of the ACD Act now permits ACDA to appoint and fix the compensation of employees without regard to civil service requirements.[2] This enables ACDA to offer competitive salaries with other excepted agencies and allows it to hire the most qualified applicant. Before, the Agency could not hire someone, regardless of his qualifications or experience, unless he was highly rated by the Civil Service Commission. Then the process could take up to twelve weeks, even if he had appropriate security clearances. Now many can be hired within a few days. By December 1977 ACDA had already acquired nine analysts under this new authority, several of whom could not have been hired under the old system.

Though precise statistics are unavailable, ACDA has always had a high personnel turnover. By late 1973 only five professionals had been with the Agency continuously since 1962–1963. It is relatively infrequent for a bright young analyst to stay more than five or six years. Two factors other than salary considerations appear to contribute to this. Arms control is a politically sensitive business. When political winds change, so do many of the presidential appointees and some of the working-level people closely associated with them. In a small agency such transitions can take a sizable percentage of the personnel. Second, ACDA's size and limited policy role can be constricting. It may be difficult for analysts to try something new. Some transfer to other departments to be closer to the policy action. To leave ACDA for this reason is often considered an advancement.

Rapid turnover has benefits. It brings new energy and ideas, perhaps particularly important for a secondary agency whose more ambitious designs are regularly frustrated. It also means that ACDA serves as a seedbed sending trained arms control experts out into government and academia. For example, three former ACDA employees later served on both the Nixon–Ford and Carter NSC staffs. One of them commented:

> Ironically, we're the ones who give ACDA the hardest time. We know where their positions are coming from. But we also appreciate and understand the arms control perspective—both the positive and negative aspects. That former ACDA people like us are in high places may not always be good for ACDA, but it's certainly good for the U.S. government.

But frequent turnover has undercut one of the reasons for establishing ACDA: creation of a permanent cadre of career civilians working in arms control. ACDA is deprived, to an extent, of long-term human memory in the field. Because rapid changeover is the norm, understood by all and welcomed by some, it does not significantly affect morale except in extreme cases like the 1973 purge. But it does contribute to a perception, especially among younger analysts, that ACDA is a good place to be for a few years, but, beyond that, career interests dictate going elsewhere.

Foreign Service Officers

FSOs and Foreign Service Reserve Officers have always been part of ACDA. Several joined the Agency in 1961 from State's Disarmament Administration. One of ACDA's four Assistant Directors has usually been an FSO, and many other senior officials were once affiliated with the State Department. Until 1977 most FSOs went to ACDA's International Relations Bureau, where they dealt with multilateral issues before the CCD or with regional concerns like MBFR.[3]

With its tie to State, ACDA is aware of able FSOs. It has an active voice, usually with the Secretary of State's support, in their recruitment. Until the late 1960s, when Samuel De Palma became Assistant Director for the International Relations Bureau, most FSOs did not welcome an ACDA assignment. It was considered outside the traditional route for career advancement, and until the Non-Proliferation Treaty ACDA had little policy responsibility. De Palma himself had not requested the assignment. But his bureau took the lead·in the Non-Proliferation Treaty negotiations. Indeed, this was when it first became widely accepted within the bureaucracy that ACDA should have broad negotiating responsibilities. After De Palma's departure (to become an Assistant Secretary of State), an ACDA tour was often requested, especially by younger FSOs. Even before De Palma, ACDA FSOs generally went on to successful careers. Several eventually rose to the rank of Assistant Secretary or Ambassador. This pattern has continued.

Under Smith, when ACDA matched or eclipsed State in most arms control areas and several negotiations were in progress, the Agency attracted the very best. But after the purge, although ACDA continued to draw good younger officers, it had difficulty recruiting at the more senior FSO 3 and 4 levels. There were two reasons for this: a perception that ACDA had been downgraded and Kissinger's new emphasis on the need for senior FSOs to gain managerial experience. A small agency offers few managerial opportunities.

Still, in 1978 ACDA was appealing to those FSO 3s and 4s to whom managerial responsibility could be offered and to junior officers. Few want to stay longer than the normal two-year tour, however. An ACDA assignment often means direct involvement in significant negotiations.

For the younger FSOs, importantly, efficiency reports are prepared by senior ACDA FSOs, not civilians. They know the games and mores of the Foreign Service, which relieves much of the anxiety about an interagency assignment. They also remain physically close to the State Department.

Fortunately (we have seen exceptions), State and ACDA are often in basic agreement on arms control questions. The Iklé–Kissinger feud over SALT did not involve ACDA's FSOs. In other areas, like nuclear exports, there has often been a split within State itself. An individual FSO seldom confronts a clear conflict in organizational loyalty. An FSO-4, nearing the end of his tour, summarized his fellows' sentiments: "We must remember where our primary loyalty is [State], but this is practically never a problem." Only once did this present a significant concern at a senior level. When Jacob Beam (later Ambassador to Moscow) headed the International Relations Bureau in the mid-1960s he was cool toward arms control and opposed the Non-Proliferation Treaty. But Fisher soon isolated Beam and worked around him. The problem vanished with his departure.

Having FSOs in ACDA symbolizes the legal prerogatives of the Secretary of State, improves coordination, tends to encourage close working relations, and mitigates tensions that otherwise might arise. FSOs have been particularly helpful in multilateral negotiations, while State acquires expertise and experience in arms control. FSOs have certainly not dominated the Agency, nor have they seriously compromised ACDA's integrity.

Military Officers

Military officers are usually assigned to ACDA for three-year tours of duty. The Agency has less voice in their recruitment than with FSOs, but it often gets the preferred officer. Until 1973 virtually all military officers went to the WEC Bureau, always headed by a senior active duty military officer. Iklé abolished WEC, and military officers were then distributed more broadly throughout the Agency. Warnke re-created the bureau, though it acquired a civilian bureau chief and different responsibilities. In 1977 twenty-three military officers were still spread throughout the Agency, though half were in WEC or the Operations Analysis Office. Since 1973 at least one of ACDA's Assistant Directors has been a senior military officer, but they were now required to retire from the service.

Before 1973 WEC performed only support functions for other bureaus. It never had the lead on important issues. ACDA's leadership avoided even a hint of undue military influence in an agency that regularly clashed with Defense. It was also feared that an active WEC would alarm the JCS, reduce their cooperation with the Agency, and perhaps jeopardize officers' careers. Most officers were content with their low profile. Some others were not. Vice Admiral John Lee, who headed WEC under Gerard Smith, complained repeatedly about WEC's tertiary policy role.

Iklé ended the military's relative apartness from crucial matters with his 1973 reorganization. For the only time in the Agency's history two of the four bureau chiefs were recently retired senior military officers. Air Force Colonel Robert Behr was Assistant Director for the Military and Economic Affairs Bureau. Rear Admiral Thomas Davies was Assistant Director for the Nuclear Weapons and Advanced Technology Bureau. The second highest official in the Plans and Analysis Bureau was an active duty Air Force officer, Major General Kermit Kaericher, who was promoted to that rank while with ACDA. Of the three, only Davies was a vigorous arms control supporter.

Iklé sought closer rapport with the military services. Early in his tenure he invited Admiral Zumwalt and the Chairman of the JCS, General George Brown, to address ACDA's senior staff. The Agency's more conservative stance seemed conducive to better relations with the military. Whether the new roles and positions acquired by ACDA's military officers further strengthened this conservative posture is conjectural. Certainly many in ACDA, State, and elsewhere thought so.[4]

But it is debatable. ACDA remained firmly in civilian hands. The prevailing political tone came from the Iklé–Lehman group, not the military. Furthermore, Behr, and particularly Kaericher, appear to have been isolated from some sensitive matters. Kaericher's bureau, headed by Amrom Katz, never acquired a clear, consistent direction, and it was later abolished. Behr was eventually sent overseas for long periods to the MBFR negotiations. An ACDA civilian official commented that Behr's absence from Washington was "no accident." Admiral Davies's bureau was central, yet his commitment to arms control was unquestioned. Finally, it cannot be convincingly demonstrated that the greater dispersion and functional integration of military officers at the working level engendered more caution than otherwise would have been the case. They continued to support and answer to civilians. Indeed (although their numbers subsequently increased) after the 1973 purge ACDA retained only thirteen military officers, several of whom were in Operations Analysis.

In 1977 Warnke erased the suggestion of improper military influence, though Major General John Ralph, promoted to that rank while with

ACDA, was retained by Warnke as Senior Military Adviser and charged with an additional arms control verification responsibility. Only the retired Admiral Davies remained an Assistant Director. Also, as part of an overall reduction in interdepartmental tours, OSD informed ACDA that it could expect only eighteen officers in FY 1979.

BENEFITS

Active and retired military officers have an advantage over civilians in three respects:

Military Experience. Superior natural scientists are vital to arms control, and ACDA is well endowed. But to comprehend armaments and their use fully the operator must be consulted. ACDA military officers bring an impressive array of technical, tactical, and operational experience. Those with an engineering background are particularly valuable. The civilian scientists cite instances when ACDA studies would have been defective or misleading had it not been for their military colleagues.

Information. Agency employees agree that the military's most important function is to gain access to information from Defense. General John Davis, who assumed the directorship of WEC in 1966 after a career in intelligence, is still warmly regarded. He opened lines of communication with DOD that had previously been closed.

Military officers, especially of higher rank, are unlikely to be considered carefree arms controllers by fellow officers, and their many personal acquaintances facilitate information flow. They have been particularly instrumental in getting data on weapons systems and the defense budget. A civilian official has said: "We often have nowhere else to go for information on weapons technology. We must have military officers." One analyst reported a not uncommon type of incident. He had driven to Edgewood Arsenal in Maryland for certain information on chemical weapons. The base commander told him, according to the analyst, that "we can't give you this information since it relates to national security and, of course, ACDA has no business in that area." This was reported to Admiral Davies, who promptly called a Lieutenant General. The information was released.

Bureaucratic Style. Military personnel can make an informational contribution of another sort. Military officers generally bring values and assumptions that, while not wholly shared by ACDA's civilians, are potentially useful. A sense of what might imprecisely be called a "military perspective" can assist civilians in their dealings with Defense.

Several officials commented that ACDA military officers provide insight into how the JCS might receive certain proposals, how ACDA's position should be presented to the military services, or who should be approached and when.

PROBLEMS

The presence of military officers within ACDA creates three potential problems:

Loyalty. There may be tension between loyalty to service and loyalty to ACDA. Until 1966 this was a serious concern, as neither of ACDA's first two senior military officers, Vice Admiral Edward Parker and Lieutenant General Fred Dean, had an affinity for arms control. During that early period some officers saw their primary function as curbing supposed ACDA excesses. This strained intra-Agency relations—to the point, in one instance, where two Assistant Directors, one of whom was a military officer, were not on speaking terms. It also ensured a minimal policy role for WEC.

Neither ACDA nor the services profit when officers see themselves as infiltrators of an alien organization. They are identified and isolated. The military's influence declines, interdepartmental relations deteriorate, and Congress may inquire into the matter. General Davis, who succeeded General Dean as head of WEC, recognized this. Davis was no passionate arms controller, but, like most military officers who come to ACDA, the experience broadened his perspective. Many officers, thus exposed, conclude that there is no necessary antipathy between arms control and national security. After leaving the Agency, General Davis recalled that his initial reaction to ACDA "was one of extreme skepticism"; he felt that "the objectives of ACDA must be exactly opposite to the objectives of the Department of Defense." His attitude later "changed completely."[5]

This kind of problem has not been significant since 1966. General Davis's successor, Admiral Lee, was specifically requested by Gerard Smith. The admiral was an arms control supporter (though his enthusiasm waned somewhat when the Navy was affected). He was followed by Retired Admiral Davies, whose services were valued by both Iklé and Warnke.

Individual active duty officers will always be sensitive to their dual role. They know they must return to their service, and this often inclines them to assume a low profile. A direct clash of loyalties arises only infrequently. When it does, many appear to handle it like one Navy officer: "It's a very individual thing. The dual loyalty problem is there, but it is certainly not great. When there is a conflict most of us give our civilian superiors both our own views and our service's views." The agency is aware of this personal dilemma and tends to assign officers to positions where there is little risk of being suspected of service disloyalty. Only if the officer's career is thus protected can ACDA expect to receive quality people.

Career. An ACDA assignment is clearly outside the normal career advancement route. Through the mid-1960s it was especially difficult to attract able officers. But when SALT became a possibility in 1967 the situation began to change. Suddenly arms control had meaning—it threatened service missions and budgets. No longer could the military afford to send poorly qualified people. Since then, ACDA has been generally pleased with the overall quality and motivation of its military officers. Indeed, by the 1970s several younger officers were requesting an ACDA tour, and some were promoted while with the Agency.

As a general rule (there are exceptions) for those who come to ACDA at or above the rank of colonel or Navy captain, the assignment is either their next to last or final tour before retirement. Below this rank, it is thought to have either a positive or a neutral career impact. Younger officers usually receive promotions and choice assignments after leaving the Agency. If arms control remains central to national security policy and ACDA continues giving active-duty military officers tasks that do not risk friction with their service, the Agency should attract good people.

Larger Policy Role. Admiral Lee and some other military officers complained about their lesser policy role within ACDA. Iklé did diversify and, perhaps, enhance the military's role, but even under Iklé they continued to perform an essentially support function. But ACDA cannot significantly upgrade the policy role of active-duty military officers without jeopardizing both the Agency's civilian character and the careers of its military officers. It is also prudent to continue to require most senior officers holding leadership positions in ACDA to retire from the service. Those who are not retired must serve in a support capacity.

In the early 1960s and subsequently (though to a lesser extent), congressional conservatives saw ACDA's military officers as a sober check on arms controllers. Liberals, on the other hand, were uneasy about a possible fifth column. Neither the fears of liberals nor the hopes of conservatives have been realized. There are loyalty considerations, but they are entirely manageable. The military has influenced yet never overruled civilians.

The services are represented in an organization that deals with issues directly affecting national security. Military officers gain useful experience and provide a generally more moderate tone on arms control than civilians. ACDA also benefits substantially. Only one of dozens of ACDA civilians queried on this subject felt that the Agency's interests would be enhanced by severing this relationship.

Size

"We are only a pisswink outfit," remarked one ACDA analyst. Even including FSOs and active-duty military officers, the Agency has never had as many as two hundred professional employees. From FY 1965 to FY 1977 the annual budget remained around $10 million. For every *civilian* employee in ACDA and State together, Defense has thirty. For every dollar spent by ACDA and State combined, Defense spends $150. Scores of congressmen are military veterans, none are former ACDA officers. ACDA simply cannot exert the political and institutional clout of, say, the Navy. It lacks the organizational bulk, budget, and constituency. Other considerations aside, it is difficult for the military to have confidence in so small a unit, especially if it seeks a leading role in important political-military questions.

Of course, there is not an invariable one-to-one ratio of size to effectiveness. The NSC staff is fairly compact. Although ACDA is not the NSC staff, it plays an important (though never dominant) role. Smith, Iklé, and Warnke all expressed a preference for keeping ACDA small, and they present a strong case.

ACDA's diminutive size partly reflects some fundamental assumptions about American national security policy and the international system. The latter part of the twentieth century is unlikely to witness a Peace Department eclipsing the Pentagon. ACDA's area of responsibility is also circumscribed by usually legitimate existing departmental jurisdictions. But smallness does have advantages. It promotes intra-Agency coordination and cohesion while allowing even very junior officers occasionally to meet with the Director. Though growth in selected areas is highly advisable, an Agency of moderate size can accomplish its assigned mission.

Only once during the 1960s (in FY 1963) did Congress grant ACDA its full requested appropriations. This changed by 1970. Most of the pressure for budgetary growth—and opposition to budget reductions— now came from Congress. ACDA not only received its requested appropriations, but Congress sometimes allocated additional funds. By 1977, when ACDA sought $13.6 million, Congress appropriated $16.5 million, a substantial real increase over the $10 million level to which ACDA was accustomed. In 1978 ACDA requested a budget of $16.4 million and Congress authorized $18.4 million. Senator Pell stated that "there is no agency where dollars would be better spent," and Senator Ernest Hollings (D–S.C.), who chaired the subcommittee of the Senate Appropriations Committee that passed on ACDA's budget, remarked, "We . . . want to make just absolutely sure you are not hampered budgetwise."[6] Few national security or foreign affairs agencies fared better.

Between 1975 and 1978 ACDA acquired several new negotiating responsibilities, and legislation was enacted giving ACDA new authority in the weapons acquisition process, conventional arms transfers, nuclear nonproliferation, and other areas. Congress also markedly increased ACDA's appropriations for contracted research and public affairs. The initiative for most of this came from Congress, not ACDA. But, sometimes belatedly, ACDA welcomed most of these congressional actions and hired more people to fulfill its new or expanded responsibilities.

The resulting modest growth in the Agency's size was salutary and came in areas that had been neglected. There is room for additional expansion. In the summer of 1977 an ACDA official in the nuclear proliferation area who regularly worked long hours complained that he was "grossly understaffed." Similar complaints come from other sections of the Agency. At one point in 1978 ACDA's personnel were severely taxed by having simultaneously to head and staff five separate negotiations in different subject areas. The number of civilian professionals could usefully rise to at least 150. This would only raise the total number of ACDA's professional employees (including FSOs and military officers) to about 200. The benefits of a smaller agency would still be preserved, an evident need for more analysts would be met, and there would be a healthier balance between permanent employees and those on temporary assignment from the State and Defense Departments.

Part III
Congress and Interest Groups

12 Outside Constituency

SEVERAL DEPARTMENTS, agencies, and even bureaus can claim an organized, well-financed, vocal, politically consequential constituency outside of government whose interests roughly parallel their own. Interest groups can importantly affect the organization's welfare, primarily through their impact on Congress. Most agency heads regularly attempt to cultivate and expand their clientele by being responsive to their concerns, often articulated by congressmen. Numerous mass membership groups like the Navy league, the National Guard Association, the American Legion, and the Veterans of Foreign Wars support the budgets, views, and interests of DOD and the military services. The 200,000-member American Security Council alone, which consistently opposes arms control efforts while advocating increased defense spending, has annual expenditures that far exceed those of interest groups supportive of arms control.[1]

ACDA does not have such a constituency and—with the partial exception of the contracted research program—has made virtually no effort to acquire or nurture one. Even a tenfold increase in its external research program would not make ACDA politically competitive with most executive branch national security actors. Some would agree with Representative Harrington that ACDA's ''single greatest obstacle [is] the absence of any constituency.'' Warnke acknowledged that this was one of ACDA's ''major problems,'' that there had to be ''an effective counter to some of the groups that are really fearful of arms control.''[2] This was a familiar subject for Warnke, as he had been associated with some arms control interest groups before becoming Director.

While there are no arms control interest groups comparable in size and funding to those which support a large military establishment, there are several significant smaller organizations (only some of which will be discussed). During the 1960s ACDA's constituency, such as it was, con-

159

sisted of a loose, fractionalized coalition of academic, scientific, religious, and "peace" groups. There were many ad hoc, short-lived groups. But following the 1969 congressional debate over the Safeguard ABM some of the older groups gained new life, and new ones were formed. The orientation and tone of these organizations range from the strident National Committee for a Sane Nuclear Policy (SANE) to the liberal-moderate United Nations Association and the even more staid Arms Control Association.

The Federation of American Scientists, founded in 1946, is among the oldest and most effective of the interest groups. It is a registered lobby composed primarily of natural scientists, including some of the most eminent in the country. It publishes a newsletter that goes to many congressional offices. In the 1970s it was regularly testifying on major arms control and defense issues, while its members met frequently with individual legislators. In 1969 the federation joined with another lobbying organization, the Council for a Livable World, to lead the ABM opposition. The latter group sponsors seminars and actively aids legislators who are supportive of arms control. Of the twenty-three senators who received financial assistance from the council between 1962 and 1970, twenty-two were consistent arms control proponents.[3]

The Brookings Institution is neither a lobby nor an interest group, but it does sponsor seminars and studies on arms control and defense policy. Its staff consults with Congress and the executive branch. Some Brookings analysts have been ACDA officers; others have left to join the Agency.

The Members of Congress for Peace through Law was established in 1966 by a bipartisan group of congressmen concerned about soaring military expenditures. Funded largely by private contributions, it has no formal standing in Congress. But it does provide a link among like-minded members of Congress, and its small staff analyzes a variety of defense issues, especially weapons systems. The organization sees itself as an overseer of the performance of authorizing committees. Its direct impact has been modest, but its studies sometimes spur committees to consider a matter carefully. For instance, the organization's comprehensive 1971 critique of proposals for a new strategic bomber probably contributed to the Senate Armed Services Committee's subsequent close scrutiny of the B-1 bomber.

The Center for Defense Information was established in 1972 with Rear Admiral Gene La Roque as director. It has a permanent staff of eight to ten and is funded by private contributors, particularly the Fund for Peace. Admiral La Roque testified often before congressional committees and met privately with legislators on defense issues. The center also prepared studies, sponsored meetings, and published *The Defense Monitor*, which went to many congressional offices. The three top officials of the center in 1977 were all retired military officers. The theme it presented to the public was stated in *The Defense Monitor*: "The Center for Defense Information supports a strong defense but opposes excessive expenditures or forces. It believes that strong social, economic and political structures contribute equally to national security."[4]

During the Center's first years of existence its services were well received by liberal and moderate legislators. Senator William Proxmire (D–Wis.), Senator Frank Church (D–Id.), and others publicly praised it. Admiral La Roque was in frequent personal contact with congressmen.[5] Subsequently, though still active, the center encountered difficulties. La Roque ran a tight ship, too tight for his staff. In a three-year period several research directors resigned, as did many professional staffers. Former staffers, one of whom called La Roque "the dove admiral," reported that the center had lost some credibility and influence with Congress partly because of factual errors in some of its publications and because of its acquired reputation for predictably saying "no" across the board to additional defense spending. A Brookings Institution analyst remarked: "Today, those who listen to the center are already convinced." This image of the organization is widely held and has alienated many who were once well disposed toward the center. Unless this image is changed, internal problems are addressed and, perhaps, new leadership secured, the center could face a troubled future.

To some extent, people acting singly, generally academics who may also be Agency consultants, have helped ACDA improve its institutional well-being and promote specific stands. Some of these individuals bring new ideas, others have potentially helpful personal relations with senior executive officials or congressmen, and many openly espouse arms control in publications and congressional testimony. President Kennedy lauded Gerard Smith for originating the notion of a Hot Line communications link between Washington and Moscow, but Thomas Schelling, who later became an ACDA consultant, is generally credited with the idea. Albert Wohlstetter was close to Iklé and shared his cautious views on some arms control issues. But Wohlstetter also had Iklé's passionate concern about nuclear proliferation and made these concerns well-known within and outside government. Matthew Meselson, a friend of Kissinger, deserves much credit for influencing the Nixon administration to support controls on biological and toxin weapons. Meselson also did much to spur ACDA's interest in this subject during the 1960s and was a leading figure in organizing an outside lobby for controlling these weapons. In 1977 the author proposed legislation affecting ACDA's personnel, subsequently enacted into law, which the Agency had wanted for some time yet was hesitant to request.[6]

The Arms Control Association

No private group has been more interested in ACDA's welfare and the promotion of arms control than the Arms Control Association (ACA). It was formed in October 1971 by several former ACDA officials. (One active middle-ranking ACDA officer also played a part, apparently without the knowledge of his superiors.) Former ACDA officials—many of whom had also served in State, Defense, or the CIA—were and continue to be among the organization's top officers. They are also heavily represented on its board of directors. ACA's first officers included William Foster, Adrian Fisher, and two former ACDA Assistant Directors—Archibald Alexander and Herbert Scoville, Jr. ACA was administered by Thomas Halsted, another former ACDA officer, who also directed the arms control program of the Carnegie Endowment for International Peace. With such an array of experienced people, ACA resembled a professional organization like the Foreign Service Association. Since these officers had served in the Kennedy or Johnson administrations, ACA also had the appearance, until 1977, of an ACDA-in-exile. That year Halsted and four board members—Gerard Smith, Adrian Fisher, Lawrence Weiler and Anne Cahn—joined the Carter administration's arms control team.[7]

ACA describes itself as a nonpartisan organization seeking to create "broad public appreciation of the need for positive steps toward the limitation of armaments and the implementation of other measures to reduce international tensions on the road to world peace."[8] In carrying out this mission it has sought to project a professional, responsible image. An ACA officer has stated that "we're definitely an establishment outfit, which gives us a certain respectability with those in government." He added that the dominant members of the board were very reluctant to identify too closely with "the crazies of the left like SANE and various quasi-populist disarmament groups." Though ACA has lent its name and support to some ad hoc groups, such as the Task Force for a Nuclear Test Ban, which published a pamphlet entitled, "Should Nuclear Weapons Tests Be Stopped?," that same officer referred to instances when ACA refused to identify with a particular disarmament cause partly for fear of losing "respectability." Its success in projecting this image varies with the audience. Some government officials see it as a "bunch of knee-jerk arms controllers," while some members of more activist groups consider ACA conservative and calcified. The truth, though a matter of perception, probably lies somewhere in between.

In late 1972 the association had only about 270 members and expenditures of $8,500. ACA remains small, though it has grown considerably. By early 1978 it had annual expenditures of about $150,000 and a membership of 750; many members have a professional or scholarly interest in arms control. The Carnegie Endowment—whose president sits on the board of directors—participates in several joint ventures with ACA, provides office space for its tiny staff, and in 1977 covered about 40 percent of ACA's expenditures. Beyond this, ACA is sustained by annual membership dues and outside contributions. ACA is a nonprofit tax-exempt organization and is careful not to participate in lobbying activities, support political candidates, or identify too closely with overtly partisan causes. Halsted personally contacted reporters and others when they erroneously described ACA as a lobby.

ACA engages in two broad categories of activity: public education and direct interaction with policymakers, especially in Congress, with an eye toward influencing policy. While ACA does promote understanding of arms control, it is education with a theme. The basic message is that arms control and national security are or should be congruous, if not synonymous; even apart from moral considerations, America's national interests are furthered and international stability is enhanced through measured and balanced restraints on armaments. This message is spread in several ways. The association sponsors, organizes, and participates in conferences and symposiums in the United States and overseas. Press briefings and luncheons are held; close touch is maintained especially, though not exclusively, with the liberal press. ACA has provided speakers for colleges and for other institutions and groups. Its members appear on radio and national television. It has challenged the accuracy of publications and films produced by organizations like the Institute of American Strategy and the American Security Council, whose products are often, according to ACA, "canned polemics" with an exaggerated "the Russians are coming" theme. Each month it publishes *Arms Control Today,* which contains a short article by a leading figure in the field as well as a current bibliography on arms control and related subjects. ACA has also lent its assistance to other publications. Beginning in 1976, for example, ACA cosponsored the annual publication of *World Military and Social*

Expenditures under the direction of Ruth Sivard, a former ACDA economist who once had responsibility for the Agency's *World Military Expenditures*.

While the association portrays itself as primarily an educational organization, only 32 percent of its membership agrees. A majority perceive ACA as an interest group.[9] Because of its tax-exempt status, ACA officially offers advice to congressmen only upon request. However, as is the practice among such groups, some members regularly advise Congress in an "individual capacity." That is, they formally divorce their personal views from those of the association, though in fact they are often—but not always—identical.

Among groups sharing interests similar to those of ACA, only the Federation of American Scientists has been asked to testify as frequently before congressional committees on arms control issues. ACA members have actually helped draft portions of major legislation affecting ACDA. For instance, at Congressman Zablocki's request, Adrian Fisher wrote a memorandum that directly contributed to sections of the 1975 arms control impact legislation.[10] Some members have personal friends in the House or Senate, and the executive director may have informal telephone conversations with legislators two or three times a week. Discussions between ACA members and individual legislators sometimes influence the latter's stands. Even prior to 1972, those who later became prominent ACA members were in contact with legislators. Senator Clifford Case (R–N.J.), for example, requested the Senate Foreign Relations Committee hearings on a comprehensive nuclear test ban, held in July 1971, following his talks with former ACDA officials who aroused his interest in the subject.[11]

The ABM issue marked a turning point. Afterward Congress demonstrated a notable tendency to lessen its dependence on the executive branch for sound analysis of national security issues. Many legislators turned to ACA and other organizations as alternative or supplemental sources of expert advice and analysis. These groups do not just address the specific military and budgetary implications of proposed security measures but often question the very assumptions underlying them. They provide ACDA with a small yet not inconsequential outside constituency, and they offer a public information service that ACDA either cannot provide or will not emphasize. Finally, they give Congress the kind of experienced professional advice that is essential if the legislative branch is to make an informed, distinctive contribution to arms control and national security policy.

13 ACDA and Congress

ACDA's RELATIONSHIP with Congress has often been referred to up to this point, but only in a piecemeal fashion. Here we examine the general nature of the relationship itself. The scope of this chapter is restricted. It does not systematically probe the intricacies of the congressional process. Nor is it a comprehensive treatment of Congress's handling of specific substantive arms control issues, an appropriate topic for a separate study.[1] Reference is made, of course, to Congress's role in particular substantive issues, but only to provide background and to illustrate the issue's impact upon or association with ACDA.

Before SALT I, the ABM controversy, détente, and the Nixon administration, congressional interest in arms control was at best sporadic. Congress never refused appropriations for any weapons system requested by a modern President; it lacked both analytical expertise and experienced staffing for arms control matters; and on those infrequent occasions when Congress noted ACDA's existence, it imposed restrictions. This began to change after 1968.

First SALT, then conventional arms sales and nuclear proliferation, made arms control a priority concern. Interest in arms control paralleled Congress's renewed overall activity in foreign and national security policy. Closer scrutiny was given to the defense budget. The Senate Armed Services Committee became more active, as did its Subcommittee on Research and Development, chaired by Senator Thomas McIntyre (D–N.H.). For the first time, the committee permitted testimony from witnesses critical of certain weapons programs. Jurisdiction over defense policy—once the exclusive preserve of the two Armed Services Committees, the two defense subcommittees of the Appropriations Committees, and the Joint Committee on Atomic Energy—became more diffuse. Now others got into the act: the House International Relations Committee, the Senate Foreign Relations Committee, the Senate Government Operations

165

Committee, the Joint Economic Committee, and others. Arms control proponents gained new strength and cohesion until they represented a formidable, if informal, coalition with a direct impact on policy outcomes. This coalition cut across both houses of Congress, though it has probably been most visible and effective in the Senate.[2] Congressional staffing for arms control and national security increased in quantity and quality,[3] while liberal-moderate legislators availed themselves of the outside advice of groups like the Council for a Livable World and the Arms Control Association. Congress enhanced its analytical capability by strengthening the arms control expertise of the General Accounting Office and the Congressional Research Service and by establishing two new organizations whose functions include the preparation of defense policy studies: the Office of Technology Assessment and the Congressional Budget Office. Congress also noticed ACDA. The coalition of arms control proponents regularly joined forces to secure for ACDA its budgetary requests, prod it to be more aggressive, give the Agency new legislative authority, and, on occasion, intercede when ACDA was thwarted by the executive branch or threatened by habitual congressional antagonists like Senator Jackson.

ACDA interacts most frequently with the committees which authorize and appropriate its budget: the House International Relations Committee and its Subcommittee on International Security and Scientific Affairs; the Senate Foreign Relations Committee and its Subcommittee on Arms Control, Oceans, and International Environment; and the subcommittees of the two Appropriations Committees. Agency officials also brief individual legislators and testify before several other committees. ACDA's congressional relations are handled by its Office of the General Counsel as well as the Offices of the Director and Deputy Director.

The two oversight subcommittees in the House and Senate have had a close, continuous interest in ACDA. Both have consistently sought to strengthen the Agency. The membership and chairmen of the Senate Foreign Relations Committee's Subcommittee on Arms Control, Oceans, and International Environment, which has had several different names, have been solicitous for ACDA's welfare. When it was chaired by Senator Humphrey, it pushed for ACDA's establishment. Subsequent chairmen, including Senators Muskie, Stuart Symington (D–Mo.), and Pell, have all been arms control advocates.

Congressman Zablocki has long chaired the House International Relations Committee's (formerly the House Foreign Affairs Committee) Subcommittee on International Security and Scientific Affairs (formerly the Subcommittee on National Security Policy and Scientific Developments).

If the Senate subcommittee has been solicitous, the House subcommittee has been virtually paternal. Following Senator Humphrey's death in January 1978 and Senator John Sparkman's (D–Ala.) announced retirement that year, Clement Zablocki, who by this time had succeeded Congressman Thomas Morgan as Chairman of the House International Relations Committee, was the only member of the 1961 Conference Committee on the ACD Act still serving in Congress. If Humphrey considered himself ACDA's "grandaddy," Zablocki was the benevolent guardian. His interest in ACDA was personal. Zablocki's subcommittee drafted much of the legislation in the 1970s affecting ACDA. It conducted the first thorough oversight review of the Agency, resisted attempts to weaken ACDA, and monitored its operations.

Gerard Smith, Dean Rusk, and others have urged Congress to create a joint committee on arms control. They argue: (1) In addition to the House International Relations Committee and the Senate Foreign Relations Committee, the Senate Armed Services Committee has a Subcommittee on Arms Control chaired by Senator Jackson, the House Armed Services Committee sprouted a Special Subcommittee on Arms Control and Disarmament in 1974 as well as a panel on SALT and a Comprehensive Test Ban Treaty in 1978, and several other committees have varying degrees of jurisdiction in the field. This leads to a duplication of effort and requires busy executive branch officials to deliver identical testimony before two or more committees. (2) A single committee should permit the executive to keep Congress more fully and currently informed since security would be improved.

But Congress has not been receptive to the idea. The reasons are not hard to find: (1) Most important, the existing committees guard their jurisdictional prerogatives closely. When the House Armed Services Committee established its Special Subcommittee on Arms Control and Disarmament, Zablocki denounced it as "an intrusion." Zablocki and other committee chairmen have been similarly cool toward intrusion by a joint committee.[4] (2) The trend has been away from joint committees. Some, like the Joint Committee on Atomic Energy, were abolished. Others, like joint committees on intelligence and on national security policy, have never been created despite efforts by their proponents. (3) A joint committee might add focus and continuity to congressional arms control efforts, but the existing arrangement, even if duplicative, serves a purpose. Arms control does affect foreign, defense, energy, and economic policy. It therefore seems proper for committees with responsibility for these diverse yet interrelated areas to consider the arms control perspective. After all, it might be neater and more efficient to consolidate all executive branch arms control authority in the State Department, but there are persuasive reasons for not doing so.

Dilemma: Executive Agent or Congressional Ally?

In 1974 George Berdes (of the Zablocki subcommittee staff) and Philip Farley coauthored a study for that subcommittee, which concluded, "As a resource for the Congress or the public, independent of the President [ACDA] has scarcely functioned."[5] ACDA is part of the executive branch and acts accordingly in its public and congressional relations. In their congressional testimony ACDA officials, like most executive branch agents, generally adhere closely to official policy. The President has ultimate responsibility for national security and the conduct of foreign relations. Naturally, he demands a high degree of discipline and conformity from subordinates. Presidents do have different styles; some will permit more leeway than others. But no President will tolerate public statements by subordinates that directly contravene established policy. Such disloyalty incurs a high risk of retribution, particularly if the transgressor is a small agency without a powerful public constituency. Also, if ACDA is thought by other departments to cooperate too closely with congressional arms controllers or, worse, to use Congress to augment its policy role, information may dry up, and the Agency could find itself excluded from some decisions. To be effective ACDA requires the backing or acquiesence of senior officials. It will not be forthcoming if this perception is prevalent.

ACDA Directors are acutely aware of this. Agency officers, like other government officials, have often delivered congressional testimony or other public statements that recited official policy but contravened their personal views. One of the more consequential examples of this occurred in 1970, when Gerard Smith, first in the spring, later in a telegram circulated on the day of the Senate vote, expressed his support for expanding deployment of the Safeguard ABM on grounds that it would not prejudice SALT. Many, including Raymond Garthoff of the SALT delegation, believed that without Smith's support the Senate would not have sustained the system.[6]

The Defense Reorganization Act of 1958 includes a provision, termed "legalized insubordination" by President Eisenhower, which permits service Secretaries and JCS members to present to Congress, on their own initiative, after notifying the Secretary of Defense, "any recommendations relating to the Department of Defense that he may deem proper.''[7] Senior military officers have often used this authority to present their personal views to Congress. ACDA Directors have not enjoyed this privilege. Fred Iklé was the most independent. He even maintained that there was a "tradition" permitting Congress "to obtain the personal opinion . . . of a director of an agency.''[8] But ACDA has no such tradition. Iklé's relative freedom resulted from an unusual combination of factors: President Ford encouraged improved relations with Congress; Iklé had considerable personal support from congressional conservatives and even some liberals; Iklé frequently allied with OSD and JCS on SALT, which endeared him to the conservatives; and most of his more outspoken statements concerned nuclear proliferation, where there was a consensus in favor of doing something.

But most of the time, Iklé adhered to the party line. So did his predecessors. For example, prior to President Johnson's decision to kill the MLF, ACDA was directed to defend it at Geneva and before Congress even though the Agency, believing it to be antithetical to the Non-Proliferation Treaty, was its most ardent in-house critic. ACDA was concerned about the Sentinnel ABM, yet in 1967 Fisher told the ENDC that its deployment would neither aggravate the arms race nor impede arms control. Foster testified in 1968 that ACDA was fully involved in decisions concerning conventional arms sales when, in fact, it was almost entirely excluded. Smith and Farley repeated the Nixon administration position that a comprehensive nuclear test ban could not be negotiated without further refinements in verification techniques and on-site inspection, though that was not their personal opinion. Iklé's deputy, John Lehman, told a West Point audience of ACDA's opposition to three items in DOD's FY 1977 budget, which had been overruled by the White House. Nonetheless, Lehman said he would testify in favor of them since, "If I tell the Congress . . . that the Agency opposes these three items, I can probably kill [them]. You might say that is in the national interest. But it will be the last time ACDA ever participates in Executive deliberations.''[9]

Chapter 14 will indicate specific hazards and real costs in fraternizing, or being thought to fraternize, too closely with Congress. But there are also risks in being too aloof. Congress expects a reasonable degree of executive cooperation and adequate information flow. An angry committee chairman or influential Senator can make life very unpleasant. Furthermore, although ACDA does not stress the point publicly, the Agency needs congressional allies. It is not so richly endowed with bargaining advantages within the executive branch that it can afford to be unresponsive to Congress. Still, ACDA has been reluctant to seek major new legislative authority; the impetus for such legislation has usually come from Congress.

Between 1974 and 1978 Congress took, or attempted to take, several actions to strengthen the Agency. Most of these actions seemed rooted in three concerns: (1) Arms control proponents were deeply disturbed by the 1973 purge, which was thought to have gravely jeopardized ACDA's effectiveness. The result was a congressional reaction intended not only to buttress the Agency but to signal other executive actors that they would have to answer to Congress if ACDA was excluded from certain matters. (2) There was a desire to see arms control more fully integrated into national security and foreign policy decisions. ACDA was the chosen instrument for effectuating this. (3) Congress wanted more accurate, complete, and timely information than it had previously received from ACDA or the rest of the executive branch.

On balance, ACDA has benefited greatly from these congressional actions. However, in some instances there was an executive reaction, predicted by ACDA officials, a feeling that ACDA was being favored at the expense of others and was, wittingly or unwittingly, a tool of Congress. This sentiment is not conducive to the degree of internal executive branch confidence ACDA must enjoy to be effective. In the summer of 1977 a congressional staffer said: "Unfortunately, in the long run, I think the Agency is doomed given its inability to clearly identify itself as an executive actor, not an arm of Congress." While this overstates the gravity of the problem, it indicates ACDA's dilemma. ACDA needs congressional allies but is sometimes threatened by their usually well-meaning attentions. Congress gave ACDA new legislative authority in several areas, but the legislation itself, in certain instances, circumscribed the Agency's ability to implement this authority. However, it was not solely a question of ACDA's ability to utilize this new authority; it was also, to a degree, a matter of the Agency's willingness, first to accept the legislation, and then vigorously to use it.

1961–1968

This dilemma acquired poignancy only in the 1970s and, despite its importance, represents an improvement for ACDA over the 1960s. The concern then was more basic. ACDA did not consider Congress particularly hospitable to arms control or arms controllers. Reflecting on that period, Mason Willrich, then with ACDA, found that Congress exercised its authority over arms control policy "primarily in a negative sense."[10] There is ample evidence to support this view. Many legislators approached arms control and ACDA with coolness and distrust. The arms control supporters in Congress had only limited influence. Thus, certain measures favored by ACDA, like a comprehensive nuclear test ban, could not have mustered necessary support in the Senate.[11] Even potentially destabilizing weapons programs were rarely scrutinized for their possible arms control ramifications. For example, Congress added enormous momentum to the Sentinnel ABM program when it appropriated $167.9 million in 1966 for procurement of ABM hardware that McNamara had neither requested nor desired.[12]

On the other hand, this picture must be balanced against other congressional actions during the 1960s. ACDA was established. The Senate ratified the Partial Test Ban Treaty and the Outer Space Treaty and encouraged U.S. efforts toward a Non-Proliferation Treaty. Individual legislators played significant roles. On May 27, 1963, Senator Thomas Dodd (D–Conn.)—who opposed a comprehensive test ban treaty—introduced a resolution, cosponsored by thirty-three other senators, calling for "an immediate agreement banning all tests that contaminate the atmosphere or the oceans."[13] This came at a crucial juncture in the test ban negotiations and demonstrated to President Kennedy that the treaty enjoyed considerable support. Senator Humphrey, a cosponsor of the Dodd resolution, had introduced a test ban resolution in 1959 that was unanimously adopted by the Senate; this probably made it difficult for the Eisenhower administration to break off negotiations without appearing to defy the sense of the Senate. On January 18, 1966, Senator John Pastore (D–R.I.), with fifty-five cosponsors, introduced Senate Resolution 179, which vigorously supported the Geneva Non-Proliferation Treaty negotiations and urged "additional efforts by the President." It was unanimously endorsed by the Senate and welcomed by President Johnson. Pastore's speech on S. Res. 179 called for amending Article III of the proposed treaty in order to strengthen the safeguard requirements. This probably exerted some pressure on those within the executive branch who were reluctant to press for more stringent safeguards, and, by the summer of 1966, the United States had adopted the Pastore position.[14] In September 1967 Senator Pell introduced S. Res. 172, which called for the initiation of arms control measures to prevent the stationing of nuclear weapons and other weapons of mass destruction on the ocean floor. After the Senate Foreign Relations Committee hearings on S. Res. 172, Pell introduced S. Res. 186, proposing a draft treaty to implement his proposal. The executive branch opposed both resolutions. Pell persisted, and by 1968 it was an ENDC agenda item. The Senator's perseverance was rewarded when the Senate ratified the Seabed Treaty in 1972.[15]

So Congress had a mixed record on arms control. But ACDA did not fare well. Adrian Fisher, whose father had been chairman of the House Military Affairs Committee, dealt adroitly with Congress, but this was not enough to offset the clout of ACDA's critics. Budgetary requests were usually cut, external research programs were criticized and reduced, security requirements were unusually restrictive, the public information program was crippled, and other constraints were imposed. ACDA's low estate was especially reflected by one amendment to the ACD Act. The National Rifle Association and its congressional spokesmen succeeded in amending section 33 of the act (PL 88-186) in 1963. It prohibited ACDA or other government agencies from interfering with the right of U.S. citizens to possess or use firearms, thereby assuring America's squirrel hunters that their Second Amendment rights would not be usurped by arms controllers. The amendment's proponents, judging from their testimony and the floor debate, had little understanding of either ACDA or arms control, but they had an abiding fear of and distaste for both.[16]

1969 to Mid-1978

ARMS CONTROL GAINS ATTENTION

Things began to change by 1969. The Senate ratified all arms control accords submitted by the Nixon and Ford administrations, and Congress took arms control initiatives in several areas. Congressional support was not automatic. For example, Senate approval of the SALT Interim Agreement was accompanied by Senator Jackson's 1972 amendment, which sent a cautionary message to the executive, and SALT critics became increasingly vocal by 1973. The Senate attached reservations to its ratification of Protocol II of the Treaty for the Prohibition of Nuclear Weapons in Latin America. Senator Fulbright delayed Senate Foreign Relations Committee action on the Geneva Protocol and the Biological Warfare Convention until the executive modified its stand on herbicides and riot control agents. But arms control had become a generally accepted component of American foreign policy.

Congressional arms control proponents lost the 1969–1970 fight over the ABM, but their efforts were not entirely fruitless. The episode marked the first time since World War II that such a formidable bloc expressed concern about a major weapons system. It was a catalyst for the formation of a large, loose coalition of congressional arms control supporters. The narrow margin in favor of the ABM also restricted the administration's SALT options.

But Congress had difficulty participating in SALT, especially during the Nixon administration. Nixon distrusted Congress. The President and Kissinger shared a penchant for secrecy and withheld vital information.[17] Their close policy control deterred ACDA officials and others from frankly advocating their views before Congress. Hence, Congress's attempts to influence the course of negotiations were ineffectual. For instance, Senator Edward Brooke's (D–Mass.) S. Res. 211 (approved by a vote of 72 to 6 in 1970), which called upon the President to propose a joint Soviet–American MIRV flight test moratorium, was ignored by Nixon.

Overall congressional activity did, however, increase. For example, it was learned in 1969 that the Army planned to ship poisonous chemical munitions across the country to the Atlantic Coast, where they were to be placed aboard old liberty ships and sunk 250 miles out at sea. Protests poured into Congress. That spring three congressional subcommittees opened investigations. This made it difficult for the administration to ignore the issue of chemical weapons; one of the congressional hearings, by the Zablocki subcommittee, was cited by an ACDA official as influencing some in the executive branch to include toxins in the Biological Warfare Convention.[18]

In 1971 Senator Pell became concerned about the Pentagon's research, development, and use of various environmental modification techniques for military purposes. At first, DOD refused to divulge requested information pertaining to its activities in this area, and Pentagon witnesses before Pell's subcommittee were uncooperative. Pell persevered. He introduced S. Res. 71, adopted by a vote of 82 to 10 in 1973, which declared the sense of the Senate to be that there be a "complete cessation of research, experimentation, and use of environmental and geophysical modification activities as weapons of war." His subcommittee, and other committees as well, held hearings on the subject, and Pell asked the President to open negotiations on the matter.[19] The resulting Environmental Modification Ban, signed by the United States in 1977, is in large measure Senator Pell's personal accomplishment.

Nixon was not enthusiastic about a comprehensive nuclear test ban, but it now had stronger backing in the Senate. There were thirty-two cosponsors of Senator Edward Kennedy's (D–Mass.) 1973 S. Res. 67 which declared the sense of the Senate to be that the President "propose an immediate suspension on underground nuclear testing."[20]

By the time of the Ford administration, much of Congress's attention had turned to conventional arms shipments and nuclear proliferation. Some individual legislators had been concerned about U.S. conventional arms transfers, but not until 1974 did they become a major issue. Several factors now combined to arouse congressional interest, including: (1) frustration with Congress's minimal policy role; (2) seeming lack of a coherent U.S. arms transfer policy; (3) the dramatic increase in the volume of sales (less than $6 billion in 1973 to more than $10 billion in 1974); (4) the advanced technology involved in certain transactions; (5) destination—by 1974 one-third of U.S. arms sales went to the volatile Middle East and Persian Gulf; and (6) concern about arms races, human rights, regional stability, sound economic development, and maintenance of adequate quantities of weapons for our own armed forces.

Senator Gaylord Nelson (D–Wis.) and Representative Bingham introduced legislation, subsequently enacted, that required the President to notify Congress of proposed foreign arms sales in excess of $25 million. Congress then had twenty calendar days to adopt an objecting concurrent resolution if it wished to overrule the President. But this authority was not exercised. Then the International Security Assistance and Arms Export Control Act of 1976 (PL 94-329) was passed. In the most general sense, it channeled most U.S. foreign arms transfers into the more easily monitored foreign military sales route; established comprehensive procedures designed to force the executive to state an overall national policy for arms sales abroad; and required fuller public disclosure in order to permit congressional deliberation on the issues. *Inter alia,* it required exhaustive reports to Congress on a variety of arms transfer matters; notification of certain commercial export licenses; the Nelson–Bingham stipulations were changed so that Congress was to be notified of all military sales of more than $7 million and now had thirty days to interpose an objection; and the President was urged to institute international negotiations to limit conventional arms traffic.[21] Despite this legislation, U.S. overseas arm sales continued to rise sharply in 1977.

After Senate ratification of the Non-Proliferation Treaty in 1969, Congress paid little attention to nuclear proliferation until the May 1974 Indian nuclear blast and Nixon's June trip to the Middle East, where, without consulting Congress, he agreed to provide Egypt and Israel with light water nuclear reactors. But from May 1974 and into the Carter administration, nuclear proliferation was a subject of intense interest and activity. Numerous hearings were held, national and international agencies with responsibility for nuclear safeguards received additional funding, and several pieces of legislation were passed. For example, Congress denied appropriations for the purpose of constructing reactors in Egypt and Israel, and the Energy Reorganization Act abolished the AEC, replacing it with ERDA and the NRC. This marked the end of a long period of congressional encouragement to international commercial activities by the U.S. nuclear industry with only minimal restrictive oversight by Congress.

Until 1976, however,more comprehensive approaches to the problem were repeatedly thwarted by the Joint Committee on Atomic Energy, which viewed itself as a guardian of the American nuclear industry. Before March 1976, the Joint Committee had held only one hearing on nuclear proliferation in five years. Of the seven nuclear export measures reported by this committee between 1971 and 1976, five authorized increases in exports and none attempted meaningfully to limit them. Hostility toward the Joint Committee grew until it was stripped of its legislative authority and, in early 1977, abolished.[22] This cleared the way for the Nuclear Nonproliferation Act of 1978, which comprehensively addressed the subject of American nuclear exports.

SMITH AND IKLÉ: RELATIONS WITH CONGRESS

Smith and Farley had generally cordial relations with most committees, but there was some dissatisfaction with their refusal to be more forthcoming with information, especially on SALT. Although ACDA briefed congressional committees (usually in executive session) at least thirty times on SALT I—nine times for the Zablocki subcommittee alone—these encounters were not always open, engaging, and wide-ranging. The requirements for full consultation were absent. Smith was under White House constraints. Specific proposals were usually unavailable. When they were available, there was little opportunity for real consideration, and congressional staff members were sometimes denied access to them.[23] Nonetheless, one House staffer remarked that the frequency of these briefings was crucial to gaining broad congressional acceptance of SALT I, not only by fostering understanding but, more subtly, by creating a "sense" of being consulted.

In addition to the Kissinger-imposed restrictions on all SALT officials, Smith and Farley conscientiously avoided the appearance of attempting an end run around ACDA's SALT opponents. Hence the formal channels of communication to Congress were usually the actual channels. Only in the last months of his directorship, after the SALT I accords were signed in Moscow, did Smith adopt a more outspoken stance. He challenged some publicly expressed views of Defense Secretary Laird and criticized the so-called bargaining chip approach to SALT, the notion that weapons systems should be deployed less for their inherent strategic rationale than as bargaining chips to be traded in negotiations.[24] But such outspokenness was exceptional. The rule in public and in private was circumspection. It is probable that the NATO allies were better briefed on SALT then was the U.S. Congress.

For reasons discussed above, Iklé enjoyed reasonably good relations with the Hill despite frequent complaints that he was too cautious and diffident. Conservatives were especially pleased with him. After all, ACDA's leadership was a product of the Jackson-sponsored purge and reflected the senator's general orientation on key national security issues. Iklé's immediate task in 1973 was to ameliorate ties with aroused liberals, who were to scrutinize ACDA's operations more closely throughout his directorship than at any other time in the Agency's history. In his first fifteen months Iklé or his staff testified at nineteen committee hearings. Iklé personally gave sixty-five briefings to individual members of Congress and hosted at least four informal sessions in his office, involving forty-three congressional staffers. He maintained this pace, often remarking that congressional relations were his "first priority." Iklé was moved by the bipartisan tributes from members of Senator Pell's subcommittee when he last appeared before Congress in an official capacity in January 1977.[25]

Iklé had to shoulder such a heavy load personally because his deputy could not be of much assistance. John Lehman's nomination hearing was heated, and he was only narrowly approved by the Senate Foreign Relations Committee. Senator Symington, who then chaired the committee's Arms Control Subcommittee, had not been consulted about the nomination, and he led the opposition. Some were concerned about Lehman's reputed conservative views. Questions were raised about his Ph.D. dissertation and his charging Senator Fulbright with "dereliction of trust and good faith." A former Deputy Assistant Secretary of State for Congressional Relations asserted that Lehman lacked a "personal commitment to consultation and cooperation with the legislative branch." This obviously created, as Senator Pell later remarked, "a very bad situation."[26] Lehman did, of course, have ties to Senator Jackson's office, though this hardly endeared him to the arms control bloc.

SUPPORT FOR ACDA

When I say "Congress" did this or that, the reader should know the caution with which such statements are made. None of our federal institutions is more complex, unpredictable, and downright cantankerous. General assertions about the legislative branch are invariably subject to exceptions or refinements. Nonetheless, generalizations can and should be made.

One generalization is that from 1969 to 1976 ACDA acquired considerable congressional backing, reflected in regularly satisfied budget requests as well as supportive hearings, investigations, and legislation. This is not to suggest that most legislators followed ACDA closely, or at all, or that it lacked critics. Representative L. H. Fountain (D–N.C.) has a point when he says that "not many Members of Congress know much about the Arms Control Agency, except the title." But general awareness of ACDA and, more important, understanding of arms control certainly did increase. Senator Jackson was not the Agency's only faultfinder. Some liberals as well as some conservatives criticized the Agency, though for different reasons. Still, ACDA acquired significant bipartisan support during this period, which, while not an entirely unmixed blessing, did afford a far more secure congressional base than in the past. Some traditional ACDA critics even changed their tune. Representative Paul Findley (R–Ill.) said that "at one time I thought the Arms Control Agency was a waste of high-priced help. . . . I have changed my view."[27]

At times, legislators were too eager to improve ACDA's lot. Senator Case introduced an amendment to the ACD Act in 1972 that would have transferred government responsibility for seismic research from the Defense Department's Advanced Research Projects Agency (ARPA) to ACDA. The bill was reported out by the Senate Foreign Relations Committee over ACDA's strenuous opposition but was defeated on the Senate floor by a vote of 45 to 34. Senator Case argued: (1) This would improve ACDA's effectiveness by adding new responsibility (which the ACD Act already permitted it to have) and by doubling its budget. (2) It would enhance prospects for a comprehensive nuclear test ban, which DOD and ARPA opposed. (3) Seismic research spending was reduced in 1971 despite the official U.S. position that on-site inspection and more research were still necessary before a comprehensive test ban would be feasible. (4) ACDA did not meaningfully participate in ARPA's program, and data had been withheld.

ACDA was alarmed that one of the Senate's most dependable arms control supporters could propose a measure, based upon a misreading of political and bureaucratic realities, that promised to harm the Agency. This concern was largely shared by the Arms Control Association. Adrian Fisher testified that he supported the amendment "in principle," though most of his testimony stressed ACA's reservations. But ACDA had difficulty convincing friends in the Senate of the sincerity of its objections.

Senator Fulbright, for one, felt that Smith was only following the administration's orders.

Smith's objections were several: (1) ACDA–ARPA relations *were* cooperative. Information flow was not a significant problem; they had worked jointly for many years, and it was ARPA research that had led to the Partial Test Ban Treaty; and ACDA had the government's top seismic expert. (2) The advantage of small size would disappear without an offsetting gain. The amendment, which stipulated a $10 million increase in ACDA's budget, would grossly distort the Agency's priorities. Seismic research was not ACDA's only interest. The real obstacle to a comprehensive test ban was neither ARPA's supposed obstinacy nor, contrary to official statements, a lack of research. It was Nixon's political decision not to proceed. Transferring seismic research to ACDA would not have altered Nixon's position. (3) It would be a needless, counterproductive affront to DOD, jeopardizing ACDA–DOD relations in other areas.[28] ACDA was relieved when the Senate defeated this well-meaning but mischievous amendment. While acknowledging congressional support, ACDA must have felt, "With friends like that, who needs enemies?"

Within months, though, ACDA needed all the support it could muster. When the leadership was purged and the budget slashed in 1973, the congressional arms control bloc reacted aggressively. First came the protests. Senator Proxmire, Chairman of the Joint Economic Committee, termed it "appalling" and vowed to "fight" to restore ACDA's funds and stature. ACDA's oldest patron, Senator Humphrey, issued statements, wrote Nixon warning that this warranted Congress's "immediate attention and corrective action," and instructed his staff to prepare a report for the Members of Congress for Peace through Law. Senator Muskie, Chairman of the Senate Foreign Relations Committee's Arms Control Subcommittee, and Senator Fulbright made it clear to Iklé at his nomination hearings that ACDA's welfare would be a primary committee concern. Senator Pastore, Chairman of the Senate Appropriations Committee's subcommittee that passed on ACDA's budget, found it "disgraceful." And thirteen senators and forty-three congressmen wrote OMB Director Roy Ash calling the budget cut a "false economy" and urging that no less than a $10 million budget be assigned ACDA for the next fiscal year.[29]

Congress restored some of OMB's budget cuts, and in the spring of 1974 the Zablocki subcommittee commenced the first complete review of ACDA since 1961. Over Iklé's protests, the Agency was given just a one-year authorization, pending the outcome of this investigation. The review was necessary, said Zablocki, because "the feeling has been growing in Congress that the initial effectiveness of the Agency has diminished.'' Zablocki was concerned that ACDA had "veered away from original congressional intentions'' and that its role in the formulation and execution of policy had declined. Iklé was assured that the "sole purpose'' of the review and the one-year authorization was to "upgrade ACDA'' by enhancing its "future status and effectiveness.'' The subcommittee then ordered a study of the Agency to provide an analytical base for subsequent legislation.[30]

In 1975 the ACD Act was amended for the express purpose of enhancing ACDA's effectiveness:

1. The most significant amendment (discussed in the next chapter) sought to give ACDA a say in the weapons acquisition process via a new arms control impact statement procedure.

2. The language of section 2 of the ACD Act, which enumerates ACDA's four "primary functions,'' was changed from "It [ACDA] must be able to'' to "It shall have the authority to'' perform these functions (PL 94-144). This, said the House report, shifts the emphasis "from capability to perform'' the enumerated functions to ACDA's "designation as the Government agency having primary authority for performing those functions'' under the President and Secretary of State.

3. Section 22 was amended to give the Director, for the first time, legal standing identical to the Chairman of the JCS as an adviser to the NSC (PL 94-145). The symbolic importance of this amendment, which permits the Director's regular attendance at NSC meetings, probably exceeds its actual significance. Its drafters sought to emphasize that many national security issues "directly or indirectly,'' potentially or in fact, relate to arms control; that arms control must be viewed broadly. But this provision may also increase the political costs to senior actors if they exclude ACDA from policy decisions, for congressmen can ask (and have asked), "Was ACDA consulted?'' An admission of nonconsultation might disturb key legislators, and, as it could imply that the NSC was not involved, it could also raise awkward questions about how the decision *was* reached.

4. Restrictive security procedures were eased, and the inhibitory prohibition against disseminating "propaganda'' was eliminated.

5. Noting that ACDA's annual report to Congress provided "little if any substantive information,'' Congress amended section 50 to require that it "include a complete and analytical statement of arms control and disarmament goals, negotiations and activities'' (PL 94-141). The report should be "analogous to the annual 'Posture Statement' provided to Congress by the Secretary of Defense.''[31]

Changes in ACDA's legal mandate extended beyond the ACD Act to the area of conventional arms transfers. A precursor of this legislation was Senator William Roth's (R–Del.) amendment to the Foreign Relations Authorization Act of 1972 (section 302, PL 92-352), requiring the Agency to submit a comprehensive report to Congress on the international transfer of conventional arms. The Agency's analysis in the submitted Roth report (1974) was justly criticized by the Congressional Research Service for its vagueness, for inadequate citations, and for essentially summarizing some of the publicly available research. However, while deficient, the report contained some useful statistical data that had hitherto been classified, and it was the first time a major nation had published detailed statistics on the arms trade.[32] ACDA had initially resisted the Roth amendment, but the exercise was later considered "very useful" by an ACDA official responsible for implementing it. Among other things, it forced the Agency to bring together previously unconsolidated material for use within the bureaucracy and suggested some new areas for future research. ACDA has continued annually to publish statistical data on the international arms trade. Its *World Military Expenditures* was retitled *World Military Expenditures and Arms Transfers* to reflect this.

By 1975 Congress was prepared to go beyond the modest reporting requirements of the Roth amendment. The House International Relations Committee stated that it was time to formalize executive procedures for consultation and cooperation concerning conventional arms transfers, because, especially regarding ACDA, existing informal procedures "have not been fully implemented or followed."[33] That is, ACDA was out of the action. Hence, Congress amended section 414 of the Mutual Security Act, section 42(a) of the Foreign Military Sales Act, and section 511 of the Foreign Assistance Act of 1961 (PL 94-150a-c) to require that the Director be consulted and his opinion considered in the issuance of arms export licenses, in military sales decisions, and in decisions to furnish military assistance. A congressional staffer described these amendments as "a statement of frustration." Congress was concerned about U.S. international arms traffic and was grasping—here by legislating a larger role for ACDA—for a way to make the executive branch face the problem. This staffer added, by way of accurate prediction, "We're offering an olive branch, but the amendments' effect will likely be pro forma. State will resist. But if they do, more stringent legislation will follow."

State resisted. The next year saw the passage of the International Security Assistance and Arms Export Control Act of 1976, which, concerning ACDA, reiterated the 1975 language and mandated that future executive submissions regarding security assistance be accompanied by reports to Congress, which must include (1) an estimate of the quantity of proposed arms transfers to each recipient country and "a detailed explanation" of how U.S. arms shipments to each recipient affected U.S. foreign policy and national security interests, and (2) "an arms control impact statement for each purchasing country" analyzing the transaction's anticipated arms control impact on the country and on regional stability. Additionally, any U.S. offer to sell more than $7 million of defense equipment must be accompanied by an arms control impact statement pertinent to that offer if the House International Relations Committee or the Senate Foreign Relations Committee so requests.[34] ACDA was given a primary role in the preparation of these statements in cooperation with the State and Defense departments.

Congress was bluntly instructing the State Department to include ACDA in the policy process. In January 1977 President Ford issued Executive Order 11958, directing the implementation of this legislation with full ACDA involvement. Simultaneously, State's Inspector General issued an internal report warning that refusal to bring ACDA into the decision-making process "prompted hostile congressional pronouncements that result in further legislative attempts to shore up ACDA's position within the executive branch."[35] Some improvement in ACDA's status did occur in 1977 and 1978, though only time will permit a conclusive judgment.

While Congress's overall attempts to bolster ACDA's executive branch position in the conventional arms area have aided the Agency (before the legislation, ACDA had no significant voice) the ultimate utility of the conventional arms transfer arms control impact statements, for ACDA and for Congress, is problematic. These statements pose the familiar predicament for an executive actor of being cast as an agent of Congress, even though they are executive branch, not ACDA, documents. This can be especially troublesome for ACDA, because the statements might be used by legislators to embarrass the administration. ACDA, State, and Defense therefore have strong incentives to submit rather bland statements to Congress, which is what happened in 1977 concerning the proposed sale of a sophisticated airborne warning system to Iran. It is also questionable, because of the subject matter, whether the statements' projections of the arms control consequences of a proposed arms transaction can be instructive to Congress. While guarded forecasts might be hazarded about the possible arms control implications of, say, a proposed U.S. mobile ICBM, forecasting becomes even more speculative for an amorphous subject like conventional arms transfers, which is so enmeshed in larger, competing foreign policy considerations and has stubbornly defied lasting international controls. On the other hand, the statements could prove productive in two ways. While the information contained in the initial statements was sparse, it is probable that future statements will have more and better data. This prospect was suggested by the improved quality of the 1978 statement on the F-16 multimission fighter. Second, by forcing the executive branch to deal directly and systematically with the arms control implications of conventional arms sales—something the executive said and maybe even thought it was doing but, in fact, was not—Congress may affect the larger decision-making climate by heightening general awareness of the problem.

A final area where ACDA enjoyed newfound congressional support was in the civilian nuclear field. When concern about nuclear proliferation increased, Congress pressured the executive to afford ACDA a greater role in nuclear export decisions. Congress and Fred Iklé prodded Kissinger and President Ford to take nuclear proliferation seriously. A top ACDA officer in this area remarked, "When we didn't have the press and Congress screaming at us, things didn't get done. Strong congressional support for nonproliferation also afforded Iklé some leeway to make outspoken public statements."

In 1976 the Senate Government Operations Committee held hearings on a bill that, *inter alia,* proposed requiring the NRC to "obtain a nuclear proliferation assessment statement" from ACDA before approving various U.S. civilian nuclear transactions. ACDA was to send the statement *directly* to the NRC, the Secretary of State, and Congress instead of processing it through the State Department bureaucracy. Both Iklé and Kissinger opposed this proposal. State, stressing its authority over foreign policy, argued that all policy-relevant actions must be coordinated through State. The Nuclear Nonproliferation Act of 1978, passed unanimously by the House and by an 88 to 3 vote in the Senate, differed substantially from the original bill. Under the Act, ACDA's Director may prepare an unclassified nuclear proliferation assessment statement covering any U.S. arrangement for nuclear cooperation with another government if he considers that arrangement to contribute significantly to proliferation. While ACDA's important role in the civilian nuclear area is expressly recognized throughout the act, the law also mandates thorough interdepartmental coordination.[36]

THE WARNKE NOMINATION

ACDA as such was hardly mentioned during the controversy surrounding Paul Warnke's nomination by President Carter in early 1977.

Except for questions about the wisdom of the Director's leading the SALT delegation (and many who criticized his wearing two hats seemed as upset about the man as the number of hats he wore), Warnke's detractors were primarily concerned about his substantive stands and normative views.

Equally important was the President's openly professed personal stake in the outcome. Carter repeatedly declared his support for Warnke and personally lobbied for his confirmation. The affair was widely portrayed as a crucial test for the new administration and, as such, received national media coverage. The entire nomination process had a heavy undercurrent of liberal-versus-conservative politics. And Carter's obvious willingness to risk his reputation for Warnke put a finer point on the debate: This Director, his critics feared, just might enjoy the President's confidence.

The pro- and anti-Warnke forces represented more or less identifiable philosophical camps. Senate liberals and moderates, including virtually the entire arms control coalition, were supportive. They dominated the Senate Foreign Relations Committee, which advised his confirmation as Director by a vote of 15 to 1 and as chief SALT negotiator by a vote of 14 to 2. Outside the Senate, Warnke's backers included, among others, former Directors Foster and Smith; the Arms Control Association; former Defense Secretaries Clark Clifford, Robert McNamara, and Melvin Laird; some labor unions; as well as George Kennan, Lawrence Eagleburger, Bernard Brodie, Herbert York, Harold Agnew, McGeorge Bundy, and William Colby. The oppostion comprised conservatives and some moderates. Their institutional base was the Senate Armed Services Committee, which took the unusual step of holding hearings on a nomination over which it lacked jurisdiction. Mindful of this, Committee Chairman John Stennis (D–Miss.) announced that it would neither vote nor issue a report on the nomination. However, all the committee's Republican members and half of its Democratic membership expressed disapproval of Warnke. They were joined by Admiral Moorer, Paul Nitze, the Liberty Lobby, the American Conservative Union, the American Security Council, and several conservative congressmen. The conservative lobby sent out more than a million pieces of mail to influence public opinion. Many Senate offices reported receiving more than five hundred anti-Warnke postcards daily.[37]

Warnke's firmest supporters, like Senator Humphrey, were delighted that, at last, ACDA was to be headed by a prominent, aggressive arms control advocate with certified liberal credentials. With his numerous publications criticizing some defense expenditures as excessive or destabilizing, affiliation with organizations like the Center for Defense Information, and a prominent role as national security adviser to Senator

George McGovern (D–S.D.) during his 1972 presidential campaign, Warnke was seen by many liberals as an ideal choice. For critics, predictably led by Senator Jackson, these credentials completely disqualified him, especially for the post of SALT negotiator. The opposition's arguments included the following.

Patriotism. No senator questioned Warnke's patriotism, but Paul Nitze did:

SENATOR McINTYRE. Are you saying that you impugn his character as an American citizen?

MR. NITZE. If you force me to, I do.

SENATOR McINTYRE. That is very interesting. Do you think you are a better American than he is?

MR. NITZE. I really do.[38]

Arms Controller. Conservatives saw Warnke as the classic arms controller—supposedly idealistic, insensitive to Soviet designs, and, of course, as Senator Jake Garn (R–Utah) concluded, "naive."[39]

Opposition to Defense Programs. Senator Jackson began his questioning by listing several military programs Warnke had opposed. Much of the Armed Services Committee's hearings revolved around this list. For Jackson and the conservatives this suggested an almost doctrinal, automatic stand against weapons systems vital to national defense.[40]

Inconsistency. When Warnke replied that he had altered his views on some of these programs, Senator Jackson and other dwelled upon the nominee's alleged inconsistency and the "suddenness" with which he changed his mind.[41]

Credibility as Negotiator. Senator Stennis and others therefore asserted that—because of Warnke's alleged inconsistency, "softness," and opposition to necessary weapons systems—he lacked the kind of toughness and credibility a SALT Ambassador must possess. Admiral Moorer summarized this view: "I believe that Mr. Warnke has already devalued his chips in this life and death poker game before he has been dealt the first hand."[42]

Warnke and his supporters argued that he was not the knee-jerk arms controller portrayed by his detractors, but a strong advocate of sound arms control; there was no incompatibility between well-conceived arms control agreements and national security, indeed, they enhance security; only ideologues never change their opinions; and therefore he was an excellent choice for SALT Ambassador and ACDA Director.

The final vote on the SALT Ambassador position was 58 to 40; for ACDA Director, 70 to 29. Warnke was confirmed, but his future effectiveness was in question. Senator Jackson (who opposed only Warnke's nomination as SALT Ambassador) said, "I cannot vote to confirm a man who has shattered my confidence." Jackson and congressional conservatives would have to be reckoned with, and perhaps mollified, concerning SALT II. Aware of this, President Carter attempted early in 1977 to establish a dialogue with Senator Jackson.[43]

TROUBLE AHEAD?

Despite the Warnke controversy, in 1977 Congress increased AC-DA's budget, augmented its funds for external research and public information, and passed several amendments to the ACD Act, which, with one notable exception, were welcomed by the Agency. ACDA was exempted from inhibiting civil service regulations; certain travel restrictions were liberalized, it was permitted to let contracts to foreign research organizations, and—at Warnke's request—a new position of Special Representative for Arms Control and Disarmament Negotiations was authorized.

The exception was the so-called Derwinski amendment. Representative Edward Derwinski (R–Ill.) introduced a bill to amend the ACD Act by requiring the Director to report to Congress on a variety of matters relating to the verification of arms control proposals and agreements. Professing support for ACDA, Derwinski stated that "the purpose behind the amendment [is the] public feeling that you can't trust the Russians." Zablocki opposed the amendment, arguing on the House floor that the assumption that the Soviet Union casually violates arms control accords was erroneous; the reporting requirement was assigned to the wrong agency, inasmuch as the intelligence community, not ACDA, has primary responsibility for verification; by law, ACDA was already charged with fully considering the verification of arms control agreements; and the reporting procedure was unnecessary because verification matters were routinely discussed both within the executive branch and before relevant congressional committees. But Zablocki's objections were overridden by a 159-to-148 vote.[44]

A similar, though not identical, bill was passed in the Senate, where Senator Jackson was a key originator and sponsor. However, it had significant liberal backing from such reliable arms control proponents as Senators Pell, Case, and Alan Cranston (D–Cal.). Cranston, in fact, introduced the amendment. His purpose was to send "a signal . . . that there is a widespread concern in the Senate . . . over the verifiability of arms control agreements, especially those dealing with strategic arms."[45]

The Conference Committee elected the Senate version, which differed in important respects from the Derwinski bill. Most significantly, the latter had declared it to be the sense of the Congress "that effective verification of compliance is an indispensable factor in any international arms control agreement." Several congressional arms control proponents and, somewhat belatedly, ACDA feared that the phrase "effective verification" might be so construed as to set a standard of compliance, especially concerning SALT, that would be impossible to meet. More bluntly, they saw the Derwinski bill as an attempt to kill SALT II. When the Senate turned its attention to the matter in late May, a senior administration official, at considerable risk to his career, offered his assistance to liberal senators. This official was personally responsible for the substitution of the phrase "adequate verification" for "effective verification" in the Senate bill.

The Senate version, which Congress adopted, unlike the House bill, also exempted ACDA from disclosing sensitive information about intelligence sources, methods, or persons working on arms control verification. The Conference Committee's report additionally stated that the provision "is not intended to interfere with the President's ability to conduct arms control negotiations."[46] This eased ACDA's concern about security and, particularly, about being forced by Congress to poach on the legitimate territory of the intelligence community. ACDA's familiar dilemma was not entirely avoided, however, as it must still draw upon the intelligence community to implement its reporting duties and it is assigned a function primarily performed by the Director for Central Intelligence. An ACDA officer commented in 1978: "All ACDA can do is receive a report from the intelligence community, stamp 'ACDA' on it, and send it over to the Hill. If the information in the report is deemed inadequate by some members of Congress, there is little ACDA can do."

Section 37 of the ACD Act (PL 95-108) requires ACDA's Director to report to Congress, on a timely basis and upon request, the following information: (1) the verifiability by existing national technical means of significant arms control proposals made to or received by the United States; (2) any significant degradation or alteration in the U.S. capacity to verify existing arms control agreements; (3) the number of professionals assigned to arms control verification throughout the government; and, (4) ACDA's research expenditures for verification. This last provision differs from the House bill, which would have required ACDA to divulge government-wide research expenditures for arms control verification. This would have invited a lively and probably fruitless bureaucratic tussle to extract secret budgetary data from the intelligence community, which ACDA would then have had to divulge to Congress.

Why did Congress pass section 37? Motivations varied, but at least four were particularly evident. First, there was a broad and growing bipartisan concern about Soviet SALT compliance. If Senator Jackson and Representative Derwinski were disturbed, so were Senators Cranston and John Glenn (D–Ohio). Senator Glenn remarked, "I will vote against anything around here that cannot be verified because I do not trust the people with whom we are dealing."[47] The theme of "not trusting the Russians" was often heard. The bloom was off détente, whether the subject was SALT, Africa, or the Middle East. Second, although it is uncertain whether section 37 will noticeably improve Congress's access to information about verification, this was certainly an objective. Third, Warnke had just abolished Iklé's Verification and Analysis Bureau, which was heavily staffed with members of the so-called Jackson underground and whose Verification Division frequently criticized the "softness" of CIA analyses of Soviet SALT compliance. There were erroneous press reports that Warnke had fired several of the bureau's permanent professionals who were not political appointees. Many did leave, but none had been asked to. Conservatives, particularly Senator Jackson, were concerned that this signaled a downgrading of the verification function. They viewed section 37 as a tool for rectifying this and for monitoring Agency verification efforts. But verification had not been deemphasized. Instead, it was returned to the respective functional units, and, of course, the Jackson people were no longer dominant.[48] Fourth and finally, for some conservatives section 37 was a personal slap at Warnke and a warning to the administration that SALT II had better be adequately verifiable.

Throughout this process ACDA maintained a very low public profile. While Warnke objected to allegations that he had downgraded arms control verification, and though ACDA privately agreed with Zablocki's objections, the Agency did not openly oppose the amendment. Warnke had just been through a bitter nomination proceeding and was probably not eager for an early second round. He also did not want his Agency to appear to oppose verification. When queried why ACDA had not resisted section 37, an ACDA officer who had followed it closely replied, "Because Warnke *knew* he'd lose; hence, why harm your reputation? By adopting ostensible neutrality, he gave ACDA a say in drafting the much more acceptable Senate version." Also, it was at least debatable whether the final version of the legislation was anti-ACDA. Except for section 37, all the 1977 amendments to the ACD Act were supportive of the Agency. Several section 37 backers were arms control proponents. Indeed, when Senator Cranston introduced the Senate bill he justified his move as one that would bolster the Agency by encouraging its greater involvement "in the formulation of intelligence requirements relating to arms control."[49]

But anti-ACDA or not, it meant more paper work and possible difficulties with the intelligence community. It also portended close, possibly explosive, congressional examination of future SALT agreements. In 1977 ACDA continued to receive benign treatment from a congressional majority, but there were clouds on the horizon. Continued moves by Congress to compel ACDA to serve congressional needs by encroaching upon the traditional jurisdictions of other departments could jeopardize ACDA's effectiveness and encourage these departments to isolate the Agency. To some extent—it varies from case to case—kindness can hurt. But the debate over Warnke's nomination, section 37, and the growing distrust of Soviet intentions suggested a much more troublesome prospect. If the Senate should reject important negotiated arms control agreements and public opinion reflect nonsupport of arms control, ACDA's future could be uncertain.

By mid-1978 the threatening clouds were no longer merely on the horizon. They were directly overhead. Though Congress that year authorized an ACDA budget of $18.4 million, $2 million more than the Agency had requested, the Carter administration's arms control program, particularly SALT, was in jeopardy on the Hill. Soviet–American relations were at their lowest point since the Soviet Union's invasion of Czechoslovakia a decade earlier. Despite (or for some legislators, *because of*) the administration's repeated but not always convincing denials that the future of SALT was not linked to Moscow's adventures in Africa or to its treatment of dissidents within the Soviet Union, the entire fabric of U.S.-U.S.S.R. relations, so laboriously constructed since 1969, was being called into question. Conservatives in particular were accusing the administration, Paul Warnke, and ACDA of "weakness" in dealing with the Soviets.

For example, in the spring of 1978 all but one of the twelve Republicans on the House International Relations Committee joined two of the committee's Democratic members in issuing a statement highly critical of Warnke and the administration's arms control policy. They castigated "the stream of concessions in Geneva," accused Warnke of noncompliance with the requirements of section 37, deplored his alleged failure to "encourage a diversity of views on arms control within the Agency," charged him with viewing arms control as "an end in itself," expressed opposition to a comprehensive nuclear test ban treaty, and warned that the Director's "single-minded predispositions" coupled with "U.S. weakness and lack of will" entailed "a grave risk that a SALT II agreement will be rejected by the Congress."[50]

These sentiments were reflected in the House vote on ACDA's authorization bill. Though the bill was overwhelmingly approved in 1977 by a vote of 395 to 15, in 1978 the vote, while still favorable, was 332 to 74. Although the charges leveled against the Carter administration and Paul Warnke were all disputable—and some were patently false (neither Warnke nor anyone else in ACDA considered arms control an end in itself)—they nonetheless reflected the deep-seated concerns of a growing number of legislators. Both ACDA and much of President Carter's arms control program now faced formidable opposition.

14 Arms Control Impact Statements

IN NOVEMBER 1975 President Ford signed into law the new section 36 of the ACD Act, which for the first time sought to *legislate* a specific arms control input into the *executive* defense budgetary process. The State Department was uneasy about the legislation. Defense, OMB, and ERDA actively opposed it. Even close observers were surprised that it survived such formidable opposition, especially as it embodied a premise that has not consistently characterized American national security policy: Arms control, properly conceived, is a vital component of national security, and the defense budget can no longer be exempt from this proposition. The legislation guaranteed intense bureaucratic infighting, executive–legislative bickering, and turmoil for ACDA. This chapter examines the implementation of section 36 through its first three years.

Legislative History

Robert Metzger of Congressman Harrington's staff, drawing upon his experience with environmental impact statements, conceived the idea of an impact statement in the arms control field. In the spring of 1974 Harrington introduced an amendment to the ACD Act that would have required ACDA's Director to issue an arms control impact statement (ACIS) to Congress for any strategic weapons program whose estimated annual cost exceeded $50 million or when the Director determined that any government agency had taken an action that would substantially impact upon strategic arms or arms control policies. Its principal announced purpose was to increase information flow to Congress in this area.[1]

Metzger subsequently acknowledged that the language of the amendment was unrefined. However, despite Harrington's strained rapport with his colleagues and strong opposition within the committee, the House Foreign Affairs Committee adopted it by a 15-to-11 vote. Opponents raised several substantive questions, but their procedural objections proved decisive. Harrington had not adequately consulted with Iklé, nor had hearings been held on the measure. That the proposal was first made in committee, without prior debate, concerned many congressmen. Important questions about its effect had been unexplored. When Iklé was fully apprised of the matter, he opposed it. He was particularly concerned that by requiring ACDA to report *directly* to Congress, without coordinating the product with the rest of the executive branch, the Agency would be placed in an untenable adversary relationship with other departments. Many of ACDA's friends therefore joined in defeating the Harrington amendment when it reached the House floor. The vote was 152 to 239. Senator Nelson had introduced a similar bill in the Senate, but the Senate Foreign Relations Committee, citing the need for hearings and further study, did not report it out. In both houses there was an understanding that the matter would be reconsidered after being restudied and reworked.[2]

This task fell primarily to the Zablocki subcommittee. But when Zablocki introduced the reformulated bill in April 1975 it still required ACDA to submit the ACISes directly to Congress. Hence Iklé and the administration again opposed it. They argued that the statements must be administration, not ACDA, documents. Faced with a certain presidential veto, Zablocki accepted a compromise suggested by the administration—process the ACISes through the NSC prior to their submission to Congress. Once the committee agreed to this substantial alteration, ACDA swung its support to the legislation.[3]

In October 1975 a senior ACDA officer confided, "It would be helpful to get that statutory club, especially to get budget information from DOD." But while ACDA officials made their views known privately, they were forbidden by the White House to express them publicly, for the executive branch was hardly of one mind. OMB did not want yet another bureaucratic layer interposed in the defense budgetary process. DOD, especially its General Counsel's Office, was adamantly opposed. Defense, as Senator Humphrey remarked, was "not exactly singing the Hallelujah Chorus when this was proposed." James Wade of ISA testified that the ACIS process would be an unwarranted intrusion into the weapons acquisition process, that it would be time-consuming, burden-some, and costly. When asked directly if there was an existing procedure "making sure" that arms control considerations were weighed in the weapons acquisition process, Wade replied that they were taken into account for those weapons systems directly related to ongoing arms control negotiations.[4] Later, contrary to the intent of Congress, DOD attempted to justify its noncompliance with the law by asserting that the ACIS requirement applied only to defense programs that related to such negotiations.

Despite DOD opposition the House passed the bill by a 382-to-28 vote. It also gained Senate approval, but only after crippling amendments were added. In October, before the bill went to Conference Committee, Defense Secretary Schlesinger spent an hour with Zablocki trying to persuade him, unsuccessfully, to accept the weaker Senate bill. This bill differed from the House version in two significant respects: it was limited to nuclear arms, and it restricted the discretion of ACDA's Director by requiring the concurrence of the Director and the agency concerned before an ACIS could be issued about a program other than one dealing with nuclear arms. Ironically, the Conference Committee—thanks in large measure to the efforts of Congressman Zablocki and Senator Humphrey—actually reported out a bill that was stronger than the House version, having incorporated the strongest provisions of both bills. The Conference Committee bill was passed by both houses and signed by the President. It was not restricted to nuclear arms or even to armaments, and the Director was given broad discretion.[5]

The legislation had four principal objectives: (1) It was an attempt to force the executive to regularize and systematize an arms control input into defense programs, particularly weapons systems. A more subtle and modest expectation, which arose only after the legislation was implemented, was that it would raise the executive's arms control consciousness, thereby encouraging a climate within the executive branch more conducive to critical appraisals of certain weapons systems. (2) ACDA's policy role was to be enhanced and it would acquire new legal leverage for prying data from other agencies. (3) Congress was to receive better information and analysis to facilitate a better-informed and more independent legislative appraisal of defense programs. (4) It was hoped that there could now be a system permitting improved executive-legislative monitoring and, if necessary, curtailing of those programs and technologies with adverse arms control implications.[6]

The legislation's backers were fully aware of the resistance it would encounter. One House staffer, in 1975, described it as "opening the door, with the hope that the door would, later, open wider.'' Another, George Berdes, writing shortly before the first batch of ACISes was issued, correctly predicted that the real work on the statements ''has only begun.''[7]

The Law

Section 36 of the ACD Act[8] requires that any government agency requesting authorization or appropriations from Congress for (1) any program of research, development, modernization, etc. relating to *nuclear* armaments *or*, (2) any program of research, development, modernization, etc. relating to other armaments or military facilities having an estimated *total* cost exceeding $250 million or *annual* cost exceeding $50 million, accompany such requests with a statement analyzing the program's impact on arms control and disarmament policy and negotiations. Additionally, regardless of cost, *any other* programs involving technology with potential military application or weapons systems that are determined by the proposing agency or ACDA's Director and, then, *by the NSC* to have a *significant* impact on arms control and disarmament policy and negotiations, must be accompanied by an ACIS.

Section 36 primarily affects DOD and DOE. Congress did not intend the law to cover routine operational deployments and redeployments, but there were some uncertainties about section 36's scope:

Arms control policy and negotiations. DOD's Office of the General Counsel took a restrictive view of what constituted ''policy'' and asserted that the law applied only to ongoing negotiations. Said one Pentagon attorney, ''Arms control means arms control negotiations. ACDA has no business, legally or otherwise, interfering with defense programs.'' Another DOD official even asserted that arms control was not part of national security. But such opinions clearly contravene congressional intent. This and other 1975 amendments to the ACD Act demonstrate Congress's very broad conception of arms control policy. Nor were ACISes to be prepared only for defense programs affecting current negotiations. Arms control considerations were to be related to the larger defense budgetary process. The House International Relations Committee's report said: ''Specifically included in the Committee's intent here is the on-going, year-long, constant procedure followed in the Department of Defense.''[9]

Research. At what stage of research and development is an ACIS required? The House International Relations Committee stated that it intended to include even items "of a 'seminal' nature, such as major philosophical or doctrinal changes in defense posture or new weapons concepts in various stages of research and development." Yet the committee qualified this: "[W]e do not wish to constrain prematurely such ideas by subjecting them in their infancy to overly exacting analytical requirements. . . . The more appropriate concern . . . is with advanced research." ACDA and DOD had different interpretations of congressional intent. DOD argued that most research programs are exempt; until a single weapons design is selected for a "program," no ACIS is necessary unless the $50 million annual program expenditure level is met. An ACDA official, observing that—prior to this legislation—the Agency rarely saw a DOD or ERDA research project before the decision to enter production was made, asserted that it is essential to raise questions at the conceptual stage if arms control is to affect the program's direction. He cited section 36, which permits the Director, on his *own* initiative, to examine *any* program he feels may have a significant arms control impact. Unfortunately the word "program" is undefined, but it clearly relates to budget presentations to authorizing and appropriating committees.[10]

Nonweapons technology. Before section 36(a)(3) was amended by Congress in 1978 (at Senator Pell's initiative), there was considerable controversy over whether the law covered certain "nonweapons technologies"—such as some civilian nuclear, laser, and space programs—which *potentially* affected defense programs. During the Ford administration ACDA sought ACISes on some nuclear energy research programs only indirectly related to weapons. The NSC refused to sanction them, arguing that section 36 was inapplicable to nonweapons technology. ACDA disagreed with this interpretation of the law, but the Agency's position did not prevail until the 1978 amendment brought "technology with potential military application" directly within the purview of section 36.[11]

Specified Funding Limits. Any request to Congress for authorization or appropriations within the specified funding limits—$250 million total or $50 million annual program costs—*automatically* requires a complete ACIS. Several officials felt that this would bring many programs into the ACIS process that had little or no arms control impact. This was not the intent of Congress, nor has it been a problem. It can reasonably be inferred that only those programs having a substantial impact are covered. The impact could be either favorable or unfavorable for arms control. It can also be assumed that the ACIS reporting system was not to be overloaded with insignificant matters whose net effect would be to impede the process.[12]

Significant Impact. In addition to programs within the specified funding limits, ACDA's Director has discretionary authority to prepare an ACIS for "any other program involving technology with potential military application or weapons systems" that he believes may have significant impact upon arms control policy and negotiations. This recognizes that even small programs could fundamentally affect arms control—for example, "scratch" money to examine ways of mobilizing ICBMs. However, before such programs can be accompanied by an ACIS, the NSC must find that their arms control impact would be "significant." By requiring NSC certification, thereby making the statements administration documents, it was hoped that ACDA would not be cast too blatantly into an overtly adversarial role with other agencies. But in the FY 1977– FY 1979 processes, ACDA was so viewed. The authors of the legislation realized not only that reasonable men could differ over what "significantly" affected arms control but that the NSC might dilute or gut the entire procedure. This is precisely what happened in FY 1977 and FY 1978. No agency will normally admit that its defense program has arms control liabilities. Therefore the NSC's role is critical. If the NSC does not adopt a more or less balanced stance between ACDA's frequent assertion that program X significantly affects arms control and DOD's contrary claim, Congress can expect tendentious ACISes.[13]

ACDA's Director has responsibility for assessing a program's arms control impact and for so advising the NSC. All agencies are to provide the Director with "full and timely" access to "detailed" information "on a continuing basis." Congress intended the Director to have virtually unrestricted informational access. The House International Relations Committee stated that the information available to the Director must "be complete, accurate and current in every respect"; that all parties are to be "cooperative and responsive"; and that the Director is entitled to any information he determines pertinent to his assessment and analysis. The phrase "on a continuing basis" expresses the committee's intent that "the Director's access to information be on a regular, on-going, uninterrupted basis."[14] Despite the law, however, ACDA encountered considerable informational problems, especially in FY 1977–FY 1978.

ACISes that are submitted to Congress must be "complete." A DOD official reported that he was "confused" by this word. But ACDA and State officials found no confusion. DOD, they said, was simply refusing to be forthcoming. In FY 1977–FY 1978 DOD prevailed and Congress received what one official called "the lowest common denominator."

ACISes are to be prepared for Congress in both classified and unclassified forms. Once an ACIS has been submitted to Congress, section

36 stipulates that, upon the request of a committee, the Director shall, after informing the Secretary of State, advise the committee of the program's arms control implications. This provision may have been influenced by Adrian Fisher's testimony. Fisher argued that ACDA's Director should enjoy the same legal prerogative as the JCS to express his own views about defense programs.[15] The actual degree of freedom the Director has to express his personal views will, however, still be governed by the preferences and style of the President and the Secretary of State.

Finally, section 36 exempts the entire ACIS process from judicial review. This meets administration concerns that, as with the National Environmental Policy Act of 1969 (PL 91-190) and its required environmental impact statements, the legislation would invite litigation, which in this instance could jeopardize the defense budgetary process. The exemption merely ratifies the usual judicial disposition not to hear national security cases.[16]

Noncompliance and Congressional Reaction: FY 1977–FY 1978

The first group of ACISes (FY 1977) were inadequate in every respect. They were submitted after Congress had already authorized the FY 1977 budget, hence were too late to serve a useful purpose. Only sixteen statements were submitted, while dozens of eligible programs were omitted. They were brief and superficial. Only one exceeded a page in length. They were not the complete, analytical statements required by law. Congress had put the executive on notice that it intended to exercise careful oversight review of the ACIS procedure. Now Senator Humphrey and Congressman Zablocki jointly wrote General Scowcroft that they were "appalled." Senate Foreign Relations Committee Chairman Sparkman and Senator Case wrote to Defense Secretary Rumsfeld and ERDA Administrator Robert Seamans, Jr., stating that the ACISes "do not comply with the law and are unacceptable."[17]

The twenty-six FY 1978 statements included the sixteen from the previous fiscal year, which the House International Relations Committee and the Senate Foreign Relations Committee had asked to be resubmitted. Though the FY 1978 statements were timely and somewhat lengthier, they, too, were completely inadequate. Again, they were neither complete nor analytical. Most programs were deemed to have no arms control impact, and there was not a single unfavorable net assessment. The GAO initiated an investigation of the ACIS process, and Congress assigned the Congressional Research Service (CRS) to assess these and future ACISes. The CRS was also asked to devise model impact statements to show the executive exactly what Congress expected. The CRS selected 108 weapons systems for which no submissions to Congress were made in FY 1978. Of these, 66 were found to require ACISes. The CRS determined that probably more than one hundred programs were eligible for ACISes. Senators Sparkman and Case again sent a letter, this time to ACDA's new Director, Paul Warnke, stating that the statements "still do not comply with the law and are unacceptable."[18]

The Process: FY 1977–FY 1978

Section 36 gives ACDA the authority to prepare draft ACISes for the NSC. The legislation's originators had briefly discussed the wisdom of having other departments prepare the statements before they were forwarded to ACDA. But this procedure was never seriously considered, because it encouraged bureaucratic foot-dragging, which could undermine the entire process; it invited statements entitled, "Why MIRVs Are Good for Arms Control"; and finally, it seemed tactically prudent to compel others to challenge ACDA's statements.

On February 20, 1976, the NSC issued a document—prepared by ACDA, ERDA, and DOD—intended to guide the process in FY 1977 and FY 1978. The document (1) defined such terms as policy, negotiations, research, and program; (2) established liaison points in ACDA, DOD, and ERDA; and (3) specified that ACDA was to receive DOD's research and procurement budget descriptions furnished to the Appropriations and Armed Services Committees as well as "associated documents." That month Senator Humphrey and Congressman Zablocki met with executive branch officials to discuss the scope and magnitude of the FY 1977 submissions. It was agreed, considering the law's enactment in late 1975, that it would be preferable to prepare a few thorough analyses rather than give casual treatment to many programs.

ACDA, DOD, and ERDA were to prepare ACISes on sixteen programs but, despite the February 20 document, they could not agree on criteria to guide their preparation. Hence that agreement broke down. DOD and ERDA particularly differed with ACDA on the interpretation of the phrase "arms control policy and negotiations." They asserted that "negotiations" referred only to formal international negotiations that were either ongoing or authorized by the President through the NSC system. ACDA, with some support from the NSC staff, argued that, in addition to current negotiations, possible future negotiations were covered by the law.[19] Concerning "arms control policy," DOD's Office of the General Council circulated an unsigned memorandum within DOD addressing its meaning. According to the memorandum, "policy" referred only to existing U.S. legal obligations (except those dealing with the use of weapons in war); presidential statements of arms control policy; and NSC documents prepared for the President's signature. ACDA responded that this definition of policy was erroneous in fact and clearly contrary to the intent of Congress. DOD officials even denied that a Secretary of State or Secretary of Defense could issue statements that would qualify as "arms control policy." These Cabinet officers, DOD insisted, merely implement policy as presidential agents. With its broader conception of "arms control policy and negotiations," it is not surprising that ACDA was the only agency that prepared thorough internal analyses.

But despite the requirements of section 36, ACDA did not prepare the government-wide draft statements for the NSC in FY 1977. Indeed, no formal administration directive detailing interagency procedures was issued until the Carter administration. ACDA analyzed DOD and ERDA programs and commented on draft statements from these departments. Within DOD each of the armed services prepared the program description portion of the statement, which was coordinated through the Joint Staff and merged with the analysis performed by ISA. ERDA also prepared its own statements. Section 36 does not specify a role for the State Department, but, by virtue of its NSC membership, State did comment on the draft statements and, beginning in FY 1978, prepared the introductory overview portion (relating arms control to foreign and national security policy) that accompanied each ACIS. It is important for State to continue to be involved, because, contrary to DOD's assertions, the whole thrust of the legislation is to avoid isolating arms control from other aspects of defense and foreign policy.[20]

Interagency coordination for the FY 1977 statements was handled by the same committee that prepared the February 20 guidance paper. With an NSC member present, the committee sought to resolve interagency differences. But ACDA did not prevail, and Congress received worthless ACISes.

The FY 1978 process began in the same manner as the prior cycle had ended, each agency going its own way. DOD and ERDA again resisted. ACDA was concerned about congressional reaction and suggested, to no avail, ways in which DOD might avoid the wrath of Congress. One ACDA analyst said, "Each time DOD's statements came back to us they were shorter than before." A stalemate ultimately developed. ACDA refused to accept DOD's assessments. In the previous cycle (FY 1977) 60 percent of the time that ACDA devoted to ACISes was consumed in interagency wrangling over legal interpretations. This time an estimated 6,400 man-hours were expanded by ACDA personnel; more than 150 programs were reviewed by the Agency; and assessments and analyses of 63 programs were prepared. About 20 percent of ACDA's time spent on ACISes was consumed by interagency disputes.[21] By November, when the date for submitting the statements to Congress was almost at hand, neither DOD nor ERDA had draft impact statements. This forced the NSC's Senior Review Group to establish new procedures. ACDA was finally assigned the authority it had by law to prepare draft ACISes (but ERDA continued to prepare its own). DOD prepared the program descriptions. The documents underwent an interagency NSC review. The NSC edited these documents and submitted the ACISes to Congress. The process had changed: DOD now had to comment on ACDA's ACISes. But despite the change, the statements that went to Congress did not improve appreciably.[22]

The ACIS process in FY 1977–FY 1978 did not measurably enhance ACDA's access to information as Congress intended. The procedure may even have reduced its access to certain defense budgetary information because of fears that ACDA could use it to threaten desired programs. Crucial documents that DOD had agreed to supply ACDA by September 1976 arrived months later, forcing ACDA to estimate which DOD programs would require FY 1978 impact statements on the basis of DOD's FY 1977 documents. A DOD official said that he would not give ACDA information on projected procurement quantities, decisions of the Defense Systems Acquisition Review Committee, phasing of procurement, or the projected cost of certain weapons systems. ACDA's requests for specific Program Decision Memoranda were refused. Informally, ISA stated that "full access does not mean that ACDA . . . has the right to review internal decision memoranda or related material." But this is precisely the kind of information ACDA requires to implement its section 36 responsibilities effectively. In large measure, ACDA was able to prepare ACISes because of the expertise it *already* had on hand. The result was to increase the formality of interdepartmental communications. Sometimes when ACDA officers were permitted to read a document at the Pentagon they were not even allowed to take notes. Iklé might have appealed directly to Kissinger, the NSC, or Defense Secretary Rumsfeld, but he did not do so, probably because he felt the appeal would have been unsuccessful.[23]

Round III and Prospects

Presidential candidate Jimmy Carter stated, "I would insure that my Administration would abide by the spirit as well as the letter of the Zablocki amendment, which requires arms control impact statements on major new weapons programs."[24] With the change of administration came new personalities; some who had obstructed the process left government. Senator Humphrey informed Warnke that he would personally oversee the ACIS process, to which Warnke replied, "I appreciate the advice . . . and the warning."[25]

Warnke took this advice seriously and saw to it that ACDA aggressively pursued its legal prerogatives. Although the 1975 House report had stated that Congress did not anticipate a need for the "formation of additional bureaucracies,"[26] ACDA officials privately felt, even before the legislation was enacted, that analytical capabilities would have to be enlarged. Warnke greatly increased his ACIS staff to between sixteen and twenty analysts, established a new Defense Program Impact Division within the WEC Bureau, and brought in Barry Blechman from the Brookings Institution to head WEC.

ACDA also enjoyed far greater White House and NSC support. In August 1977 the NSC said that it had "no major disagreement" with a GAO report highly critical of the FY 1977–FY 1978 processes. The NSC even acknowledged that the executive "may have failed to satisfy the intent of Congress."[27] The White House was concerned lest congressional unhappiness with past statements lead to additional legislation. That spring Warnke had testified that if DOD and DOE continued to obstruct the process he might request such legislation.[28] To avoid this unwanted development the NSC gave written assurance that ACDA would assume the leading role in preparing the FY 1979 ACISes; that it was considering preparing ACISes on programs that might affect "potential" and "future" as well as current negotiations; and that an NSC interagency group had been established for developing criteria for program selection and for analyzing a program's arms control impact.[29]

An NSC memorandum was signed by President Carter in October 1977. It gave ACDA prime authority for the "analysis" component of the

ACISes while the NSC retained ultimate responsibility for approving specific topics for analysis and for reviewing ACISes before their submission to Congress. The memorandum sanctioned analyses of more than seventy programs; set a schedule for ACIS preparation; formalized interagency coordinating procedures; and authorized general criteria to guide the preparation of internal analyses and ACISes submitted to Congress. Each ACIS was to address such topics as the program's technological implications, impact on international and regional stability, bearing upon current and future negotiations, verifiability, consistency with American arms control policy, and relationship with other defense programs.

Lack of authoritative, uniform criteria had plagued the earlier process. In its 1977 review of the ACISes the CRS had drafted "model" impact statements, which, it suggested, could serve to guide future analyses. The NSC and ACDA drew liberally from the CRS model in establishing criteria for the FY 1979 statements. Warnke also acquired the services of a CRS analyst who had helped develop this model.[30]

CRS-inspired criteria were incorporated by ACDA into two special ACISes requested by Congress in 1977 for the air-launched cruise missile and the enhanced radiation (neutron) warhead for the Lance missile. They were a distinct qualitative improvement over past ACISes. Though both statements might have been more complete, they were analytical and detailed. The air-launched cruise missile was found to have potential arms control problems but the ACIS concluded that, if quantitatively limited by a SALT II accord, it "should not adversely affect arms control."[31] The debate over the neutron warhead was the first time an ACIS was used by Congress as an instrument of policy. Because ERDA had failed to accompany its budget request for the warhead with an ACIS, opponents of that program, led by Senators Mark Hatfield (R–Ore.) and Pell, charged failure to comply with the law. They forced a delay in voting in both chambers until an ACIS was presented. The hastily prepared statement forwarded to Congress in July was extremely critical, concluding that "this weapon system has no arms control advantages."[32]

The third batch of ACISes, those for FY 1979, were submitted to Congress by ACDA in March 1978, seven weeks past the time required by law for their submission; two of those weeks were spent haggling over whether ACDA would be the one to submit them. Congressman Zablocki and Senator Sparkman issued a joint statement deploring the "unacceptable delay," which "reduced the potential value of the fiscal year 1979 arms control impact statements." They insisted that future ACISes be submitted in January together with authorization and appropriations requests.[33]

There were thirty-two ACISes encompassing seventy-six programs.

Because of DOE resistance, a nonweapons technology program—the breeder reactor—was submitted as a separate ACDA study instead of as an NSC sanctioned ACIS. The ACISes covered such obvious candidates as cruise missiles, advanced ballistic reentry systems, and the ICBM M-X warhead, as well as a variety of nonnuclear weapons programs like high-energy lasers, biological research, and chemical warfare. Though all the defense programs to be carried out by DOD in FY 1979 were officially found to be generally consistent with U.S. arms control policy and negotiations—a finding that is politically and bureaucratically mandatory—they were far more numerous, analytic, detailed, and "balanced" than past ACISes. They were not documents with a single point of view or a single recommendation. Rather, they were studies that elaborated both the positive and negative arms control ramifications of a defense program. Critics as well as supporters of specific programs could find ample ammunition to buttress their respective positions.

The ACISes' timeliness of submission as well as their scope and depth of coverage can be improved, but one of the legislation's principal objectives was substantially realized—for the first time ACISes gave Congress fairly detailed information on specific defense programs. However, as a congressional staffer who was "delighted" with the improvement remarked, "If we were to grade them, it's unlikely that they'll *ever* get a better grade than B or B+." Any administration will generally put a high premium on presenting a united front to Congress. No President will be entirely content to have his Secretary of Energy seeking funds for a neutron warhead while his ACDA Director castigates the program. President Carter, at least from 1977 to mid-1978, was clearly more tolerant of such "diversity" than President Ford. But he paid a price for not having a uniform public administration position. The debate over the neutron warhead caught Carter in a crossfire between its critics and its supporters, which probably contributed to his adopting a "wait and see" stance on the program. Of course, the decision not to issue an ACIS for the Lance warhead in 1977 was made by the Ford Administration (ACDA had prepared one, but it was overruled by the NSC).

This kind of unpleasant experience was not repeated in 1978 with the FY 1979 statements since, publicly, they were presented as consensus administration documents expressly approved by President Carter. Again, however, the administration paid a price for not issuing an ACIS on a controversial program. In May 1978, after the administration had failed to issue an ACIS on the W-81 nuclear warhead for the Navy's Aegis missile, despite a specific request from Senator John Culver, the Senate Armed Services Committee voted to delete funds for the system from the FY

1979 defense authorization bill. This was the first time a congressional committee used the lack of an impact statement, which, of course, is required by law, to cut a weapon's funding. The action was even more significant in view of the fact that the Armed Services Committee regularly supports defense projects. Clearly, there were now strong incentives for subjecting all key programs to the ACIS procedure.

But once the White House sanctions a defense program that has been through the ACIS process it is extremely unlikely, even if it has arms control problems, that the ACIS for that program will be completely forthcoming. Still, the overall improvement recorded in 1978 was directly attributable to a Carter administration that had a notably greater commitment to faithfully implementing the law than did its predecessor.

It was also attributable to unrelenting pressure from congressional arms control proponents who—as Senators Hatfield, Pell, and Culver demonstrated—were willing to demand administration compliance with Section 36. Active congressional oversight must continue if the process is to be successful. But the ability of Congress to review executive activities does not confer a capacity to manage. Congress cannot manipulate bureaucratic processes; it can only reveal and prohibit. It is still premature to speculate on the ACISes' ultimate policy significance for Congress. The mere existence of something called an ACIS will not influence voting behavior, but its official character may imbue it with a certain authority. ACISes of the caliber of the FY 1979 statements have the potential for becoming policy tools for both the critics and the supporters of defense programs.

Criticisms of this tool are many and varied: ACISes will not be frank or "balanced"; Congress should not become overly dependent on the executive's analysis of a program's arms control implications; they will be abused by fervent critics of the defense budget; Congress will leak classified information for political purposes; ACISes deal with an inherently plastic subject where reasonable men can always differ. But the ACIS can serve a useful purpose. All political phenomena have a certain ambiguous or amorphous quality. If "arms control" is plastic, so is "national security." Many ACISes have been "balanced" and can be helpful, not only to those who might allegedly misuse them, but to a Congress that has long played a far too distant role in the weapons acquisition process. And ACISes give Congress a means, via ACDA, for pressuring the executive branch to give genuine consideration to the arms control implications of defense programs.

In addition to providing more information to Congress, there was some modest movement toward meeting the other objectives of the legislation during the FY 1979 cycle. The arms control ramifications of new weapons technologies were subjected to somewhat closer scrutiny within the executive branch. OMB reviewed some FY 1979 defense programs with reference to their accompanying ACISes. The FY 1979 ACISes also, for the first time, referred to the previously classified "insertable nuclear components" (INCs) being developed by all three military services, which would permit the insertion of a nuclear explosive device into a conventional bomb or warhead. In 1977 Senator Culver raised questions about the arms control implications of such weapons, which had prompted the executive to consider the matter. An ACIS for the Navy's Harpoon missile tended to confirm Culver's concern. This ACIS further revealed that such systems were the object of an interagency study and stated, "No further funds will be spent on INC's unless the President decides to go ahead. In that event, a supplementary ACIS will be provided to Congress."[34] These developments suggest that the ACIS process had some impact on the executive's review of defense programs, though it was only a beginning.

The process for integrating arms control factors into defense program decisions was now institutionalized. A firm government organization and procedure for coordinating and processing ACISes was in place and functioning. Disputes that could not be settled at either the working level or among agency principals were referred to the NSC's Special Coordinating Committee, chaired by Assistant for National Security Affairs Zbigniew Brzezinski. In the FY 1979 cycle at least eight contested draft ACISes reached the Special Coordinating Committee. When necessary, disputes were finally resolved by the President.

While ACDA's policy role may actually have declined during the FY 1977–FY 1978 cycles, it improved in the early Carter administration. There was still a reluctance to give ACDA needed information. On some issues, for example, the Department of Energy resisted ACDA's informational requests to the level of the Secretary. But, with greater White House support, overall access to information improved significantly, and neither DOD nor DOE could count on prevailing in the Special Coordinating Committee. Nor did either of these departments complain to the Zablocki subcommittee, as they had in the past, about ACDA's role in the process. ACDA now took the initiative for drafting ACISes for the NSC and, indeed, for managing the process. Though the NSC retained ultimate authority over the statements' contents, NSC participation declined primarily because of staff reductions.

But it is far too early to make final judgments.[35] Controversy continued over interpretation of the law, and participants characterized the

FY 1979 process as "particularly bloody." Many officials continued to feel that Congress was playing favorites with section 36. This engendered suspicion and hostility toward ACDA. More important, many in Defense saw ACDA as an agent of Congress menacing DOD's traditional sovereignty over "its" budget. Most of these officials resented an outsider's poaching on the exclusive preserve of the armed services, OSD, and the Defense Systems Acquisition Review Council. Section 36 tended to make ACDA an adversary whose loyalty to the executive team was questioned.

The ACISes vividly illustrate ACDA's (and the executive's) dilemma. Unsatisfactory ACISes invite congressional retribution. If the statements are inadequate, or even if they are adequate, Congress might enact additional legislation to clarify and strengthen section 36—which is precisely what happened in 1978 concerning nonweapons technology. Should the executive habitually refuse to be forthcoming, Congress could consider using the CRS, the GAO, the Office of Technology Assessment, or the Congressional Budget Office to prepare its own statements. But ACISes deemed satisfactory by Congress strain ACDA's relations with senior executive branch actors who are not anxious to release damaging information about their programs to hostile legislators.

While the outcome of the ACIS process will vary with the administration in power, its central purpose is essential for sound national security. For too long critical defense budget decisions have been made without systematic reference to arms control considerations. Under any administration the process will plunge ACDA into potentially costly bureaucratic struggles. But the possible benefits could be substantial. Prior to this legislation ACDA had virtually no voice in the weapons acquisition process. It is unlikely, regardless of section 36's ultimate fate, that ACDA's influence can sink below zero. The Defense Department's budget fundamentally affects foreign policy and arms control policy as well as defense policy. To permit the Pentagon to exclude ACDA, State, or other actors representing legitimate interests from meaningfully affecting the direction of key defense programs is a dangerous and costly abdication of national responsibility.

Part IV
Conclusion

15 ACDA's Role and Effectiveness

THIS STUDY has examined ACDA's policy role and the factors that bear upon its effectiveness in carrying out that role. Much of the American arms control policy process since 1961, as it relates to ACDA, has been covered. Here, following the framework of the preceding chapters, the findings concerning overall Agency effectiveness are presented.

Origins. The Arms Control and Disarmament Act of 1961, which established ACDA, was a compromise between those seeking a vigorous, independent advocate for an arms control approach to national security and those who considered arms control, and especially disarmament, suspect or even antithetical to national defense. ACDA acquired considerable legal authority to affect U.S. arms control policy and negotiations, while its Director was designated the principal arms control adviser to the President and Secretary of State. But this authority was offset by several limiting provisions, the most significant of which placed the Director squarely "under the direction of the Secretary of State." ACDA is neither a bureau of the State Department nor wholly independent. It is quasi-independent. Though the ACD Act was later amended to upgrade ACDA's legal authority, the Agency cannot aspire to the stature of more senior policy actors. To prevail, or sometimes even to be heard, ACDA needs allies. The support or acquiescence of the Secretary of State is usually mandatory.

Still, ACDA is the only executive agency whose exclusive mission is to promote arms control policy and negotiate arms control agreements. It is generally the first to raise arms control issues within the executive branch. And it deserves much of the credit for the professionalism that characterizes U.S. arms control efforts.

Image. Because of its mission ACDA has acquired a distinct image within government, which is widely, though not universally, perceived. ACDA officers and analysts are often pejoratively referred to as "arms controllers." This term (for those who use it) connotes naivete, softness, and idealism. The arms controller image led Congress to insist that ACDA employees be held to the government's most stringent security requirements. This image partly explains why certain categories of sensitive information have sometimes been withheld from the Agency and why the JCS and congressional conservatives are uneasy when ACDA's Director heads a SALT delegation.

Arms control has lost its mystery. It is now a recognized component of U.S. foreign and national security policy. But the negative image persists. ACDA cannot shed its essential mission, yet effectiveness may be jeopardized if it arouses the fears of powerful actors. The severity of this dilemma depends upon the issue and the constellation of forces. For example, it is a factor when the Agency seeks a role in defense budgetary matters, but it is a lesser concern in the nuclear proliferation area.

Effectiveness demands that ACDA identify to a considerable degree with prevailing bureaucratic norms lest it be isolated. Likewise, an appropriate balance must be struck between assertiveness and reticence. But if ACDA is to fulfill its purpose, minimize criticism from potential congressional allies, and maintain Agency cohesion, it must be an advocate for arms control within the executive branch. When Fred Iklé adopted a cautious stance toward SALT, cohesion declined, congressional liberals were aroused, and there were accusations that ACDA was straying from the spirit of the ACD Act. Arms control will always encounter formidable opposition. But it will not always have a champion, particularly if ACDA is habitually unassertive. The continuing challenge for ACDA and those who support its efforts is to demonstrate the identity of pragmatic arms control with sound national security policy. While this identity is now widely acknowledged, it must gain even greater credence.

Leadership and Cohesion. Organizational effectiveness requires able leadership and a reasonable degree of internal cohesion. This is particularly so for a small unit lacking institutional clout. The Navy will be influential even if it has a mediocre Chief of Naval Operations and its airmen feud with the submariners. But ACDA cannot afford such luxury.

An ideal Director should possess or should foster the following qualities and conditions: (1) an outgoing, flexible personality that interacts easily with people of differing persuasions, particularly the President and Secretary of State; (2) good relations with Congress; (3) a sharp intellect and thorough grasp of substantive arms control issues; (4) past government experience and a talent for operating within the bureaucracy; (5) an able Deputy Director and a say in this as well as other ACDA political appointments; (6) a primary presence in Washington, instead of spending excessive time at overseas arms control negotiations; (7) a sense, depending on issues and personalities, for when to push the case for arms control aggressively and when to hold back; (8) an ability to promote Agency cohesion, which largely relates to his personality and style, and a perception from below that the Agency's leadership is committed to arms control; (9) a civilian, not a military, background.

William Foster had personality clashes with key senior actors, sometimes held dogmatically to positions when this was counterproductive, and did not always play the bureaucratic game astutely. Gerard Smith spent too much time away from Washington and had mixed relations with Congress. Fred Iklé's personality and disposition meant that he could not operate well within the bureaucracy, he had strained relations with important senior actors, and Agency cohesion was severely strained under his directorship. Paul Warnke's outspoken advocacy invited a formidable backlash from the Pentagon and from congressional conservatives, which threatened to dilute or negate some of his efforts for arms control.

My purpose is not to denigrate these dedicated men, all of whom brought special qualities to a difficult task. A Director who satisfied all of the above conditions would walk on water. But these criteria do provide a suggestive checklist for assessing one's qualifications and performance.

President: Confidence and Access. The Director must enjoy the President's confidence and have access to the Oval Office. However, at least before Paul Warnke, no Director had ready access to the White House. Presidential confidence is personal. It flows to the individual. Hence, a case can be made that the Director should be a person of stature who can command the President's confidence, preferably someone who knew the President before he assumed office.

Hearing on Policy Issues. To be effective one must first be heard. The most desirable hearing within the executive branch is an informal one with the President or other senior officials. Formal hearings via ad hoc or fixed-membership interagency committees are generally of less consequence. Nonetheless, they perform an important coordination function, and attendance is particularly useful for a secondary actor like ACDA. The Agency's ability to gain a hearing is substantially affected by two additional factors—Congress and an issue's proximity to another department's mission or budget. Hence, DOD excluded ACDA from the weapons acquisition process until the 1975 legislation and persistent congressional pressure finally gave the Agency a precarious toehold on the outermost perimeter of this vital area by 1977-1978. During the Kennedy and Johnson administrations the formal mechanism for arms control matters was the Committee of Principals, chaired by Secretary of State Dean Rusk. While the committee performed a coordinating function, it atrophied after 1963. Important decisions were made elsewhere. The only major issue where ACDA had a leading role was the Non-Proliferation Treaty. ACDA had no meaningful say in key defense programs affecting arms control, conventional arms sales, or the use of chemical weapons in Vietnam. Though heard, its voice in SALT was muted.

Despite an early hint of openness, the Nixon NSC system soon revolved around Henry Kissinger. But this more formal system, featuring several fixed-membership and ad hoc committees, had some advantages for ACDA. The Director was represented on the Verification Panel, which had responsibility for SALT and some other arms control issues. The panel's frequent meetings during the 1969–1972 period afforded ACDA a forum. The Agency sometimes attended meetings of other NSC committees, like the Senior Review Group. The NSSM process also ensured involvement in arms control issues, certainly at lower levels, and the Agency had good relations with the NSC's Program Analysis staff. ACDA eclipsed the State Department in SALT I, and its analytical input was significant.

ACDA's SALT role declined in 1973–1974 with the purge of the Agency, Watergate and the resultant temporizing in foreign policy, Kissinger's nearly sovereign dominance, his lengthy absences from the country, and the infrequent convening of the Verification Panel. By 1975 ACDA began to recover from the purge. President Ford was more open and accessible than Nixon. Secretary of Defense Donald Rumsfeld, with whom Iklé was often allied on SALT, had the President's ear and was therefore able to challenge Kissinger's preeminence in SALT. Ultimately, of course, the quality of ACDA's hearing depends on the President. If he assigns a high priority to arms control and insists that his Director play a central role, ACDA will be heard. President Carter did this, thereby enabling Warnke to express his views at the highest level.

In other arms control areas ACDA's hearing was either adequate or improving by the mid-1970s. It was fully involved in MBFR negotiations, nuclear test ban deliberations and related issues, controls on chemical and biological weapons, and the Environmental Modification Ban. ACDA has always had a voice in the nuclear proliferation area, though its involvement in nuclear export policy was slight until Congress urged, then mandated, a role for the Agency. Only in 1977 did ACDA begin to acquire a significant say in conventional arms transfer decisions. Legislation in 1975 and 1976 requiring ACDA's participation in this latter area encountered persistent resistance from the State Department.

Access to Information. To withhold, delay, or only partially comply with informal requests from a bureaucratic competitor is part of the game. Ability to obtain complete, timely information from other policy actors is an important determinant of effectiveness. This is especially true when, like ACDA, an organization is small; operates in an essentially staff capacity; lacks independent data collection systems like those possessed by State, Defense, the JCS, and the intelligence community; and therefore must rely heavily on the cooperation of others.

Many factors affect information flow: (1) Cordial personal relations help immensely. (2) Similarly, someone in DOD is more likely to confide in an ACDA officer whom he knows to be "responsible." Hence, AC-DA's retired and active duty military officers are important conduits of information between DOD and the Agency. (3) When the foreign policy process systematically *requires* an input from all pertinent actors as it did, for example, during the first Nixon administration concerning the Biological Warfare Convention, information flow improves. (4) When a request for data seems to threaten a department's budget or mission, satisfactory compliance is unlikely. So DOD often rejects ACDA's inquiries about key defense programs, and the Department of Energy resists informational requests concerning peaceful nuclear explosive devices. (5) Congress—through legislation, hearings, resolutions, and private meetings with executive branch officials—has freed much information for ACDA, though this avenue can be blocked or impeded if the President sanctions or tolerates noncompliance with these congressional actions. (6) ACDA obtains necessary technical data relating to current negotiations but informational difficulties do arise concerning possible future negotiations. Also, particularly during the Kissinger era, ACDA (and others) were often denied access to high policy decisions and developments even when they fundamentally affected ACDA's responsibilities. (7) But ACDA's relations with the CIA have, with some exceptions, been cooperative.

Over the years there has been a gradual improvement in ACDA's access to information. While this will always be a concern, by 1978—with the principal exception of several DOD programs—the problem appeared manageable.

ACDA–State Department Relationship. While ACDA has a legal connection to the State Department, its relative freedom of action has varied considerably depending in large part on the operating style of the Secretary of State and his personal relationship with the Director. Under

Gerard Smith, who was on excellent terms with William Rogers, ACDA had virtual autonomy, at least in SALT. Iklé's relations with Kissinger were strained. Kissinger tried, with mixed success, to keep ACDA tethered. Neither extreme, too much or too little control, is desirable. Smith was so far removed from Rogers that he was even instructed to keep certain information about the SALT negotiations from the Secretary. On the other hand, excessively close control could deprive ACDA of its legitimate, distinct voice in arms control policy. By law, the Director can go directly to the President, but in practice this prerogative is infrequently exercised, especially if the Secretary of State objects.

Those concerned about inhibiting State Department controls have sometimes suggested establishing a completely independent ACDA. Others, troubled about an unhealthy distance between ACDA and State, have advocated merger. Neither alternative is advisable. Independence would not necessarily improve the Director's access to the President. That depends on a personal relationship that has little to do with ACDA's organizational location. Autonomy will impede interdepartmental coordination and aggravate ACDA's image problem. Arms control's close association with foreign policy is appropriately symbolized by the present arrangement.

Incorporation into State, that is, abolition of ACDA, would negate image concerns and improve coordination. But it would be extremely unwise for three reasons. Above all, it would reduce—and in some cases eliminate—the kind of clearly identified voice for arms control that ACDA represents. The Secretary of State cannot and should not devote excessive time to arms control. He has other pressing duties. Merger would invariably mean that arms control issues would receive inadequate attention, particularly if the Secretary himself was cool toward arms control. In some areas, like conventional arms exports, State—especially in the regional bureaus—is often not disposed toward restraint. ACDA is a catalyst for arms control. Without incessant noise from Iklé, the government would not have acted expeditiously in the nuclear proliferation area. ACDA ferrets out attempts by State and others to suppress data. These functions could not be effectively performed if the Agency were abolished. Merger would also eliminate one more voice for arms control on interagency councils. Second, the stodgy ambience of the State Department could stifle ACDA's high-quality, often innovative analysis. Finally, abolition of ACDA would be interpreted for what it was, a sharp downgrading of the policy priority assigned to arms control.

ACDA's quasi-independent status should be retained. With few exceptions, coordination with State has been adequate. Kissinger's tight control was unique. ACDA, even with Kissinger to a considerable degree, enjoyed sufficient leeway vis-à-vis State to carry out its mission.

Negotiations, Research, and Public Information. ACDA has a policy implementation function because of its role, often a leading one, in formal bilateral and multilateral arms control negotiations. Its activities are well coordinated with the State Department, and FSOs on assignment to ACDA are intimately involved in negotiations.

The most debated issue, concerning negotiations, relates to the advisability of a Director's heading the American delegation to a major negotiation like SALT. Smith and Warnke led the SALT delegation; Iklé did not. The title of SALT Ambassador brings certain policy and symbolic advantages, but it can also take the Director away from the Washington policy action and expose him to critics. This matter was at least partially resolved in 1977 when Congress authorized a new ACDA position—a "most-of-the-time" negotiator who could lead the delegation in the Director's absence—thereby permitting him to be in Washington. When it is imperative for the Director to attend the negotiations, he can do so. Then he heads the delegation.

A President may conduct negotiations in any manner deemed appropriate. He may elect to circumvent formal procedures in favor of more direct, "backchannel" contacts with foreign leaders. But as a rule ACDA should be represented in all formal arms control negotiations; it should continue to backstop such negotiations; and the Director should at least be notified of informal high-level discussions.

Rigorous, high-quality analysis is ACDA's metier. Outside of DOD, its cross-disciplinary defense expertise is among the most impressive in government. This enables the Agency to confront issues directly and intelligently. Without this capability ACDA is disarmed.

Analytical efforts are divided between in-house and contracted research. Analysts are exceptionally well qualified. Most hold a Ph.D. or other advanced degree. Many have prior government experience in arms control. Others come from faculties of distinguished universities. ACDA has one of the largest systems analysis capabilities in the national security field, apart from the Pentagon. There are few arms control issues for which ACDA has not accounted for most of the analytical work. Its research is regularly utilized by the NSC, State, and (less frequently) DOD. The task for in-house analysts is simply to maintain quality performance.

Contracted research is conducted in the technical/scientific and social science areas. The former category has often been exceedingly valuable and deserves priority attention. But external social science research, while it has sometimes served a public-education function, has been less successful in a policy sense. Much of the early work was ill conceived, poorly done, and—ACDA's main complaint—unrelated to policy concerns. By the late 1970s, however, ACDA expanded outside social science research, primarily because of congressional pressure. Questions can be raised about the wisdom of compelling sponsored research that experience indicates is of minimal policy utility. It is not even clear whether ACDA is the best governmental unit to subsidize external research whose major justification is educational. On the other hand, the ACD Act encourages ACDA to further public education in the arms control field. Because of this, and since congressional liberals are insistent, it seems prudent to be judiciously responsive. Such research might be helpful if contracts are well designed. It might provide analysts with illuminating background information, challenge assumptions, assist ACDA to evaluate its own in-house analysis, and inject something that is absent from U.S. arms control efforts: planning and thinking about the future. The program should be monitored closely and its results carefully assessed.

Dissemination of public information about arms control is one of ACDA's four primary functions under the ACD Act. Yet the public affairs effort was pedestrian and virtually invisible for fifteen years. The program was criticized and restricted by congressional conservatives in the 1960s. Prior to FY 1976 ACDA seldom allotted more than about $300,000 annually to this function. But the congressional mood changed in the late 1970s, and Congress had tripled this figure by FY 1979. The increase was long overdue. Arms control is respectable, and ACDA should spread the word.

General Advisory Committee on Arms Control and Disarmament. The ACD Act permits the President to appoint a GAC to advise him and the Director on arms control and disarmament matters. Every President since Kennedy has done so, but the committee has seldom been a factor in policy deliberations. It has also outlived one of its original purposes, to police suspect arms controllers. The GAC will be used only if it offers the President a perspective not otherwise available and if he has confidence in its chairman. Despite its unimpressive record, the committee probably should be retained. Presidents should be free to consult the GAC when they believe this would be fruitful.

Personnel and Size. About two-thirds of ACDA's professional employees are civilians, and they have always controlled the Agency. The remainder are active duty military officers and FSOs on temporary assignment to the Agency. Most temporary employees leave when their tour of duty ends. But there is a high turnover rate even among civilians. To some extent this is beneficial. It brings in new ideas. ACDA also serves as a seedbed for producing arms control specialists who, when they leave, usually go to other government agencies or academia. But the constant changeover deprives ACDA of a long-term human memory and, more important, vitiates one of the reasons for its establishment: creation of a permanent corps of arms control professionals.

Staffing the Agency with FSOs and military officers should be continued. FSOs bring negotiating experience, reflect the union of arms control and foreign policy, encourage cordial relations with State, and facilitate coordination. Military officers bring field experience, knowledge of weaponry, and an ability to extract information from the Pentagon. Since 1966 there have been few significant "loyalty" problems with these officers, and their caliber has been generally high. It is, however, prudent to ask those officers considered for senior ACDA positions to retire from the service first.

Until FY 1978–FY 1979, when it almost doubled, ACDA's total budget hovered around $10 million. The Agency has usually had fewer than a hundred civilian professionals. In short, ACDA lacks the kind of institutional clout that often accompanies sheer bulk. But there is little justification or need for a massive Peace Department. Nor is there an inherent relationship between size and effectiveness. The NSC staff is quite small. And smallness has advantages: It promotes intra-Agency coordination, encourages organizational cohesion, and affords even junior officers an opportunity to meet with the leadership. Although ACDA should remain small, there is a need to increase the number of civilian professionals to about 150. ACDA has been severely overloaded since 1975 because of multiple arms control negotiations and several new responsibilities mandated by Congress.

Outside Constituency. Unlike some departments and agencies, ACDA lacks a powerful, mass-membership outside constituency that would lobby in its behalf before Congress. There are, however, several noteworthy smaller interest groups like the Federation of American Scientists and the Arms Control Association. They provide information about arms control, counter those heavily financed groups hostile to arms control, testify before Congress, and offer legislators an important alternative source of expertise and analysis on national security affairs. These organizations deal with the press and have an influence on liberal-moderate congressmen that is disproportionate to their numbers.

Congress. Prior to the opening of the SALT I negotiations Congress showed only sporadic interest in arms control and imposed several constraints on ACDA. This changed after 1969, when a succession of arms-control-related issues gained prominence; a new congressional arms control coalition formed; Congress improved its capability to assess defense matters independently; and ACDA received unprecedented support. Interest in arms control was never uncritical. This was increasingly apparent as Soviet–American relations deteriorated after 1973. But arms control ceased to be the plaything of supposedly fuzzy arms controllers. It was a tenet of U.S. foreign policy.

Congress, led by ACDA's oversight subcommittees in the House Foreign Affairs Committee and the Senate Foreign Relations Committee, was alarmed when the Nixon administration, at Senator Jackson's urging, slashed the Agency's budget and purged several of its most dedicated people in 1973. This prompted Congressman Zablocki's subcommittee to launch the first thorough review of ACDA since 1961. The result was the 1975 legislation to upgrade ACDA's effectiveness and policy role. For the first time ACDA was specifically directed to involve itself in the weapons acquisition process through a new arms control impact statement procedure; the Director gained formal advisory status on the NSC; the ACD Act was amended to eliminate various constraints and to clarify the Director's authority; and the State Department was required to consult with ACDA on conventional arms export decisions. Much stiffer legislation, this time mandating Agency involvement in conventional arms transfers, was passed in 1976. In 1977–1978 ACDA's appropriations were sharply increased, funds for external research and public information were augmented; and certain restrictions affecting personnel and travel were lifted. In March 1978 President Carter signed the Nuclear Nonproliferation Act into law. Among other things, it recognized ACDA's role in nuclear export decisions and authorized the Director to prepare nuclear proliferation assessment statements. Between 1969 and 1978 ACDA's budget requests were regularly granted and, particularly after 1973, sometimes increased.

There were three principal reasons for this concern about ACDA: (1) The purge angered and disturbed the arms control bloc and highlighted the need for a comprehensive evaluation of Agency operations. ACDA was found wanting in several respects. (2) By the 1970s there was strong sentiment in Congress for meshing arms control more fully with foreign and national security policy. ACDA was an obvious vehicle for doing this. (3) ACDA was also used as a tool for prying data from the executive branch. Much of the legislation had an informational objective.

Most of this legislation did not originate with ACDA, though it was, sometimes belatedly, welcomed. When Congress requires ACDA to examine categories of weapons systems or participate in nuclear export decisions, the Agency, ipso facto, intrudes into another department's jurisdiction. When ACDA is the chosen messenger for relaying to Congress information that could potentially jeopardize the programs of DOD and the Department of Energy, the Agency encounters suspicion and resistance. ACDA's ability to perform depends upon the confidence and cooperation of other executive actors. The requisite level of cooperation may not be forthcoming if ACDA is thought to be an agent of Congress. Yet ACDA needs congressional support. Refusal by the executive branch to comply with the law invites the wrath of Congress, which can mean (and sometimes has meant) even more stringent actions to bolster ACDA's position.

If Senator Case had had a better feel for bureaucratic realities he might have reconsidered his 1972 attempt to transfer responsibility for seismic testing from DOD to ACDA. Proposed legislation must be sensitive to the organizational environment it seeks to affect. Nonetheless, most of the legislation has been beneficial. Without it, there would be little, if any, arms control input into conventional arms export or weapons program decisions, and ACDA's role in some other areas would be slight. Agency involvement is worth the risk of a bureaucratic tussle or two.

While ACDA continued to fare well in Congress during the early Carter administration, there were signs of possible trouble. Paul Warnke, perhaps ACDA's most activist Director, faced fierce conservative opposition to his 1977 nomination as SALT Ambassador. There was no indication in 1978 that this group—which could threaten ratification of a SALT II treaty—had softened its attitude toward him. Indeed, Warnke's detractors appeared to be using him as a surrogate target for attacking the evolving SALT II treaty. Also, Congressman Derwinski's amendment to the ACD Act, which required the Director to report to Congress on the verifiability of arms control proposals and agreements, reflected (among other things) a growing anti-Soviet mood and concern about Moscow's compliance with the SALT I accords. If Soviet–American relations degenerate, so will the prospects for arms control. Should this occur, ACDA could suffer.

Arms Control Impact Statements. In 1975 Congress enacted legislation that might significantly affect both ACDA and U.S. defense policy. Briefly, section 36 of the ACD Act requires any government department requesting authorization or appropriations for a wide variety of defense programs to accompany such requests with a statement detailing the program's impact on arms control policy and negotiations. ACDA has primary responsibility for implementing the legislation.

Resistance to section 36 within the executive branch was widespread, yet President Ford signed the bill. For the first two years (FY 1977–FY 1978) DOD and ERDA failed to comply with the law. Hence, ACISes issued during this period were inadequate in every respect and ACDA's access to information about defense programs may have actually declined. Key committee chairmen warned the executive that continued noncompliance would not be tolerated and that the ACIS process would be closely monitored. When President Carter assumed office things began to change. The process acquired presidential and NSC backing. There were important personnel changes in DOD. Warnke asserted his legal prerogatives and enlarged his ACIS staff. The result, influenced by the administration's fear of further legislation, was a marked improvement in the quantity and quality of the FY 1979 ACISes submitted to Congress in March 1978.

One of the legislation's principal objectives was substantially realized. Congress received detailed, informative, analytical statements; several of them were quite critical of the programs' arms control implications. While there is room for further improvement, and while it is unlikely that a defense program with firm presidential backing will ever be entirely candid, the FY 1979 ACISes were an encouraging beginning.

There was also some movement toward meeting the legislation's other objectives, but here the improvement was less striking. The Departments of Defense and Energy continued to resist ACDA's "interference," and arms control considerations are still not satisfactorily integrated into defense program decisions at an early enough stage to make a difference. But a workable procedure for producing the statements was established, one that recognized ACDA's authority to prepare ACISes for the NSC. The Agency still had difficulty procuring needed information, and there was controversy over the legal interpretation of section 36, although neither of these problems was as great as in the first two years.

The ACIS process presents ACDA with its familiar dilemma. If the statements are deemed unsatisfactory by the congressional arms control coalition, ACDA and other executive branch units face criticism, investigatory hearings, and possible additional legislation. None of this will necessarily improve either the ACISes or ACDA's position (though continued congressional oversight is essential if the process is to succeed). Much depends on the administration in power. On the other hand, if the ACISes are judged satisfactory by Congress—they are frank, timely, and "balanced"—ACDA's status as a trusted member of executive team may be jeopardized. This can also be costly. Even if the President himself sanctions the issuance of a candid statement on a particular defense program, exposure of this program's arms control problems to congressional critics is hardly conducive to cordial ACDA relations with the affected department or military service.

But political choices are seldom clear-cut, never value free. It is imperative that a defense program's impact on arms control policy and negotiations be carefully scrutinized. This has been a fundamental failing of American national security policy that must be corrected. A modest step toward this end has finally been taken.

Epilogue
The Carter Administration and Paul Warnke: A Further Look

OCTOBER 31, 1978, marked the end of Paul Warnke's brief twenty-month term as ACDA's Director. As the farewell party that day progressed into the evening hours, Warnke sang a few songs for the assembled ACDA employees, most of whom felt a real sense of loss. There may have been singing elsewhere in government that night. Two weeks earlier President Carter, in announcing Warnke's resignation, had praised him as "a very good man," but Warnke later remarked, "I'm sure there will be those who will be able to contain their regret."[1]

When Warnke first accepted the office he told the President that, for personal reasons, he probably would be able to serve only through 1978. Among other considerations, he knew it would be difficult to finance his children's college expenses on a government salary. In June 1978 he informed the President that he would resign by Labor Day, but in August Carter persuaded him to stay on for two more months. Warnke left for personal reasons; he was not asked to resign. However, a ranking ACDA official commented: "By 1978 there were those in the White House who were urging the President to facilitate the timely implementation of the original understanding [that Warnke would not serve out his full term]. They felt this would help SALT II's prospects for Senate ratification."

As this is being written (early December 1978) I am too near the event to assess the Warnke directorship with full confidence. Indeed, some ramifications of his tenure may not be evident for years. Still, it seems fitting to round out a book on ACDA and the American arms control

222

policy process with some guarded commentary on this important period. Particularly striking in late 1978 was the contrast between the immediate past and a possible immediate future. While ACDA had an unprecedented arms control policy role—virtually across the board—from March 1977 to October 1978, there was a sense of foreboding about the future.

ACDA's Policy Role under Warnke

Unlike any of his predecessors, Paul Warnke joined the select inner circle of senior policymakers. Hence ACDA experienced a previously unknown degree of activity across an unusually broad spectrum of issues. Warnke's role was primarily attributable to three factors: (1) a cordial and mutually respectful relationship with President Carter; (2) his own stature, style, ability, and dedication; and, (3) his warm personal relations with Secretary of State Cyrus Vance.

A government official involved at a high level in American arms control policy since the Eisenhower years said, "Carter knows an awful lot about arms control and SALT; he has a truly active interest." Though no ACDA Director, including Warnke, can normally expect better access to the Oval Office than the Secretaries of State and Defense or the Assistant for National Security Affairs, Carter was the first President actually to treat ACDA's Director as a principal adviser on a wide variety of issues. The President told Warnke to see him "any time" he needed to. Sometimes they met with Vance and/or Zbigniew Brzezinski. At other times the two met alone, though Vance was informed of their discussions. Carter initiated some of these sessions with Warnke, and often they were consequential sessions. Occasionally, after seeing Warnke, the President would support an ACDA position even though it was opposed by much of the rest of the national security bureaucracy.

Paul Warnke was someone to be reckoned with even apart from his relationship with the President. He had a certain presence, partly related to his past service in the Pentagon, his thorough knowledge of arms control, and his skill in one-to-one and small group encounters. Also, though he left most intra-Agency administrative matters to his deputy, Spurgeon Keeny, Warnke was ACDA's strongest leader. Many were in agreement with the view of one ACDA officer that "Paul brings out the best in people. He has a loyal, devoted, and competent staff." The pervasive internal dissent of the Iklé period, which was partly grounded in a feeling that the Agency was not being faithful to its mission, was gone.

Finally, while Warnke was a legal advocate by profession, he was a policy advocate by inclination. He entered eagerly into debates over arms control policy, so eagerly that he once admitted that "I tend sometimes to get carried away with my advocacy." When he felt strongly about something he was not afraid to be alone. Indeed, there were instances when he led others toward consensus even though, initially, almost no one had agreed with his position. At other times he persuaded Vance to take certain issues to the President, particularly those relating to a comprehensive nuclear test ban and certain conventional arms transfers, when the Secretary otherwise might not have been inclined to do so. But Warnke picked his cases carefully, concentrating on those where there was a prospect of prevailing. Although, internally, ACDA opposed Carter's "package" arms sale to Israel, Egypt, and Saudi Arabia in the spring of 1978 on arms control grounds, Warnke testified in favor of the transaction. There were, he felt, compelling foreign policy reasons for supporting it. Similarly, some of the nongovernmental arms control community was disturbed that ACDA did not fight harder against the enhanced radiation warhead. But Warnke personally believed that, from an arms control standpoint, apart from possibly lowering the nuclear threshold (and this was arguable), the weapon did not make much difference one way or the other.

Cyrus Vance and Secretary of Defense Harold Brown had known Warnke for more than twelve years, and the three men had an excellent rapport. Keeny also had a close, long-standing relationship with Brown. Vance and Warnke were generally (not always) allied on policy issues, while OSD and ACDA had the normal disputes. Despite predictable policy differences, Warnke got along well with the JCS on a personal level. For ACDA's Director, the most crucial relationship, below the President, is with the Secretary of State. The easy, open Vance–Warnke tie greatly facilitated ACDA's overall policy role.

Before rejoining government in 1977, Warnke had not known Brzezinski well. It soon became apparent, as several officials remarked, that the two had "different world views." Unlike Warnke, Brzezinski sought to gear the pace of the SALT talks and some other arms control negotiations to the warmth of Soviet–American relations. Brzezinski did not want to cancel SALT, but he argued that a slowing of the negotiating process would signal U.S. concern about, for example, the Soviet Union's incursions into Ethiopia and its human rights violations at home. There were instances when Brzezinski sat on policy papers that Warnke thought should have gone up to the President.[2] While ACDA's relations with the NSC staff were good (and Keeny got along reasonably well with

Brzezinski), the Director and the Assistant for National Security Affairs often clashed. For instance, they had different assessments of the domestic political ramifications of some arms control issues and of the utility of the ACISes. Though Warnke felt the impact statements were issued too late in the weapons acquisition process to have maximum effect, he nonetheless viewed them as giving ACDA an opportunity for "weighing in" on the process. Brzezinski, however, was sometimes attentive to the Pentagon's view that an ACIS constituted an unwarranted intrusion by Congress and ACDA into DOD's domain. An ACDA officer remarked, concerning the FY 1980 ACISes: "Brzezinski is blocking full implementation of ACDA's legislative mandate."

Specific Arms Control Issues

SALT. Warnke, unlike Fred Iklé, not only enjoyed warm personal relations with the President and Secretary of State but was also chief U.S. SALT negotiator. Not surprisingly, then, ACDA's influence in SALT was more substantial than it was during the Ford administration. However, before the controversy over the advisability of linking SALT progress to various other Soviet foreign policy activities first became public in the spring of 1978, Carter had never discussed such "linkage" with Warnke. The President had, of course, spoken with Brzezinski about it. When Warnke did meet with Carter on the matter, he argued that SALT was valuable to the United States in itself; it furthered American interests wholly apart from what the Soviets were doing in the Horn of Africa. Carter then urged Warnke to press forward with the negotiations.

Many who had opposed his nomination as SALT Ambassador feared that Warnke would not be a vigorous champion of American interests. These fears were not borne out. One government official in touch with all arms control negotiations during this period characterized Warnke as a "terrifically tough negotiator." He added, "The Soviets seem afraid of him. He makes them nervous. Sometimes they appear to avoid him." The same individual cited an incident when a Soviet official remarked to him: "We always wondered why Americans would pay so much for good trial attorneys. Now we know."

At first Warnke thought it essential that ACDA's Director also wear the second hat of chief SALT negotiator. But he soon recognized the inherent difficulties of doing this (see Chapter 9) and before resigning proposed that the two positions, while remaining within ACDA, be split.[3]

The proposal was accepted. After Warnke left, Carter designated AC-DA's Ralph Earle as U.S. SALT Ambassador. Earle had served as ACDA's representative at the SALT talks from 1973 to 1977, and after May 1977, when he became the Special Representative for Arms Control and Disarmament Negotiations, he functioned as alternate U.S. SALT negotiator. It seems probable (and advisable) that future Directors will not wear both hats. Yet it is desirable, though less certain, that the SALT Ambassador and the top negotiator for most other major arms control talks continue to be from the Agency.

Comprehensive Test Ban. For two decades much of the arms control community had urged a comprehensive ban on the testing of all nuclear explosive devices, but this did not become a live, sustained American policy option at the highest level until 1977. Even before Warnke came aboard, Carter unequivocally indicated his desire for a comprehensive test ban, a position he later reiterated. DOE, the JCS, and some in DOD—especially the weapons laboratories—had strong reservations and asked the President to consider instead another Threshold Test Ban Treaty. But Carter rejected this proposal after Warnke (who dealt directly with the President on this issue) and Vance reiterated the case for a comprehensive agreement.[4] A senior ACDA official commented that "the comprehensive test ban would be dead without Warnke."

In early 1977 the most important issue within the U.S. government that was still flexible was the duration of the agreement—would it be for an indefinite or a fixed term? It was subsequently decided that a fixed term (apparently three years) was necessary primarily for three reasons: (1) Moscow was concerned about nonparties to the agreement—France and, particularly, China. (2) Although the Soviets were still interested in nuclear explosions for peaceful purposes, in September 1977 Brezhnev proposed a moratorium on all underground tests. This tended to reinforce arguments for a fixed term. (3) There was some concern about retaining high confidence in the reliability of the U.S. nuclear stockpile without periodic testing.

By October 1978 the negotiations, which Warnke led, had made significant headway, though several hurdles remained. The principle of on-site inspection was established, although there were many outstanding problems with implementation, including the precise number of seismic stations each country would accept. In addition, a Soviet–American agreement would have to go to the CCD for multilateral negotiations. Still, the world had never been closer to a comprehensive (or nearly comprehensive) test ban.

Nuclear Proliferation. ACDA retained and even enhanced its role in the nuclear proliferation area, although the focal point of U.S. policy in 1977–1978 was Joseph Nye's office in the State Department. The change in personnel in 1977 and Carter's interest in the subject encouraged better integration between State and ACDA than at any previous time. Carter appointed Gerard Smith as his Special Representative for Nonproliferation Matters as well as U.S. representative to the International Atomic Energy Agency. Philip Farley was Smith's deputy. OES retained an important voice, while the Bureau of Politico-Military Affairs under Leslie Gelb sharply increased its policy authority in this and several other arms control areas.

ACDA probably had the best nuclear safeguards specialists in government, and State continued to rely heavily on ACDA for scientific expertise. By November 1978 ACDA had about thirty professionals (technical and political) in the nuclear proliferation field, and many of the leading people in this area in State, DOE, the NRC, and the NSC had formerly worked under the government's top nuclear proliferation expert, ACDA's Charles Van Doren. The Agency was fully involved in all relevant issue areas, had an active voice in nuclear export decisions, was represented on all pertinent interagency committees, had few significant problems in gaining access to necessary information, and in the summer of 1978 issued the first Nuclear Proliferation Assessment Statement (concerning Iran) under the Nuclear Nonproliferation Act of 1978. Warnke did not get involved too deeply in this area, because ACDA already had a central role and Keeny had special expertise here. Keeny, before reentering government in 1977, had a prominent part in producing the Ford Foundation–Mitre Corporation study, which set the tone for the Carter administration's overall approach to nuclear proliferation.[5]

Conventional Arms Transfers. Finally by 1978 a senior Agency official could report that ACDA was "actively involved in *all* arms transfer decisions over $7 million." Although most of the working groups of the Arms Export Control Board, including the one chaired by ACDA, never met, ACDA officers attended meetings of the board. The NSC's Policy Review Committee set U.S. arms transfer ceilings, and when it met for this purpose it was chaired by Vance. ACDA was represented on this body by Warnke, the first Director to take an active interest in the subject. His involvement was prompted partly by ACDA's new legal authority here, but it also stemmed from the fact that this was an area of concern to both Congress and the President. Congress would ask, as it did in 1978 with the sale of aircraft to Israel, Egypt, and Saudi Arabia, about AC-

DA's policy role. It learned that for the first time an ACDA Director spoke with the President about some important arms sales. For instance, in October 1978, concerning a proposed sale of F-5Gs to Taiwan, Carter decided against it after seeing Warnke. Vance, Brown, and Brzezinski all favored the sale. Also that fall, following a heated interdepartmental debate, Carter opted for the position supported by ACDA and decided not to authorize an early sale of F-16s to South Korea.[6]

Other Issues. ACDA was fully involved in a variety of other arms control issues and chaired several working groups, including one that coordinated U.S. policy on a possible Soviet–American treaty limiting antisatellite capabilities. Although the Agency lost the chairmanship of the interagency coordinating committee on MBFR, which it had held in the Ford administration, it was represented on all formal MBFR committees. MBFR was centralized under Reginald Bartholomew of the NSC staff, who, with Brzezinski, spoke of linking these talks to other areas of Soviet behavior. While Moscow did make a significant new proposal in June 1978, formidable impediments to agreement remained, and few officials were optimistic about their early resolution.

Naval limitations in the Indian Ocean were the subject of three rounds of negotiations between the United States and the Soviet Union in 1977. Though the American base on Diego Garcia promised to be a stumbling block, Moscow showed great interest in an agreement that, it was generally thought, would involve a two-step process: first a freeze on existing naval deployments in the region, then possible reductions. But by 1978 Brzezinski and others argued that it would be unseemly to move these negotiations forward while the Soviets and Cubans were meddling in the Horn of Africa. Warnke concurred with this position.

Warnke and Congress

Relations with Congress were decidedly mixed and, with a few exceptions, divided roughly along ideological lines.[7] Warnke's ties to liberals and many moderates were cordial, while most conservatives remained cool to him. At the time most observers read his resignation as, on balance, improving the likelihood of a favorable congressional reception for the SALT II agreements.

Although some friendly legislators complained that he spent too much time out of the country and not enough on the Hill, Warnke gave priority attention to congressional relations. He testified regularly and, on SALT, appeared far more often than the previous SALT Ambassador, U. Alexis Johnson. At one hearing Warnke turned to an aide and said, "When I write my book on my time as ACDA Director, I'm going to call it 'Witness.'" He also had greater latitude than either Johnson or Smith to testify frankly in closed sessions. In addition, he appeared regularly before an ad hoc SALT group of about twenty liberal-moderate senators convened by his friend, Senator Cranston. Other senior Agency officials periodically briefed legislators on SALT; for instance, in September–October 1978 Ambassador Earle and another officer briefed twenty-nine liberal and conservative senators. Some thirty legislators visited the SALT delegation in Geneva, and, like Iklé, Warnke met with groups of congressional staffers in his office.

Warnke found considerable (though hardly universal) support on both the House International Relations and the Senate Foreign Relations committees. He, not Vance, was their principal SALT briefer, and a majority of their members welcomed ACDA's expanded policy role. Keeny, however, was never comfortable dealing with Congress. This was soon evident to several members of the House International Relations Committee, and that committee informed the Agency in 1978 that Keeny was not to appear before it again.

Opposition to Warnke centered in the House and Senate Armed Services Committees. Prior to 1977, when he testified twice before the House committee, no ACDA Director had ever appeared before it. Still, ACDA's association with this committee was not harmonious. It was no better with the Senate Armed Services Committee, though Warnke was on good terms with the liberal Democratic members and eventually cultivated a rapport with Senators Sam Nunn (D–Ga.) and Dewey Bartlett (R–Okla.). Warnke did not overcome the opposition of its other members. Conservatives of both parties throughout Congress criticized him on substantive and occasionally personal grounds. Some Republican fundraising literature for the 1978 congressional elections referred to both Warnke and the SALT verification issue. Senator Jackson's hostility was unremitting; he never invited Warnke to testify before his Subcommittee on Arms Control. And it was Jackson who set the tone on arms control for the full Armed Services Committee. Warnke was prepared, even eager, to meet with Jackson, but the Senator never asked. While the two had obvious policy differences, Warnke was perplexed as to why Jackson's antagonism ran so deep, especially insofar as the only time in his life he had ever spoken with the Senator was during his confirmation hearings. Whatever the reasons, it cast a shadow over both ACDA and SALT II.[8]

The Future

Perhaps the only certainty about the political future is that it will eventually become the political past, and as such will be analytically much safer to examine. Still, despite several encouraging arms control initiatives and accomplishments during 1977–1978, there was a growing sense of uneasiness within the governmental and nongovernmental arms control communities about the future of arms control and ACDA. Inhibiting the global dissemination of nuclear weapons was a herculean task. Weapons systems like the cruise missile were outstripping the capabilities of national technical means of verification. The continued growth of Soviet conventional and strategic military power and Moscow's assertiveness in international affairs were a source of genuine concern, which will not bolster Congress's enthusiasm for arms restraint even if a SALT II accord is ratified.

Similarly, while President Carter made several decisions in the fall of 1978 clearly designed at least in part to sweeten SALT II before presenting it to the Senate, these actions also reflected the President's perception that it was necessary to counter an increasingly threatful Soviet Union. Carter's actions included a substantial rise in defense spending for FY 1980; closer attention to civil defense; approval for the production of elements of the enhanced radiation warhead; and a decision to ask Congress for funds to begin full-scale development of a mobile MX ICBM. While a world without SALT would hardly be preferable to one with at least some adequately verifiable restraints on strategic weapons, those who argued that SALT has been a de facto cover for an escalating strategic arms race would be given additional fuel for their position.

In October Carter took another step designed to enhance Congress's receptivity to SALT II. He announced that the President of the Citadel, Lieutenant General George Seignious, would become ACDA's new Director.[9] General Seignious was given a recess appointment, effective December 1, under which he could serve for up to a year or until the Senate elected to act upon his nomination. The reaction to the appointment within ACDA, the congressional arms control coalition, and the broader arms control community was, as might be expected, less than ecstatic.

In the past ACDA had sometimes been well served, at lower levels, by active duty or retired senior military officers. Indeed, the worst-case scenarios painted by many liberals in the fall of 1978 may prove to have been somewhat overdrawn. But never had a retired military officer held either of the Agency's top two positions, and it was not surprising that several groups, after Seignious's appointment, began pressing for a law for ACDA similar to the one that prohibits appointing a retired military officer as Secretary of Defense.

ACDA was destined to have a lower profile as long as Seignious was Director. The general had no prior relationship with the President. Though he was an at-large member of the SALT delegation after September 1977 (Warnke recommended his appointment to this position) and had occasionally differed with JCS SALT representative General Rowny, he lacked experience and knowledge in most other arms control areas. He once held the top post in the Pentagon's weapons sales program, but arms control supporters were unconvinced that this qualified him to lead an Agency whose mission is to seek reasonable restraints on the arms trade. The fundamental concern about Seignious was, of course, rooted in the evident incongruity of appointing a military officer, one who from 1972 to 1974 was staff director for the JCS, to head an organization whose ethos clashed directly with that of the JCS. Arms control proponents were hardly encouraged by Seignious's first personnel decision: He replaced ACDA's civilian Executive Secretary, who had served ably under both Democratic and Republican administrations, with another retired military officer.

These concerns were heightened, and another was added—lack of political tact—when it was revealed that in July General Seignious had joined the American Security Council's Coalition for Peace Through Strength, whose declared objective was to "stop SALT II." Though Seignious dismissed his association with that anti-SALT lobby as the result of administrative errors, he did not resign from it until October 17, after he was first queried about the ACDA directorship by Brzezinski. He then compounded his problems by displeasing John Fisher, head of the American Security Council, whose "stop SALT" lobby claimed to have the support of 175 members of Congress, by writing a letter of resignation that Seignious himself later admitted was "entirely too strong."[10] Clearly, Seignious's relationship with both congressional liberals and conservatives did not begin under the most propitious of circumstances (though his confirmation by the Senate was virtually certain). It was questionable whether he would, in fact, be an asset to the administration in the forthcoming SALT debate.[11]

Once again government "arms controllers" were forced to beat a retreat precisely when their accomplishments were most pronounced. In late 1972 and into 1973, following SALT I, ACDA was purged. In late

1978 on the (apparent) eve of the SALT II accords to which Warnke had contributed so much, the presumptively unreliable arms controllers were placed in the charge of a retired lieutenant general who, apparently because he had worn three stars, was thought "responsible" in matters of national security.[12]

ACDA will be permitted to be effective only to a degree. Beyond that point it is thought to be politically hazardous, even for an administration committed to arms control, to permit arms control professionals to play too active or too public a policy role. Warnke was ACDA's most effective Director in executive branch deliberations. Ironically, in being effective, he invited what is now, in light of the Agency's history since 1961, a familiar reaction. This does not imply that ACDA or arms control is necessarily best furthered by a low-key Director, though a case to that effect can be made. What it does mean is that ultimately the future of arms control, and hence the future of policy actors like ACDA, is partly, though critically, anchored in the attitudes of the American people and their elected representatives about arms control, defense expenditures, the Soviet Union, and the role of the United States in world affairs.[13] Only time and circumstances will reveal the evolution of these attitudes.

Notes

Throughout the notes, three abbreviations will be frequently used: Senate Foreign Relations Committee (SRFC); House Foreign Affairs Committee (HFAC); House International Relations Committee (HIRC). Each source receives a full citation the first time it appears in a chapter, and abbreviated citations on subsequent appearances. When ten or more notes intervene between a short citation and the last previous reference to the same work, the location of the full citation is indicated as follows: "(n. 1 above)."

Chapter 1: Introduction

1. Donald P. Warwick, *A Theory of Public Bureaucracy: Politics, Personality, and Organization in the State Department* (Cambridge, Mass.: Harvard University Press, 1975), pp. 186, 198.
2. See Robert Rothstein, *Planning, Prediction and Policymaking in Foreign Affairs* (Boston: Little, Brown, 1972).
3. U.S. Congress, HIRC, Subcommittee on International Security and Scientific Affairs, *Hearings: The Arms Control and Disarmament Agency Authorization for Fiscal Year 1978,* 95th Cong., 1st sess., 1977, p. 52.

Chapter 2: Origins

1. See U.S. Congress, HFAC, Subcommittee on National Security Policy and Scientific Developments, *The Baruch Plan: U.S. Diplomacy Enters the Nuclear Age,* Committee Print, 92d Cong., 2d sess., 1972.
2. U.S. Arms Control and Disarmament Agency, *Documents on Disarma-*

ment, 1961, pp. 405–408; U.S. Congress, SFRC, Subcommittee on Disarmament, *Hearings: Disarmament and Foreign Policy,* 86th Cong., 1st sess., 1959, p. 410; and Robert W. Kastenmeir, "United States Machinery for Disarmament," in Seymour Melman, ed., *Disarmament: Its Politics and Economics* (Boston: American Academy of Arts and Sciences, 1962), p. 178.

3. Saville Davis, "Recent Policy Making in the United States Government," in Donald G. Brennan, ed., *Arms Control, Disarmament, and National Security* (New York: Braziller, 1961), pp. 382–383, 387, and Robert A. Divine, *Blowing on The Wind* (New York: Oxford University Press, 1978), pp. 146, 178.

4. U.S. Congress, HFAC, Subcommittee on National Security Policy and Scientific Developments, *Report: Review of Arms Control Legislation and Organization,* 93d Cong., 2d sess., 1974, p. 3.

5. Senator Hubert H. Humphrey, "Government Organization for Arms Control," in Brennan, *Arms Control,* p. 397, and *Documents on Disarmament,* 1961, p. 407.

6. Harold K. Jacobson and Eric Stein, *Diplomats, Scientists, and Politicians: The United States and the Nuclear Test Ban Negotiations* (Ann Arbor: University of Michigan Press, 1966), pp. 87, 371–372, 471, and Divine, *Blowing on The Wind,* pp. 314–318.

7. U.S. Congress, SFRC, Subcommittee on Disarmament, *Report: Control and Reduction of Arms,* No. 2501, 85th Cong., 2d sess., 1959; SFRC, Subcommittee on Disarmament, *Report: Control and Reduction of Arms,* No. 1167, 85th Cong., 1st sess., 1958; and SFRC, Subcommittee on Disarmament, *Hearings and Report: Control and Reduction of Arms,* 85th Cong., 1st sess., 1956–1958.

8. John McClaughry, "The United States Arms Control and Disarmament Agency," unpublished, Department of Political Science, University of California, 1963, ch. 5, pp. 15–18. McClaughry's paper is the only detailed analysis of ACDA's early legislative history.

9. U.S. Congress, Senate, *Report: Strengthening the Government for Arms Control,* by the National Planning Association's Special Committee on Security Through Arms Control, presented by Mr. Humphrey, Sen. Doc. No. 123, 86th Cong., 2d sess., August 27, 1960, and McClaughry, "U.S. Arms Control and Disarmament Agency," ch. 6. pp. 1–4, 18–20; ch. 8, p. 16.

10. *Documents on Disarmament,* 1960, pp. 59–64.

11. Graham T. Allison, *Essence of Decision: Explaining the Cuban Missile Crisis* (Boston: Little, Brown, 1971), p. 93.

12. ACDA "clearly was meant to express . . . a perspective that could provide some balance to the views propounded by military planners." Senator Hubert H. Humphrey, *Report on the U.S. Arms Control and Disarmament Agency,* Members of Congress for Peace through Law, April 9, 1973, p. 7. See also Kastenmeier, "United States Machinery," pp. 180–181.

13. Gerard C. Smith, "Should There Be a Larger U.S. Role for Policies and

Programs of Arms Control and Disarmament?'' unpublished statement, Aspen Institute for Humanistic Studies, Aspen, Colorado, August 13, 1976, p. 3.

14. Graham Allison and Peter Szanton, *Remaking Foreign Policy: The Organizational Connection* (New York: Basic Books, 1976), p. 22. The authors cite Thomas Hughes as describing ACDA, USIA, and the Agency for International Development as ''monuments to the State Department's disinterest in their functions.''

15. U.S. Congress, Senate, *Report: Strengthening the Government,* p. 17.

16. U.S. Congress, SFRC, *Hearings: Disarmament Agency,* 87th Cong., 1st sess., 1961, p. 15.

17. U.S. Congress, SRFC, *Hearings: Review of Operations of the Arms Control and Disarmament Agency,* 87th Cong., 2d sess., 1962, p. 3.

18. *Documents on Disarmament,* 1961, p. 364.

19. SFRC, *Hearings: Disarmament Agency,* pp. 117, 120.

20. *Ibid.,* pp. 148, 153, and Kastenmeier, ''United States Machinery,'' p. 179.

21. Kastenmeier, ''United States Machinery,'' p. 178.

22. See Bernard G. Bechhoefer, *Postwar Negotiations for Arms Control* (Washington: Brookings Institution, 1961), pp. 589–591.

23. Humphrey, ''Government Organization for Arms Control,'' (n. 5 above), p. 395.

24. Arthur M. Schlesinger, Jr., *A Thousand Days* (Boston: Houghton Mifflin, 1965), p. 472; see also Chalmers M. Roberts, *The Nuclear Years* (New York: Praeger, 1970), p. 53.

25. McClaughry, ''U.S. Arms Control and Disarmament Agency'' (n. 8 above), ch. 7, pp. 20–21.

26. U.S. Congress, HFAC, Subcommittee on National Security Policy and Scientific Developments, *Hearings: Arms Control and Disarmament Agency,* 93d Cong., 2d sess., 1974, pp. 3, 13.

27. *Ibid.,* pp. 3, 35.

28. *Ibid.,* pp. 4, 13, 34, 107, and Schlesinger, *A Thousand Days,* pp. 472–473.

29. *Documents on Disarmament,* 1961, pp. 158, 197–198, 214–216.

30. *McClaughry, ''U.S. Arms Control and Disarmament Agency,'' ch. 8, pp. 19–20.*

31. SFRC, *Hearings: Disarmament Agency* (n. 16 above), pp. 15, 20. Rusk (p. 19) was additionally concerned that placement of the agency in State would increase interdepartmental tensions: ''We must avoid any possibility that disarmament would be looked upon as an effort, say, by the State Department to put the Defense Department out of business.'' It also appears (p. 94) that William Foster, ACDA's first Director, may have insisted on a measure of independence from State as a precondition to taking the job.

32. *Ibid.,* pp. 40, 16–17, 34.

33. HFAC, *Hearings: Arms Control and Disarmament Agency,* pp. 3–4.

34. SFRC, *Hearings: Disarmament Agency,* p. 87.

35. *Ibid.,* pp. 70–81. The level of understanding of arms control and disarma-

ment was evidently no higher in the military services than elsewhere in the country. General Lemnitzer defined disarmament as "the complete elimination of arms," thereby failing to note distinctions between partial and general disarmament or between various forms of disarmament and the far broader concept of arms control. See U.S. Congress, HFAC, *Hearings: To Establish a United States Arms Control Agency,* 87th Cong., 1st sess., 1961, p. 86.

36. U.S. Congress, HAFC, *Report: To Establish a United States Arms Control Agency,* No. 1165, 87th Cong., 1st sess., 1961, p. 1.

37. SFRC, *Hearings: Review of Operations* (n. 17 above), p. 44.

38. U.S. Congress, SFRC, *Report: United States Disarmament Agency for World Peace and Security,* No. 882, 87th Cong., 1st sess., 1961.

39. *Congressional Record* 107, 87th Cong., 1st sess., September 8, 1961, pp. S17520–S17561.

40. PL 87-297. The ACD Act has been amended many times. Subsequent amendments will be discussed in later chapters. Here we deal only with PL 87-297.

41. Most nations, including the Soviet Union, look to units in their foreign ministries for disarmament activities, with support from defense and technical agencies. ACDA's status interested some governments. In 1964, for example, Great Britain established a Ministry of State for Disarmament, and its first Minister, Lord Chalfont, came to Washington to study ACDA's staff and organization. Subsequently, an expert group to perform functions similar to ACDA's was organized within the British Foreign Office. *Documents on Disarmament,* 1964, p. 536. In December 1978 the Bundestag of the Federal Republic of Germany debated the question of creating a "German ACDA."

42. U.S. Congress, House of Representatives, Conference Committee, *Report: Arms Control and Disarmament Act,* No. 1263, 87th Cong., 1st sess., 1961, pp. 1–2.

43. U.S. Congress, HIRC, Subcommittee on International Security and Scientific Affairs, *Hearings: Arms Control and Disarmament Act Amendments,* 94th Cong., 1st sess., 1975, p. 48.

44. George Bunn, "Missile Limitations: By Treaty or Otherwise?," *Columbia Law Review* 70 (January 1970): 11–12.

45. *Documents on Disarmament,* 1961, p. 416.

46. *Ibid.,* p. 418.

47. HFAC, *Report: Review of Arms Control Legislation* (n. 4 above), p. 5.

Chapter 3: Image

1. U.S. Arms Control and Disarmament Agency, *Documents on Disarmament,* 1963, p. 197.

2. Statement of Fred Iklé to the Commission on the Organization of the Government for the Conduct of Foreign Policy (Murphy Commission), February 21, 1974, pp. 1–2. Emphasis added.
3. U.S. Congress, SFRC, *Hearings: Warnke Nomination,* 95th Cong., 1st sess., 1977, p. 15, and U.S. Congress, Senate, Committee on Armed Services, *Hearings: Consideration of Mr. Paul C. Warnke to Be Director of the U.S. Arms Control and Disarmament Agency and Ambassador,* 95th Cong., 1st sess., 1977, p. 6. After only a few weeks on the job Warnke said that "the number one attribute" required for "greater effectiveness ... is a recognition by the government itself of the importance of ACDA's role." U.S. Congress, HIRC, Subcommittee on International Security and Scientific Affairs, *Hearings: The Arms Control and Disarmament Agency Authorization for Fiscal Year 1978,* 95th Cong., 1st sess., 1977, p. 17.
4. *Documents on Disarmament,* 1961, p. 745, and 1962, pp. 351–382.
5. For example, U.S. ACDA, *Disarmament: Two Approaches,* publication 1, November 1, 1961; U.S. ACDA, *Toward a World Without War,* publication 10, October 1962; and U.S. ACDA, *Progressive Inspection for Disarmament,* publication 13, January 1963.
6. After the GCD phase passed, the following carol was reportedly sung at ACDA Christmas parties. The composer went on to a distinguished academic and government career.

Smash the Guns
(tune: "Deck the Halls")
Smash the guns and let's be jolly,
Fa-la-la-la-la, it's GCD;
It's not treason, it's not folly,
Fa-la-la-la-la, it's GCD.

First the nukes and then the missiles,
Break them up, smash them up, 1-2-3;
Then we'll get the rest, by golly,
Fa. . . . . . , 'til GCD.

Nations live in peaceful concert,
Not-a-war, no-one's-sore, glory be!
But there'll be no need for ACDA!
FOO-FOO-FOO-FOO-FOO on GCD.

7. William C. Foster, "Ban All Nuclear Testing," *The Atlantic Community Quarterly* 9 (Summer 1971): 175.
8. Ted Greenwood, *Making the MIRV: A Study of Defense Decision Making* (Cambridge, Mass.: Ballinger, 1975), p. 109.
9. U.S. Congress, HFAC, *Hearings: Arms Control and Disarmament Act Amendments, 1968,* 90th Cong., 2d sess., 1968, pp. 250–251.
10. *Congressional Record* 109, 88th Cong., 1st sess., November 20, 1963, pp. S22506–S22538, and James Duscha, *Arms, Money and Politics* (New York: Ives Washburn, 1965), pp. 134–135.

11. U.S. Congress, HFAC, *Hearings: To Amend Further the Arms Control and Disarmament Act,* 89th Cong., 1st sess., 1965, pp. 61–62, and HFAC, *Hearings: Arms Control and Disarmament Act Amendments,* 1968, pp. 94, 100.

12. Statement of A. M. Christopher to the Murphy Commission, July 23, 1974.

13. Nicholas Ruggieri, interview of William Foster, "The Man Who Made Arms Control 'Respectable'," *Foreign Service Journal* 48 (February 1971): 15, and Gerard C. Smith, "Should There Be a Larger U.S. Role for Policies and Programs of Arms Control and Disarmament?" unpublished statement, Aspen Institute for Humanistic Studies, Aspen, Colorado, August 13, 1976, p. 6.

14. ACDA's 11th annual report to Congress (1972) announced that the Agency "has taken a pragmatic approach, seeking step-by-step measures which are . . . practically attainable." *Documents on Disarmament,* 1971, p. 919.

15. Even a conservative subcommittee conceded that arms control is no longer "an academic toy." U.S. Congress, House of Representatives, Committee on Armed Services, Special Subcommittee on Arms Control and Disarmament, *Report: Review of Arms Control and Disarmament Activities,* No. 93-72, 93d Cong., 2d sess., 1974, p. 8.

16. U.S. Congress, HFAC, Subcommittee on National Security Policy and Scientific Developments, *Hearings: Arms Control and Disarmament Agency,* 93d Cong., 2d sess., 1974, pp. 75, 86, 91, 97, 134 ff.

17. U.S. Congress, SFRC, *Report: Arms Control and Disarmament Act Amendments of 1977,* No. 95-193, 95th Cong., 1st sess., 1977, p. 14.

18. For example, see the exchange between Admiral Thomas Moorer and Senator Thomas McIntyre (D–N.H.). U.S. Congress, Senate, Committee on Armed Services, *Hearings: Consideration of Mr. Paul C. Warnke* (n. 3 above), p. 243.

19. Congressional staffers as well as others familiar with Congress were unanimous on this point. See also, Jonathan E. Medalia, "The U.S. Senate and Strategic Arms Limitation Policymaking, 1963–1973," Ph.D. dissertation, Stanford University, 1975, pp. 108–109, 245.

20. Marvin Kalb and Bernard Kalb, *Kissinger* (Boston: Little, Brown, 1974), p. 112.

21. John Newhouse, *Cold Dawn: The Story of SALT* (New York: Holt, Rinehart & Winston, 1973), pp. 43, 159.

22. HFAC, *Hearings: Arms Control and Disarmament Agency,* pp. 23, 49–50. The only serious security breach I personally observed occurred in DOD's ISA when I was left alone in an office for thirty minutes with several top secret documents, including National Intelligence Estimates.

23. Morton Halperin, *Bureaucratic Politics and Foreign Policy* (Washington: Brookings Institution, 1974), p. 185.

24. PL 94-141, and U.S. Congress, HIRC, Subcommittee on International Security and Scientific Affairs, *Hearings: Arms Control and Disarmament Act Amendments,* 94th Cong., 1st sess., 1975, p. 15.

25. For the full text of the agreement see *Congressional Record* 123, 95th Cong., 1st sess., August 4, 1977, pp. H8678–H8679, and U.S. Congress, House of Representatives, *Conference Report: Arms Control and Disarmament Act Amendments of 1977,* No. 95-563, 95th Cong., 1st sess., 1977, pp. 6–7.

Chapter 4: Leadership and Cohesion

1. See Graham T. Allison, *Essence of Decision: Explaining the Cuban Missile Crisis* (Boston: Little, Brown, 1971), pp. 168–169; Graham T. Allison and Morton H. Halperin, "Bureaucratic Politics: A Paradigm and Some Policy Implications," in Richard H. Ullman and Raymond Tanter, eds., *Theory and Policy in International Relations* (Princeton, N.J.: Princeton University Press, 1972), pp. 50, 56; and Morton H. Halperin, *Bureaucratic Politics and Foreign Policy* (Washington: Brookings Institution, 1974), pp. 28, 151–154.
2. U.S. Congress, HFAC, Subcommittee on National Security Policy and Scientific Developments, *Hearings: Diplomatic and Strategic Impact of Multiple Warhead Missiles,* 92st Cong., 1st sess., 1969, pp. 208–209.
3. Duncan L. Clarke, "The Arms Control and Disarmament Agency: Effective?" *Foreign Service Journal* 52 (December 1975): 29.
4. Perceptions of an individual's personality are, of course, extremely sensitive and highly subjective. In all cases, the alleged personal traits of officials discussed in this chapter are based upon interviews with several people; often at least ten interviewees were in agreement on a particular individual, with few or none in disagreement. Still, this is an imperfect exercise where reasonable men can differ. It is nonetheless vital to our subject. All senior ACDA officials were, without exception, cooperative, generous with their time, and hospitable. Only the consensus views of interviewees, not those of the author, are presented.
5. John Newhouse, *Cold Dawn: The Story of SALT* (New York: Holt, Rinehart & Winston, 1973), p. 115.
6. Ted Greenwood, *Making the MIRV: A Study of Defense Decision Making* (Cambridge. Mass.: Ballinger, 1975), pp. 119, 123.
7. See Newhouse, *Cold Dawn,* p. 43.
8. *Washington Post,* March 8, 1973.
9. Four ACDA officials, two of whom worked closely with Iklé, commented: "His rigidity in dealing with the bureaucracy is a problem"; "Things get done through informal contacts. . . . You do *not,* as Iklé did, send a memo over to the Secretary of Defense: His staff will bury it. You *hand* carry it over to him personally"; "When he first arrived his attitude was—'rational men can rationally agree.' Naturally, he received a rude jolt. . . . One of his greatest failings . . . is that he is not sufficiently 'political'." "He does not

understand how to operate. . . . He antagonizes people. . . . Often his memos are sent at improper times or to the wrong people." Iklé himself occasionally hinted at the problem. See, U.S. Congress, SFRC, *Hearings: ACDA Authorization*, 93d Cong., 2d sess., 1974, p. 7.

10. Three ACDA officials, two of whom worked closely with Iklé, remarked: "He is the world's worst communicator"; "The poor morale is not so much for policy reasons. It is due to lousy administration and constant reshuffling of offices"; "He runs ACDA like a liberal arts college [and] calls up people at lower levels directly without first going through their superiors."

11. U.S. Congress, SFRC, *Hearings: Nomination of John F. Lehman, Jr., to Be Deputy Director, ACDA*, 94th Cong., 1st sess., 1975, pp. 11, 40. After Lehman had left ACDA, Senator Pell, while praising Iklé, stated that Lehman "was a dead loss." U.S. Congress, SFRC, *Hearings: Warnke Nomination*, 95th Cong., 1st sess., 1977, p. 36.

12. SFRC, *Hearings: Nomination of John F. Lehman*, p. 15.

13. Typical of the remarks of ACDA officers were the following: "very heavy handed"; "brutal"; "very heavy boots"; "reckless and consciously so—both as a tactic and because it *is* his style . . . a lust for battle"; "no, he is not a good bureaucratic player. Sure he knows the levers to pull but, unless you're Henry [Kissinger], a good player plays by the rules. Lehman does not."

14. U.S. Congress, HFAC, Subcommittee on National Security Policy and Scientific Developments, *Report: Review of Arms Control Legislation and Organization*, 93d Cong., 2d sess., 1974, p. 13. Emphasis added. Iklé denied the accuracy of this assertion. U.S. Congress, HFAC, Subcommittee on National Security and Scientific Developments, *Hearings: Arms Control and Disarmament Agency*, 93d Cong., 2d sess., 1974, p. 151.

15. U.S. General Accounting Office, *Statements That Analyze Effects of Proposed Programs on Arms Control Need Improvement*, ID-77-41, October 20, 1977, pp. 21–22.

16. Iklé indicated his strong support of the official rationale for U.S. security assistance. This prompted Congressman Michael Harrington (D–Mass.) to "question the reasons for the Agency's existence." *Congressional Record* 120, 93d Cong., 2d sess., July 17, 1974, p. E4805.

17. Paul Warnke later remarked, "Of course, the question remains, were there more than 67 in which objections should have been interposed." U.S. Congress, HIRC, Subcommittee on International Security and Scientific Affairs, *Hearings: The Arms Control and Disarmament Agency Authorization for Fiscal Year 1978*, 95th Cong., 1st sess., 1977, p. 16.

18. HFAC, *Hearings: Arms Control and Disarmament Agency*, p. 154.

19. U.S. Arms Control and Disarmament Agency, *Documents on Disarmament*, 1974, p. 864.

20. U.S. Congress, SFRC, Subcommittee on Arms Control, International Organization and Security Agreements, *Hearings: Nonproliferation Issues*, 94th Cong., 1st–2d sess., 1975–1976, pp. 358–359.

21. SFRC, *Warnke Nomination,* pp. 10, 127; U.S. Congress, Senate, Committee on Armed Services, *Hearings: Consideration of Mr. Paul C. Warnke to Be Director of the U.S. Arms Control and Disarmament Agency and Ambassador,* 95th Cong., 1st sess., 1977, p. 154; and *Washington Post,* February 9, 1977.

22. Raymond Garthoff, State's senior SALT delegation representative, was also removed, apparently at Senator Jackson's request. U.S. Congress, Senate, Committee on Armed Services, *Hearings: Military Implications of the Treaty on the Limitation of Anti-Ballistic Missile Systems and the Interim Agreement on Limitation of Strategic Offensive Arms,* 92d Cong., 2d sess., 1972, especially pp. 333–339; Peter J. Ognibene, *Scoop: The Life and Politics of Henry M. Jackson* (Briarcliff Manor, N.Y.: Stein & Day, 1975), pp. 205, 213–214; Elizabeth Drew, "A Reporter At Large: An Argument over Survival," *The New Yorker,* April 4, 1977, pp. 110–111; and *Washington Post,* December 14, 1976. Ognibene's account of Senator Jackson's role in the purge largely corresponds to those of interviewees.

23. Ognibene, *Scoop,* pp. 210–211; Drew, "Reporter at Large," 111; Joseph Kruzel, "SALT II: The Search for a Follow-On Agreement," *Orbis* 17 (Summer 1973): 337; *Washington Post,* February 23, 1977; and Alton Frye, *A Responsible Congress: The Politics of National Security* (New York: McGraw-Hill, 1975), p. 89. One senior official commented, "Spiers, Garthoff, Allison, and the ACDA people were really, and unjustly, scapegoats for Nixon and Kissinger. Also, it's no secret that Jackson intensely dislikes Kissinger. Henry's the real object of Jackson's tirades." There is no evidence that Kissinger was involved in the purge, though he did not attempt to impede it.

24. Jackson had told Smith, "I know it [minimum deterrence] is not your view." Committee on Armed Services, *Hearings: Military Implications,* p. 394, and Ognibene, *Scoop,* p. 211.

25. General Rowny, like most senior military officers, was acutely aware of General Allison's demise. In addition to having Senator Jackson's blessing, the Navy and Air Force found Rowny attractive because with the ABM Treaty the Army was effectively excluded from a role in strategic weaponry. Hence the Army had no presupposed pro-Navy or pro-Air Force bias. Additionally, Rowny had an outgoing personal manner and good relations throughout the Pentagon. Like General Allison, General Rowny was a candid and loyal spokesman for JCS interests. He served on the delegation under Presidents Nixon and Ford and was asked to stay on by President Carter.

26. *Washington Post,* March 8, 1973.

27. In May 1973 the Civil Service Commission had scheduled a one-week review of ACDA's personnel program but decided on a briefer review because of the absence of so many of the top management staff and because "there was some question about the future of the agency." U.S. Civil Service Commission, Bureau of Personnel Management Evaluation, *Re-*

port: Review of Personnel Management in the Arms Control and Disarmament Agency, April 1975, p. 4.

28. U.S. Congress, Senate, Committee on Appropriations, Hearings: Departments of State, Justice, ... Appropriations for Fiscal Year 1974, 93d Cong., 1st sess., 1973, pp. 922–924; U.S. Congress, House of Representatives, Committee on Appropriations, Hearings: Departments of State, Justice, ... Appropriations for Fiscal Year 1974, 93d Cong., 1st sess., 1973, pp. 563–574; U.S. Congress, SFRC, Hearings: ACDA Authorization (n. 9 above), pp. 6–7; U.S. Congress, SFRC, Hearings: Foreign Relations Authorization, Fiscal Years 1976 and 1977, 94th Cong., 1st sess., 1975, pp. 137, 142.

29. Though John Lehman downplayed the impact of the cuts, calling them "therapeutic," he acknowledged that they were "a blow to ACDA and did diminish its effectiveness." When the White House directive was issued Lehman was on the Nixon NSC staff. He apparently had no part in the Jackson–Nixon exchange, but he did supply White House Chief of Staff H. R. Haldeman with the names of "qualified people" to replace those who were fired. SFRC, Hearings: Nomination of John F. Lehman (n. 11 above), pp. 13–14.

30. See Paul Nitze's testimony, HFAC, Hearings: Arms Control and Disarmament Agency (n. 14 above), pp. 64–65, 68; U.S. Congress, Senate, Select Committee on Presidential Campaign Activities, Book 4, 93d Cong., 1st sess., 1973, p. 1683; and Harold Seidman, Politics, Position, and Power: The Dynamics of Federal Organization, 2d ed. (New York: Oxford University Press, 1975), pp. 107, 119–120.

31. Robert G. Kaiser, "Senate Staffer Richard Perle: Behind-Scenes Power over Arms Policy," Washington Post, June 26, 1977, and Washington Post, November 8, 1977. A CIA analyst was summarily fired by Director of Central Intelligence Stansfield Turner after he leaked papers relating to Soviet SALT compliance and strategic capabilities to Perle. The documents, containing eight classification categories above top secret, were later returned, with apologies, after Turner (unsuccessfully) demanded that Jackson fire Perle. New York Times, November 13, 1978.

32. SFRC, Hearings: Nomination of John F. Lehman, p. 12.

33. John F. Lehman, "The Carter Comprehensive Proposal: Verification and Gray Area Systems," in Paul H. Nitze, John F. Lehman, and Seymour Weiss, The Carter Disarmament Proposals: Some Basic Questions and Criticisms (Miami: Center for Advanced International Studies, University of Miami, 1977), pp. 18, 23–24. The following were representative remarks commonly heard within the bureaucracy among those who disagreed with Lehman's views (those who agreed with him confirmed his cautious orientation but in laudatory terms). An ACDA officer: "Hardline! That man scares me!" An ACDA analyst: "Frankly, he's a product of his university [Pennsylvania], always fighting the protracted war with communism." A

Kissinger staffer: "DOD is nervous because Lehman is trying to tell *them* how to structure our military forces: don't reduce theater nuclear forces in Europe, *more* carriers, etc. It's really a disgrace."

34. Fred Iklé, "Can Nuclear Deterrence Last Out the Century?" *Foreign Affairs* 52 (January 1973): 267–285 (This article impressed high administration officials as well as key congressional conservatives and influenced the decision to offer Iklé the ACDA directorship.); Gerard Smith, "SALT and Strategies," *Congressional Record* 120, 93d Cong., 2d sess., May 20, 1974, pp. S8580–S8584; *Washington Post*, February 1, 1974; Lynn Etheridge Davis, *Limited Nuclear Options*, Adelphi Paper No. 121 (London: International Institute for Strategic Studies, Winter 1975/76), p. 4; and U.S. Congress, SFRC, Subcommittee on Arms Control, Oceans and International Environment, *Hearings: United States/Soviet Strategic Options*, 95th Cong., 1st sess., 1977, pp. 15–16.

35. See SFRC, *Hearings: United States/Soviet Strategic Options*, pp. 32, 37, 96.

36. *Washington Post*, January 2, 1977.

37. One of its leading analysts said, "U.S.–Soviet relations may very well be a zero-sum game. ACDA's role has been to pull the U.S. closer to the Soviet position. . . . Congress never intended ACDA to bludgeon DOD into accepting the Soviet position."

38. U.S. ACDA, *Verification: The Critical Element of Arms Control*, publication 85, March 1976, p. 32.

39. See Jan Lodal, "Verifying SALT," *Foreign Policy* 24 (Fall 1976): 41–42. Iklé, a strong supporter of cruise missile deployment, repeatedly stressed that attempts to control it would be undermined by the inability to verify compliance. SFRC, *Hearings: Nonproliferation Issues*, (n. 20 above), pp. 279–281.

40. U.S. Congress, HFAC, *Hearings: Proposed Expansion of U.S. Military Facilities in the Indian Ocean*, 93d Cong., 2d sess., 1974, pp. 3–4, 13, and SFRC, *Hearings: ACDA Authorization*, pp. 11, 28.

41. Halperin, *Bureaucratic Politics* (n. 1 above), p. 54.

42. Gerard C. Smith, "Should There Be a Larger U.S. Role for Policies and Programs of Arms Control and Disarmament?" unpublished statement, Aspen Institute for Humanistic Studies, Aspen, Colorado, August 13, 1976, p. 5, and HFAC, *Hearings: Arms Control and Disarmament Agency* (n. 4 above), p. 119.

43. Louis C. Gawthrop, *Bureaucratic Behavior in the Executive Branch* (New York: Free Press, 1969), pp. 58–59.

44. William Safire, "Mr. Warnke's Hit List," *New York Times*, April 21, 1977. A State Department spokesman called Safire's allegations "a lie." *Washington Post*, April 21, 1977.

45. U.S. Congress, SFRC, *Report: Arms Control and Disarmament Act Amendments*, No. 95-193, 95th Cong., 1st sess., 1977, pp. 39–40, 46–49,

55–56, and U.S. Congress, Senate, Committee on Appropriations, *Hearings: Departments of State, Justice, . . . Appropriations for Fiscal Year 1978*, 95th Cong., 1st sess., 1977, pp. 360, 460. Warnke's options were severely limited. Some of the Jackson people in the Agency, fearing for their positions, had gone to Richard Perle with allegations of a purge even before Warnke had had an opportunity to consider certain personnel changes. The erroneous press reports appeared shortly thereafter. By way of a tacit threat, Senator Jackson's Subcommittee on Arms Control asked ACDA to provide a list of all people hired during the first six months of 1977.

Chapter 5: The President: Confidence and Access

1. For an insightful discussion of this subject see, I. M. Destler, *Presidents, Bureaucrats and Foreign Policy: The Politics of Organizational Reform* (Princeton, N.J.: Princeton University Press, 1974), pp. 90–93, 266–267.
2. See I. M. Destler, "National Security Advice to U.S. Presidents: Some Lessons from Thirty Years," *World Politics* 29 (January 1977): 143–176.
3. Richard E. Neustadt, *Presidential Power: The Politics of Leadership* (New York: John Wiley & Sons, 1960), p. 145.
4. Some have suggested that a powerful political figure from the President's party would be most suitable as Director—a Melvin Laird or Hubert Humphrey. Caution seems advisable here lest such a figure be considered a rival by the President or threaten the essential mission of the Agency. Also, some grounding in national security affairs may be a more important qualification than the proponents of this proposal generally concede.
5. U.S. Congress, HFAC, *Hearings: To Amend the Arms Control and Disarmament Act*, 88th Cong., 1st sess., 1963, p. 166; Jerome Wiesner, *Where Science and Politics Meet* (New York: McGraw-Hill, 1965), p. 11; Arthur M. Schlesinger, Jr., *A Thousand Days* (Boston: Houghton Mifflin, 1965), pp. 503, 902; Harold K. Jacobson and Eric Stein, *Diplomats, Scientists, and Politicians: The United States and the Nuclear Test Ban Negotiations* (Ann Arbor: University of Michigan Press, 1966), p. 475; and Neustadt, *Presidential Power*, p. 200.
6. Elinor Langer, "After the Pentagon Papers: Talk with Kistiakowsky, Wiesner," *Science* 174 (November 26, 1971): 924.
7. Humphrey recalled that he "had to be the advance man to get Mr. Foster in to see . . . Mr. Johnson. . . . [H]e didn't get over there very often. I know that for every time he was there the Secretary of Defense was there a hundred times." U.S. Congress, SFRC, *Hearings: Nomination of Fred Charles Iklé of California to be Director of the United States Arms Control and Disarmament Agency* [no committee print], 93d Cong., 1st sess., 1973, pp. 78–79.

8. U.S. ACDA, *Documents on Disarmament,* 1968, pp. 695–700, and 1969, p. 735.

9. Gerard C. Smith, "Should There Be a Larger U.S. Role for Policies and Programs of Arms Control and Disarmament?" unpublished statement, Aspen Institute for Humanistic Studies, Aspen, Colorado, August 13, 1976, p. 6.

10. *Ibid.,* p. 4.

11. Nixon also had unflattering views of Foreign Service Officers. In 1969 he reportedly told key aides that foreign policy was to be handled by the White House, not by "the striped-pants faggots" at Foggy Bottom. *Washington Post,* October 18, 1974.

12. Destler, *Presidents, Bureaucrats* (n. 1 above), p. 153.

13. *Washington Post,* January 25, 1977, and April 11, 1977.

14. "Arms Control and the 1976 Presidential Elections," *Arms Control Today* 6 (October 1976): 2.

15. *Washington Post,* February 9, 1977; February 22, 1977; March 10, 1977; and March 15, 1977.

16. U.S. ACDA, *Seventeenth Annual Report to Congress of the U.S. Arms Control and Disarmament Agency,* 1978.

Chapter 6: Hearing on Policy Issues

1. Harold Seidman, *Politics, Position and Power: The Dynamics of Federal Organization,* 2d ed. (New York: Oxford University Press, 1975), p. 197.

2. Graham T. Allison, *Essence of Decision: Exploring the Cuban Missile Crisis* (Boston: Little, Brown & Co., 1971), p. 177.

3. Two of the best treatments of the Kennedy–Johnson NSC systems are Keith C. Clark and Laurance J. Legere, eds., *The President and the Management of National Security* (New York: Praeger, 1969), and I. M. Destler, *Presidents, Bureaucrats and Foreign Policy: The Politics of Organizational Reform* (Princeton, N.J.: Princeton University Press, 1974), pp. 96–118.

4. Herbert F. York and G. Allen Greb, "Military Research and Development: A Postwar History," *Bulletin of the Atomic Scientists* 33 (January 1977): 24–26.

5. Ted Greenwood, *Making the MIRV: A Study in Defense Decision Making* (Cambridge, Mass.: Ballinger, 1975), pp. 114, 119, and Paul G. Conway, "An Analysis of Decision Making on U.S. Chemical and Biological Warfare Policies in 1969," Ph.D. dissertation, Purdue University, 1972, pp. 138–141, 192; and *New York Times,* January 15, 1970.

6. Arthur M. Schlesinger, Jr., *A Thousand Days* (Boston: Houghton Mifflin, 1965), p. 504.

7. Letter to the author from William Foster, July 17, 1972.

8. Executive Order No. 11044, 27 Fed. Reg. 8341 (1962).

9. U.S. ACDA, *Documents on Disarmament,* 1963, pp. 670–672; U.S. Congress, Senate, Committee on Armed Services, Preparedness Investigating Subcommittee, *Hearings: Arms Control and Disarmament,* 87th Cong., 2d sess., 1962, pp. 4–9; U.S. Congress, SFRC, *Hearings: Renewed Geneva Disarmament Negotiations,* 87th Cong., 2d sess., 1963, p. 12; *Washington Post,* February 10, 1962; Schlesinger, *A Thousand Days,* pp. 893–913; and Harold K. Jacobson and Eric Stein, *Diplomats, Scientists and Politicians: The United States and the Nuclear Test Ban Negotiations* (Ann Arbor: University of Michigan Press, 1966), pp. 315, 347, 381–385.

10. For case studies of the MLF policy process, see John D. Steinbruner, *The Cybernetic Theory of Decision* (Princeton, N.J.: Princeton University Press, 1974), chs. 8–9, and Henry A. Kissinger, *The Troubled Partnership* (Garden City, N.Y.: Doubleday, 1966), ch. 5.

11. Gerard C. Smith, "The Nuclear Defense of NATO," address, *Department of State Bulletin* 50 (May 18, 1964): 785.

12. U.S. Congress, HFAC, Subcommittee on National Security Policy and Scientific Developments, *Hearings: Chemical-Biological Warfare: U.S. Policies and International Effects,* 91st Cong., 1st sess., 1969, pp. 190–191, and Forrest R. Frank, "CBW: 1962–67; 1967–68; 1969–72," in Commission on the Organization of the Government for the Conduct of Foreign Policy (hereinafter cited as Murphy Commission), *Adequacy of Current Organization: Defense and Arms Control,* Appendices, 4 (Washington: Government Printing Office, June 1975), pp. 308, 318, 322.

13. U.S. Congress, SFRC, *Staff Study: Arms Sales and Foreign Policy,* 90th Cong., 1st sess., 1967; *Documents on Disarmament,* 1967, pp. 32, 756.

14. Raymond Garthoff, "Negotiating with the Russians: Some Lessons from SALT," *International Security* 1 (Spring 1977): 3–4; John Newhouse, *Cold Dawn: The Story of SALT* (New York: Holt, Rinehart & Winston, 1973), pp. 87–91, 111–132; and Burton R. Rosenthal, "Formulating Negotiating Positions for SALT: 1968, 1969–72," in Murphy Commission, *Adequacy of Current Organization,* Appendices, 4, pp. 327–329. Newhouse and Rosenthal credit the Halperin group with the central SALT role and deemphasize ACDA and the Committee of Deputies. Senior ACDA officials involved in the process took specific exception to this aspect of the Newhouse and Rosenthal accounts.

15. For extended analyses of the Nixon NSC system see Chester A. Crocker, "The Nixon–Kissinger National Security Council System, 1969–1972: A Study in Foreign Policy Management," in Murphy Commission, *Making Organizational Change Effective: Case Studies,* Appendices, 6, pp. 79–99; Wilfred L. Kohl, "The Nixon–Kissinger Foreign Policy System and U.S.-European Relations: Patterns of Policy Making," *World Politics* 28 (October 1975): 1–43; I. M. Destler, "National Security Advice to U.S. Presidents: Some Lessons from Thirty Years," *World Politics* 29 (January 1977):

143–176; and Destler, *Presidents, Bureaucrats* (n. 3 above), pp. 118–153, 295–319.

16. David K. Hall, "The 'Custodian-Manager' of the Policymaking Process," in Murphy Commission, *The Use of Information,* Appendices, 2, p. 115.
17. Statement of Fred Iklé to the Murphy Commission, February 21, 1974, p. 4.
18. Destler, "National Security Advice," pp. 150, 155.
19. See Newhouse, *Cold Dawn,* pp. 148–149, 159–161. Newhouse's account of SALT I caused considerable controversy because of the highly sensitive information it revealed. Kissinger denied that Newhouse had been his "chosen instrument" and praised the book as "distinguished." U.S. Congress, SFRC, *Hearings: Nomination of Henry A. Kissinger,* 93d Cong., 1st sess., 1973, pp. 110–111. After the book's appearance Newhouse joined ACDA. In 1977, with the Carter administration, he became one of ACDA's four Assistant Directors.
20. Elmo R. Zumwalt, Jr., *On Watch* (New York: Quadrangle, 1976), pp. 348, 403.
21. U.S. Congress, House of Representatives, Committee on Armed Services, Special Subcommittee on Arms Control and Disarmament, *Report: Review of Arms Control and Disarmament Activities,* No. 93-72, 93d Cong., 2d sess., 1974, pp. 10–11.
22. Zumwalt, *On Watch,* pp. 501, 504–505.
23. State Department frustration was reflected in an internal document: "The Department's role in foreign affairs formulation... has become circumscribed by the extensive involvement of the NSC machinery not only in broad policy but also in operational considerations. The direct involvement ... of the NSC staff... in the SALT talks... has diverted attention and resources from the policy planning process. Yet, it has proven difficult for State to fill this void under the current system in which policy initiatives cannot proceed far without NSC involvement. Another side of the problem is the close-holding of information at the NSC level on key policy matters, e.g., SALT [and] Incidents at Sea." U.S. Department of State, *PARA Review for the Bureau of Politico-Military Affairs,* undated, p. 7.
24. See Newhouse, *Cold Dawn,* pp. 26, 36–43, 80, 164, 194–195, 223–231, 246–247.
25. Thomas W. Wolfe, *The SALT Experience: Its Impact on U.S. and Soviet Strategic Policy and Decisionmaking* (Santa Monica: Rand Corporation, September 1975), R-1686-PR, pp. 138–148, 240–243, and *Washington Post,* February 23, 1977.
26. Former ACDA Deputy Director John Lehman asserted that "never in its history has ACDA had such a policy impact" as under Iklé. ACDA, Lehman claimed, "led SALT policy, MBFR policy, nonproliferation initiatives, and strategic doctrine." Letter to the editor, *Washington Post,* March 16, 1977. Except for the nonproliferation area, and then with important qualifications, virtually nobody interviewed concurred in Lehman's assess-

ment. Said one NSC staffer: "ACDA was very useful in SALT *despite* Iklé and Lehman. People like [reference to lower-level ACDA officers] were on the interagency SALT group and could make their voices heard. They were invaluable to the NSC in insuring that views other than DOD's were heard."

27. See Duncan L. Clarke and Joseph Grieco, "The United States and Nuclear-Weapon-Free Zones," *World Affairs* 139 (Fall 1976): 155–161.

28. U.S. Congress, Senate, Committee on Government Operations, *Hearings: Export Reorganization Act of 1976,* 94th Cong., 2d sess., 1976, pp. 764–765; U.S. Congress, HIRC, Subcommittee on International Organizations and Subcommittee on the Near East and South Asia, *Hearings: U.S. Foreign Policy and the Export of Nuclear Technology to the Middle East,* 93d Cong., 2d sess., 1974, pp. 93, 101; and Senator Stuart Symington, "The Washington Nuclear Mess," *International Security* 1 (Winter 1977): 74.

29. Robert Gillette, "Nuclear Exports: A U.S. Firm's Troublesome Flirtation with Brazil," *Science* 189 (July 25, 1975): 269.

30. Executive Order No. 11902, 41 Fed. Reg. 23 (1976).

31. *Washington Post,* April 20 and 28, 1978.

32. U.S. Congress, HIRC, Subcommittee on International Security and Scientific Affairs and Subcommittee on International Economic Policy and Trade, *Hearings: The Nuclear Antiproliferation Act of 1977,* 95th Cong., 1st sess., 1977, pp. 9, 43, 61, 281, and U.S. General Accounting Office, *Assessment of U.S. and International Controls Over the Peaceful Uses of Nuclear Energy,* September 14, 1976, p. 53.

33. *Presidential Documents—Jimmy Carter,* Vol. 13, No. 15, April 18, 1977 and Vol. 13, No. 18, May 2, 1977, and U.S. General Accounting Office, *An Evaluation of the Administration's Proposed Nuclear Non-Proliferation Strategy,* ID-77-53, October 3, 1977.

34. U.S. Congress, SFRC, Subcommittee on Foreign Assistance, *Staff Report: U.S. Military Sales to Iran,* 94th Cong., 2d sess., 1976, pp. 38–41.

35. *Ibid.*; "Decision Making Process for Allocating Appropriated Military Aid," prepared by State's Politico-Military Affairs Bureau, in U.S. Congress, SFRC, *Hearings: Department of State Appropriations Authorization, Fiscal Year 1973,* 92d Cong., 2d sess., 1972, pp. 407–409; Col. M. T. Smith, "U.S. Foreign Military Sales: Its Legal Requirements, Procedures and Problems," paper for the Conference on Implications of the Military Build-Up in Non-Industrial States, Fletcher School of Law and Diplomacy, Tufts University, May 1976; and U.S. General Accounting Office, *Foreign Military Sales—A Potential Drain on the U.S. Defense Posture,* LCD 77-440, September 2, 1977, pp. 13–20.

36. U.S. Congress, HIRC, Subcommittee on International Security and Scientific Affairs, *Hearings: Foreign Assistance Legislation for Fiscal Year 1978,* 95th Cong., 1st sess., 1977, p. 67. The Congressional Research Service speculated that ACDA "does not possess the influence to move other executive branch machinery to action [and] ACDA has not done suffi-

cient work in the field of controlling international arms transfers to develop an independent set of proposals for dealing with this problem.'' U.S. Congress, HFAC, *ACDA Report: The International Transfer of Conventional Arms,* Committee Print, Appendix, 93d Cong., 2d sess., 1974, p. CRS-18.

37. U.S. Congress, HIRC, Special Subcommittee on Investigations, *Hearings: The Persian Gulf: The Continuing Debate on Arms Sales,* 94th Cong., 1st sess., 1975, p. 191.
38. U.S. Congress, SFRC, Subcommittee on Foreign Assistance, *Hearings: Foreign Assistance Authorization: Arms Sales Issues,* 94th Cong., 1st sess., 1975, pp. 128, 216.
39. HIRC, *Hearings: Foreign Assistance Legislation for Fiscal Year 1978,* p. 70, and John Lehman, address, in *Arms Transfers,* final report of senior conference, U.S. Military Academy, West Point, New York, 1976, p. 18.
40. The memoranda are contained in HIRC, *Hearings: Foreign Assistance Legislation for Fiscal Year 1978,* Part 2, pp. 143–146.
41. *Ibid.,* pp. 158, 161.
42. *Ibid.,* pp. 162–163. See pp. 72–75 for a summary of ACDA–State procedures in the arms transfer field and for the ACDA document sent to other agencies explaining its evaluative criteria for arms transfers.
43. Executive Order No. 11958, 42 Fed. Reg. 4311 (1977).
44. U.S. Congress, SFRC, *Report: Arms Control and Disarmament Act Amendments of 1977,* No. 95-193, 95th Cong., 1st sess., 1977, p. 29. Emphasis added.
45. While Warnke was optimistic, his chief arms transfer officer was more guarded: ''I don't want to imply that there are not some questions as to the point at which we get involved, and this is a non-trivial problem because there is no specific point at which a foreign military sales possibility arises.'' HIRC, *Hearings: Foreign Assistance Legislation for Fiscal Year 1978,* Part 2, p. 94. Also, the Secretary of State's report to Congress on arms transfer policy on June 30, 1977, noted that there was still no single, formally established means for policy control over all arms transfer programs. The report found the existing system characterized by fragmentation; a multiplicity of decision channels; a lack of coherent policies, planning, and procedures; inadequate control of decision points; and poor interagency planning. The Secretary announced that a new interagency Arms Export Control Board (with ACDA membership) had replaced the Security Assistance Program Review Committee. It was to be an advisory body with policy planning and review functions. The board had five working groups, one of which— concerned with the arms control impact of arms transfers—is chaired by ACDA. U.S. Congress, SFRC, *Report to Congress: Arms Transfer Policy,* Committee Print, 95th Cong., 1st sess., 1977, and U.S. Congress, HIRC, Subcommittee on Europe and the Middle East, *Report: United States Arms Transfer and Security Assistance Programs,* Committee Print, 95th Cong., 2d sess., 1978, pp. 74–78. The Standard Operating Procedure for Inter-

departmental Clearance of Arms Transfers, endorsed by all members of the
Arms Export Control Board and issued in January 1978, expressly stipulated: "Particular attention is invited to the specific statutory requirements
for taking ACDA opinions into account, and the resulting importance of
maintaining audit trails demonstrating effective compliance with those requirements." U.S. Congress, HIRC, Subcommittee on International Security and Scientific Affairs, *Hearings: Review of the President's Conventional Arms Transfer Policy,* 95th Cong., 2d sess., 1978, p. 59.
46. Conway, "Analysis of Decision Making" (n. 5 above), pp. 58–63, 137–
138, 152–158, and Frank, "CBW" (n. 12 above), pp. 320–321.
47. Zumwalt, *On Watch* (n. 20 above), pp. 496–497, 503.
48. See Graham T. Allison and Frederic A. Morris, "Armaments and Arms
Control: Explaining the Determinants of Military Weapons," *Daedalus* 104
(Summer 1975): 123.
49. U.S. Congress, HIRC, Subcommittee on National Security Policy and Scientific Developments, *Hearings: Arms Control and Disarmament Agency,*
93d Cong., 2d sess., 1974, p. 43.
50. *Ibid.,* pp. 99–100, and Rosenthal, "Formulating Negotiating Positions" (n.
14 above), p. 342.
51. Herbert Scoville, Jr., "The Politics of the ABM Debate: The View from the
Arms Control and Disarmament Agency," paper prepared for the American
Political Science Association Convention, Los Angeles, September 1970,
pp. 2–4, 7–8, and Rosenthal, "Formulating Negotiating Positions," pp.
332–335.
52. Graham Allison and Richard Huff, "MIRV," in Murphy Commission,
Appendices, 4 (Washington: Government Printing Office, June 1975), pp.
158–160, and Greenwood, *Making the MIRV* (n. 5 above), pp. 107–119,
and Secretary of State Henry A. Kissinger, transcript of press backgrounder,
December 3, 1974.
53. Barry Carter and John Steinbruner, "TRIDENT," in Murphy Commission,
Appendices, 4, p. 181.
54. *New York Times,* December 17, 1973, and Henry D. Levine, "Some Things
to All Men: The Politics of Cruise Missile Development," *Public Policy* 25
(Winter 1977): 117–167. Kissinger had urged research and development on
strategic cruise missiles, partly so they might be used as SALT "bargaining
chips." In 1976 he wondered: "How was I to know the military would come
to love it [strategic cruise missile]?" Raymond Garthoff, "SALT I: An
Evaluation," *World Politics* 31 (October 1978): 22.
55. U.S. Congress, Senate, Committee on Armed Services, *Hearings: Weapons
Acquisition Process,* 92d Cong., 1st sess., 1971, p. 351, and J. P. Crecine,
"Making Defense Budgets," in Murphy Commission, Appendices, 4, pp.
88–89. Crecine concludes (p. 89): "Without Presidential interest, involvement and backing, people outside the Defense Department find it nearly
impossible to adequately analyze or influence the details of the Defense

budget. Policy mechanisms like the DPRC work only if Presidential authority is applied. Even then success is not certain.''

56. Lawrence J. Korb, ''The Secretary of Defense and the Joint Chiefs of Staff: The Budgetary Process,'' in Sam C. Sarkesian, ed., *The Military–Industrial Complex: A Reassessment* (Beverly Hills, Calif.: Sage Publications, 1972), p. 326, and *idem.* ''The Secretary of Defense and the Joint Chiefs of Staff in the Nixon Administration: The Method and the Men,'' in John P. Lovell and Philip Kronenberg, eds., *New Civil–Military Relations,* New Brunswick, N.J.: Transaction Books, 1974), p. 262. The Murphy Commission's final report concluded: ''Charged with an extraordinarily difficult assignment made even harder by the resistance of the DOD to the exercise of that responsibility at any level short of the President, the DPRC has fallen into disuse. The result has been that the recent record of our government in reviewing the totality of its defense activity in light of the nation's overseas policy and security requirements has been—in the words of Secretary Kissinger's testimony before this Commission—'not distinguished.' '' Murphy Commission, *Report* (Washington: Government Printing Office, June 1975), p. 77.

Chapter 7: Access to Information

1. Forrest Russell Frank, ''U.S. Arms Control Policymaking: The 1972 Biological Weapons Convention Case,'' Ph.D. dissertation, Stanford University, 1974, p. 267.
2. For example, the Comptroller General reported that ACDA obtains ''information from other agencies about arms control . . . research completed or in progress . . ., but that information about the other agencies' research plans . . . has not been supplied them.'' U.S. General Accounting Office, *Need for Improved Review and Coordination of the Foreign Affairs Aspects of Federal Research,* May 27, 1971, p. 46.
3. See also, Barry M. Casper, ''Laser Enrichment: A New Path to Proliferation,'' *Bulletin of the Atomic Scientists* 33 (January 1977): 37.
4. U.S. Congress, HIRC, Subcommittee on International Security and Scientific Affairs, *Hearings: Foreign Assistance Legislation for Fiscal Year 1978,* Part II, 95th Cong., 1st sess., 1977, pp. 158, 162. U.S. Congress, HIRC, Subcommittee on International Security and Scientific Affairs, *Hearings: The Arms Control and Disarmament Agency Authorization for Fiscal Year 1979,* 95th Cong., 2d sess., 1978, p. 17.
5. U.S. Congress, SFRC, Subcommittee on Oceans and International Environment, *Hearings: Prohibiting Military Weather Modification,* 92d Cong., 2d sess., 1972, pp. 32–33.

6. Betty Goetz Lall, "Disarmament Policy and the Pentagon," *Bulletin of the Atomic Scientists* 20 (September 1964): 38.
7. U.S. Congress, HIRC, Subcommittee on International Security and Scientific Affairs, *Hearings: Arms Control and Disarmament Act Amendments,* 94th Cong., 1st sess., 1975, p. 30.
8. J. Ronald Fox, *Arming America: How the U.S. Buys Weapons* (Cambridge, Mass.: Harvard University Press, 1974), pp. 87, 90, 100.
9. Elmo R. Zumwalt, Jr., *On Watch* (New York: Quadrangle, 1976), p. 496.
10. Raymond L. Garthoff, "Negotiating with the Russians: Some Lessons from SALT," *International Security* 1 (Spring 1977): 8–9.
11. As of 1978 ACDA was *not*, in fact, a member of this group, although its relations with it were good and it did receive the group's verification report.

Chapter 8: The ACDA–State Department Relationship

1. U.S. Congress, HFAC, Subcommittee on National Security Policy and Scientific Developments, *Hearings: Arms Control and Disarmament Agency,* 93d Cong., 2d sess., 1974, pp. 127–128.
2. *Ibid.*, p. 127.
3. U.S. Congress, SFRC, *Hearings: Nomination of Henry A. Kissinger,* 93d Cong., 1st sess., 1973, p. 90.
4. For an official, yet instructive, description of the relationship, see U.S. Congress, HIRC, Subcommittee on International Security and Scientific Affairs, *Hearings: The Arms Control and Disarmament Agency Authorization for Fiscal Year 1978,* 95th Cong., 1st sess., 1977, pp. 28–29.
5. But Adam Yarmolinsky argues that ACDA's quasi-independent status isolates it "from the decision-making process within the Defense Department, to which the bulk of its energies are addressed." He concedes that if ACDA was within DOD "it might not have been allowed to function." Yarmolinsky joined ACDA's staff in 1977. Adam Yarmolinsky, "The President, The Congress and Arms Control." in Sam C. Sarkesian, ed., *The Military–Industrial Complex: A Reassessment* (Beverly Hills, Calif.: Sage Publications, 1972), p. 297.
6. About 10 percent of ACDA's professionals favored merger. Only two State Department officers interviewed supported it, while a middle-ranking official in DOD's ISA said, "Except for a few, perhaps in JCS, even those who are not by nature disposed towards arms control, think ACDA should continue to exist. It represents a point of view which, without ACDA, would likely not be adequately represented."
7. I. M. Destler, *Presidents, Bureaucrats and Foreign Policy: The Politics of Organizational Reform* (Princeton, N.J.: Princeton University Press, 1974),

p. 197; see also Mason Willrich, "Factors Influencing U.S. Arms Control Policy," paper delivered at Fourth International Arms Control Symposium, Philadelphia, October 18, 1969, pp. 13–14.

8. Fred C. Iklé, "ACDA: Catalyst and Conscience," address to the Strategy for Peace Conference, The Stanley Foundation, October 7–10, 1976.

9. *Ibid.*

10. Destler, *Presidents, Bureaucrats,* p. 197.

11. U.S. Congress, HIRC, Subcommittee on International Security and Scientific Affairs, *Hearings: Arms Control and Disarmament Act Amendments,* 94th Cong., 1st sess., 1975, p. 42.

Chapter 9: Negotiations, Research, and Public Information

1. U.S. Congress, SFRC, *Report: Arms Control and Disarmament Act Amendments of 1977,* No. 95-193, 95th Cong., 1st sess., 1977, p. 41.

2. U.S. Congress, SFRC, *Hearings: Warnke Nomination,* 95th Cong., 1st sess., 1977, pp. 142, 155, and Raymond L. Garthoff, "Negotiating with the Russians: Some Lessons from SALT," *International Security* 1 (Spring 1977): 17.

3. U.S. Congress, Senate, Committee on Armed Services, *Hearings: Consideration of Mr. Paul C. Warnke to Be Director of the U.S. Arms Control and Disarmament Agency and Ambassador,* 95th Cong., 1st sess., 1977, pp. 245–246.

4. U.S. Congress, HIRC, Subcommittee on International Security and Scientific Affairs, *Hearings: Arms Control and Disarmament Act Amendments,* 94th Cong., 1st sess., 1975, p. 82.

5. ACD Act (PL 95-108), section 27, and SFRC, *Report: Arms Control and Disarmament Act Amendments of 1977,* pp. 4, 9, 61.

6. See Arnold J. Meltsner, *Policy Analysts in the Bureaucracy* (Berkeley: University of California Press, 1976), pp. 18–21, 268, 270.

7. See Howard Margolis, *Technical Advice on Policy Issues* (Beverly Hills, Calif.: Sage Publications, 1973), pp. 47–48, 52.

8. U.S. Congress, Senate, Committee on Appropriations, *Hearings: Departments of State, Justice, . . . Appropriations for Fiscal Year 1973,* 92d Cong., 2d sess., 1972, pp. 2236–2240.

9. This was one of the reasons the Ford Foundation announced a $4.5 million program in 1973 to support arms control programs at selected American universities. U.S. Congress, HFAC, Subcommittee on National Security Policy and Scientific Developments, *Hearings: Arms Control and Disarmament Agency,* 93d Cong., 2d sess., 1974, pp. 109–110.

10. SFRC, *Report: Arms Control and Disarmament Act Amendments of 1977,*

p. 6, and U.S. Congress, House of Representatives, Conference Committee, *Report: Arms Control and Disarmament Act Amendments,* No. 95-563, 95th Cong., 1st sess., 1977, pp. 7–8.

11. HFAC, *Hearings: Arms Control and Disarmament Agency,* pp. 28, 30.
12. In FY 1974, following the purge, the number of analysts fell to ten.
13. Forrest Russell Frank, "U.S. Arms Control Policymaking: The 1972 Biological Weapons Convention Case," Ph.D. dissertation, Stanford University, 1974, p. 42, and Ted Greenwood, *Making the MIRV: A Study of Defense Decision Making* (Cambridge, Mass.: Ballinger, 1975), p. 111. In 1977 Congress amended section 31 of the ACD Act (PL 95-108) to permit ACDA to deal with foreign contractors. ACDA was especially eager to tap foreign experts concerning alternate uses of spent nuclear fuel, heavy water reactors, seismic detection methods, and testing certain nuclear safeguard techniques and equipment.
14. SFRC, *Report: Arms Control and Disarmament Act Amendments of 1977,* p. 39.
15. U.S. ACDA, *Documents on Disarmament,* 1974, p. 855.
16. U.S. ACDA, *An Evaluation of the ACDA Field Operations Program,* Field Study No. 2, Vol. 1, December 1968, p. A-5. My discussion of field testing draws partly upon this report.
17. *Documents on Disarmament,* 1963, p. 675.
18. Several conservative and some liberal legislators complained about wastefulness, irrelevance to policy, and vague contract definition and results. Senate Foreign Relations Committee Chairman J. William Fulbright (D–Ark.) was a persistent critic. In 1968 his committee imposed a $7 million ceiling on ACDA's entire external research budget for FY 1969–FY 1970. At Gerard Smith's nomination hearings Fulbright stated that "the only serious quarrel . . . that we had with your predecessor was . . . research in subjects . . . that were not altogether appropriate for this agency." U.S. Congress, SFRC, *Hearings: Nomination of Gerard C. Smith to Be Director, Arms Control and Disarmament Agency,* 91st Cong., 1st sess., 1969, p. 15. A carol sung at ACDA Christmas parties began:

> Senator Fulbright, don't fly into rage
> 'Cause one of ACDA's contracts cost a thousand per page,
> It never should have happened, it's not what you supposed,
> Our research program is hard-nosed.
> (It's hard-nosed, it's hard-nosed,
> Like Pinocchio's
> Our research program is hard-nosed.)

19. U.S. ACDA, *Arms Control and Local Conflict,* WEC-135, vols. 1–9, MIT, 1970, and U.S. ACDA, *CASCON: Computer-aided System for Handling Information on Local Conflicts,* WEC-141, vols. 1–2, MIT, 1970.
20. For a summary of ACDA's economic impact studies see, U.S. ACDA, *The*

Economic Impact of Reductions in Defense Spending, publication 64, July 1972. Two excellent studies are U.S. ACDA, *Adjustments of the U.S. Economy to Reductions in Military Spending,* E-156, Graham Allison *et al.,* December 1970, and U.S. ACDA, *The Economic Consequences of SALT I: A National Assessment,* E-224, General Research Corporation, August 1973.

21. U.S. Congress, SFRC, *Report: Foreign Relations Authorization Act of 1972,* No. 92-754, 92d Cong., 2d sess., 1972, p. 89.

22. U.S. ACDA, *Utilization of the Behavioral Sciences by the U.S. Arms Control and Disarmament Agency,* E-221, Ohio State University, 1974, vol. 1, pp. 2, 8 and vol. 2, p. 48. At least one graduate student appears to have benefited: William A. Buckingham, Jr., "Client-Oriented Social Research: How Could Social and Behavioral Scientists Contribute to the U.S. Arms Control and Disarmament Agency?" Ph.D. dissertation, Ohio State University, 1974. Despite the title, Buckingham states (p. 3) that his dissertation "will probably be of little or no use to ACDA."

23. Richard J. Heuer, Jr., "Adapting Academic Methods and Models to Governmental Needs: The CIA Experience," paper presented at the International Studies Association Convention, St. Louis, March 1977, pp. 15–16.

24. Morris Janowitz, *Military Conflict: Essays in Institutional Analysis of War and Peace* (Beverly Hills, Calif.: Sage Publications, 1975), pp. 299–303.

25. *Congressional Record* 123, 95th Cong., 1st sess., 1977, p. S10149, and U.S. Congress, HIRC, Subcommittee on International Operations, *Hearings: National Academy of Peace and Conflict Resolution,* 95th Cong., 2d sess., 1978.

26. PL 94-141.

27. U.S. ACDA, *Final Report: Study of the Impact on Military Expenditures of Arms Control Measures Mutually Agreed To by the United States and the Soviet Union,* 1977, p. 133.

28. U.S. Congress, HIRC, *Report: Authorization of Appropriations Under the Arms Control and Disarmament Act, Fiscal Year 1979,* 95th Cong., 2d sess., 1978, p. 9. For a summary of the Ford Foundation's long-term interest in and extensive support of education and research in the arms control field, see Enid Schoettle's testimony in U.S. Congress, HIRC, Subcommittee on International Security and Scientific Affairs, *Hearings and Markup: The Arms Control and Disarmament Agency Authorization for Fiscal Year 1979,* 95th Cong., 2d sess., 1978, pp. 26–32. Ms. Schoettle supported a stronger government effort in this area. While some will dispute my assertion that the field is "reasonably well covered," few informed individuals would predict that, given the financial crisis afflicting higher education, continuance of activity at the present level and with the present scope of coverage will be possible. The ACDA study requested by Congress concluded: "With regard to the general infrastructure of academic study and education in this field . . . arms control is a 'cottage industry,' though a growing one." This

finding was based, in part, on an estimate (both too low and misleading) that there are fewer than 200 "full-course offerings in arms control" at American colleges and universities. A reading of the full report does not settle the matter—reasonable men can still differ over the adequacy of coverage. U.S. ACDA, *Report to Congress on Arms Control Education and Academic Study Centers,* January 1979, p. 27.

29. A discussion group composed of past and present ACDA officers, congressional staffers, and academics evinced no support for this view. "ACDA: A Re-appraisal," *Report: Sixteenth Strategy for Peace Conference,* Stanley Foundation, October 9–12, 1975, p. 13.

30. Meltsner, *Policy Analysts* (n. 6 above), p. 8.

31. HFAC, *Hearings: Arms Control and Disarmament Agency* (n. 9 above), p. 31. However, a senior ACDA official who worked on the Seabed Treaty denied that the study had any meaningful impact. Commenting on Brennan's assertion, he stated: "We got far more talking to good Navy scientists."

32. Joint statement of Amelia Leiss and Lincoln Bloomfield, *Ibid.,* p. 180. Bloomfield served on ACDA's Social Science Advisory Board.

33. James G. March and Herbert A. Simon, *Organizations* (New York: John Wiley & Sons, 1958), p. 185. See also Robert L. Rothstein, *Planning, Prediction, and Policymaking in Foreign Affairs* (Boston: Little, Brown, 1972).

34. *Documents on Disarmament,* 1964, p. 559; U.S. Congress, House of Representatives, Committee on Appropriations, *Hearings: Department of State, Justice, . . . Appropriations for Fiscal Year 1963,* 87th Cong., 2d sess., 1962, pp. 1028–1029; U.S. Congress, Senate, Committee on Appropriations, *Hearings: Departments of State, Justice, . . . Appropriations for Fiscal Year 1964,* 88th Cong., 1st sess., 1963, p. 2051; and U.S. Congress, House of Representatives, Committee on Appropriations, *Hearings: Departments of State, Justice, . . . Appropriations for Fiscal Year 1965,* 88th Cong., 2d sess., 1964, p. 857.

35. National Citizens Commission, Report of the Committee on Arms Control and Disarmament, *The White House Conference on International Cooperation,* Washington, November 28–December 1, 1965; U.S. Congress, HFAC, *Hearings: To Amend the Arms Control and Disarmament Act,* 88th Cong., 1st sess., 1963, p. 24; and U.S. Congress, House of Representatives, Committee on Appropriations, *Hearings: Departments of State, Justice . . . Appropriations for Fiscal Year 1964,* 88th Cong., 1st sess., 1963, pp. 1031–1033.

36. U.S. Congress, HFAC, *Hearings: Arms Control and Disarmament Act Amendments, 1970,* 91st Cong., 2d sess., 1970, pp. 25–27, and U.S. Congress, HFAC, *Hearings: Arms Control and Disarmament Act Amendments,* 92d Cong., 2d sess., 1972, pp. 12–14.

37. U.S. Congress, HFAC, Subcommittee on National Security Policy and Scientific Developments, *Report: Review of Arms Control Legislation and*

Organization, 93d Cong., 2d sess., 1974, p. 18; U.S. Congress, HFAC,*Report: The International Transfer of Conventional Arms,* 93d Cong., 2d sess., 1974, p. CRS-3; and *New York Times,* June 9, 1970.

38. U.S. Congress, HFAC, Subcommittee on National Security Policy and Scientific Developments, *Hearings: U.S. Chemical Warfare Policy,* 93d Cong., 2d sess., 1974, p. 190; *New York Times,* December 17, 1973; U.S. Congress, SFRC, *Hearings: ACDA Authorization,* 93d Cong., 2d sess., 1974, pp. 6-10; *Newsweek,* February 25, 1974, p. 17; *Washington Post,* February 1, 1974; and U.S. Congress, Senate, Committee on Government Operations, *Hearings: Export Reorganization Act of 1976,* 94th Cong., 2d sess., 1976, p. 780.

39. PL 95-108 and U.S. Congress. SFRC, *Report: Arms Control and Disarmament Act Amendments of 1977,* No. 95-193, 95th Cong., 1st sess., 1977, p. 7.

40. See U.S. Congress, HIRC, Subcommittee on International Security and Scientific Affairs, *Hearings: The Arms Control and Disarmament Agency Authorization for Fiscal Year 1978,* 95th Cong., 1st sess., 1977, pp. 31, 67-68. ACDA's Office of Public Affairs prepared an exceedingly ambitious, detailed internal memorandum in the spring of 1977 concerning possible future public affairs activites.

Chapter 10: General Advisory Committee on Arms Control and Disarmament

1. U.S. Congress, HFAC, *Hearings: Arms Control and Disarmament Act Amendments, 1968,* 90th Cong., 2d sess., 1968, pp. 215, 239.

2. The GAC did make a minor contribution. In 1968, at Foster's request, it agreed to support U.S. ratification of the 1925 Geneva Protocol. This, combined with other factors, helped put the issue on the agenda of the Nixon NSC. Forrest R. Frank, "CBW: 1962-67; 1967-68; 1969-72," in Commission on the Organization of Government for the Conduct of Foreign Policy (Murphy Commission), *Adequacy of Current Organization: Defense and Arms Control* Appendices, 4 (Washington: Government Printing Office, June 1975), p. 311.

3. Duncan L. Clarke, "Ups and Downs of Arms Control," *Bulletin of the Atomic Scientists* 30 (September 1974): 44-49; Chester A. Crocker, "The President's External Advisors in Foreign Policy," in Murphy Commission, *Advisory Panels,* Appendices, 6, p. 427; and U.S. Congress, HFAC, Subcommittee on National Security Policy and Scientific Developments, *Hearings: Arms Control and Disarmament Agency,* 93d Cong., 2d sess., 1974, pp. 5-6.

4. U.S. Congress, *Report: The Role of Advisory Committees in U.S. Foreign Policy*, Joint Committee Print, prepared by the Congressional Research Service, 94th Cong., 1st sess., 1975, p. 92, and *Atlanta Constitution*, June 23, 1974.

5. Testimony of Fred Iklé before the Murphy Commission, July 23, 1974. The advice was well taken. Congressman Zablocki, whose subcommittee passed on ACDA's authorization, took a personal interest in the GAC. In 1975 he suggested legislation to increase its membership by adding two senators and two congressmen. But Zablocki hesitated when the administration and members of the Arms Control Association argued against his proposal. He raised the matter again in 1977, and similar objections were voiced. U.S. Congress, HIRC, Subcommittee on International Security and Scientific Affairs, *Hearings: Arms Control and Disarmament Act Amendments*, 94th Cong., 1st sess., 1975, pp. 2, 19; U.S. Congress, HIRC, *Report: Arms Control and Disarmament Act Amendments of 1975*, No. 94-281, 94th Cong., 1st sess., 1975, p. 8; and U.S. Congress, HIRC, Subcommittee on International Security and Scientific Affairs, *Hearings: The Arms Control and Disarmament Agency Authorization for Fiscal Year 1978*, 95th Cong., 1st sess., 1977, pp. 58–60.

6. HFAC, *Hearings: Arms Control and Disarmament Agency*, p. 5.

7. On this point Chester Crocker contrasts the GAC with the little-known "Doty Group" (named after its leading figure, the scientist Paul Doty), an ad hoc group of experts who, though they often differed with Kissinger, were given a hearing by him, partly because of their impressive scientific credentials. Crocker, "President's External Advisors," p. 427. In 1977 President Carter appointed Doty to the GAC.

Chapter 11: Personnel and Size

1. U.S. Civil Service Commission, Bureau of Personnel Management Evaluation, *Report: Review of Personnel Management in the Arms Control and Disarmament Agency*, April 1975, pp. 5–8.

2. PL 95-108; U.S. Congress, HIRC, Subcommittee on International Security and Scientific Affairs, *Hearings: The Arms Control and Disarmament Agency Authorization for Fiscal Year 1978*, 95th Cong., 1st sess., 1977, pp. 46–47, 52, and U.S. Congress, SFRC, *Report: Arms Control and Disarmament Act Amendments*, No. 95-193, 95th Cong., 1st sess., 1977, pp. 64–66. There are several safeguards against abuse of this new authority.

3. The International Relations Bureau was abolished in Warnke's 1977 reorganization. Except for those attached to the Director's Office, FSOs were then assigned to two new bureaus: International Security Programs and Multilateral Affairs. Their functional activities were essentially unchanged.

4. That this perception has substance is suggested by the views expressed by a

senior retired ACDA military officer who served in a responsible position
during this period:

"ACDA's role is to help DOD. Take security assistance. . . . We must help
Defense present a strong and persuasive rationale for security assistance to
Congress and the public."

"ACDA has no business meddling in the defense budget . . . We should help
DOD, not needlessly irritate them."

"I am satisfied with ACDA's present, limited policy role. We must guard
against being considered arms controllers and pay attention to national
security."

(Question: "Are you concerned that such views might be construed as
inhibiting movement in arms control?")

"Yes, they may be vulnerable to Congress."

5. Nicholas Ruggieri, interview of Lieutenant General John Davis, "Arms Control and the Military Man," *Foreign Service Journal* 48 (February 1971): 19;
Duncan L. Clarke, "Role of Military Officers in the U.S. Arms Control and
Disarmament Agency," *Military Review* 54 (December 1974): 50; and Captain Stephen R. Norton, "The Role of the Military in the Arms Control and
Disarmament Agency," unpublished paper, 1978. In 1976 ACDA and DOD
negotiated an agreement, which read: "A military member appointed, detailed or assigned to ACDA shall not be subject to direction by or control by
his armed force or any officer thereof directly or indirectly with respect to
ACDA responsibilities exercised in the position to which appointed, detailed,
or assigned." U.S. ACDA, *Memorandum of Agreement Between Department of Defense, the Army, the Navy, and the Air Force, and United States
Arms Control and Disarmament Agency,* Washington, D.C., May 14, 1976.

6. U.S. Congress, SFRC, *Report: Arms Control and Disarmament Act Amendments of 1977,* No. 95-193, 95th Cong., 1st sess., 1977, p. 38, and U.S.
Congress, Senate, Committee on Appropriations, *Hearings: Departments of
State, Justice, . . . Appropriations for Fiscal Year 1978,* 95th Cong., 1st
sess., 1977, p. 353. The budget is sometimes authorized for a two-year
period. For ACDA's budget authorization and appropiations from FY 1962 to
FY 1976, see U.S. Congress, HIRC, Subcommittee on International Security
and Scientific Affairs, *Hearings: Arms Control and Disarmament Act
Amendments,* 94th Cong., 1st sess., 1975, p. 16.

Chapter 12: Outside Constituency

1. *Washington Post,* June 2, 1977, and *Wall Street Journal,* August 1, 1972.
2. U.S. Congress, HIRC, Subcommittee on International Security and Scientific Affairs, *Hearings: The Arms Control and Disarmament Agency Authorization for Fiscal Year 1978,* 95th Cong., 1st sess., 1977, pp. 16–17.
3. Jonathan Medalia, "The U.S. Senate and Strategic Arms Limitation

Policymaking, 1963–1972," Ph.D. dissertation, Stanford University, 1975, p. 53.

4. *The Defense Monitor* 6 (February 1977): 1.

5. Duncan L. Clarke, "Congress, Interest Groups, and the U.S. Arms Control and Disarmament Agency," paper prepared for International Studies Association Convention, New York, March 14, 1973, pp. 26–31.

6. U.S. Congress, SFRC, *Hearings: To Amend the Arms Control and Disarmament Act,* 88th Cong., 1st sess., 1963, pp. 31–32; U.S. Congress, SFRC, *Hearings: Nomination of Gerard C. Smith to Be Director, Arms Control and Disarmament Agency,* 91st Cong., 1st sess., 1969, p. 2; Paul G. Conway, "An Analysis of Decision Making on U.S. Chemical and Biological Warfare Policies in 1969," Ph.D. dissertation, Purdue University, 1972, p. 159; Forrest Russell Frank, "U.S. Arms Control Policymaking: The 1972 Biological Weapons Convention Case," Ph.D. dissertation, Stanford University, 1974, p. 272; U.S. Congress, SFRC, *Report: Arms Control and Disarmament Act Amendments of 1977,* No. 95-193, 95th Cong., 1st sess., 1977, pp. 64–65; and U.S. Congress, HIRC, Subcommittee on International Security and Scientific Affairs, *Hearings: The Arms Control and Disarmament Agency Authorization for Fiscal Year 1978,* 95th Cong., 1st sess., 1977, pp. 46–47, 52.

7. Arms control interest groups are in touch with one another and sometimes coordinate activities. Several ACA officers, board members, and general members serve on other groups in either a formal or an informal capacity.

8. *Arms Control Today,* 7 (October 1977): 2. For an account of ACA's first eighteen months of existence, see Clarke, "Congress, Interest Groups," pp. 31–35.

9. For a survey of the attitudes of ACA members see William H. Kincade, "Arms Control, Interest Groups, and Public Opinion," unpublished paper, 1973, Appendices 4 and 5. Kincade became ACA's Executive Director in 1977.

10. U.S. Congress, HFAC, Subcommittee on National Security Policy and Scientific Developments, *Hearings: Arms Control and Disarmament Agency,* 93d Cong., 2d sess., 1974, pp. 39–40, and U.S. Congress, HIRC, Subcommittee on International Security and Scientific Affairs, *Hearings: Arms Control and Disarmament Act Amendments,* 94th Cong., 1st sess., 1975, pp. 19, 34, 44, 68–69, 75–86.

11. Medalia, "U.S. Senate," p. 190.

Chapter 13: ACDA and Congress

1. See Alan Platt and Lawrence Weiler, eds., *Congress and Arms Control* (Boulder, Colorado: Westview Press, 1978); Alan Platt, *The U.S. Senate and Strategic Arms Policy, 1969–1977* (Westview Press, 1978).

2. Jonathan Medalia, "The U.S. Senate and Strategic Arms Limitation Policymaking, 1963–1972," Ph.D. dissertation, Stanford University, 1975, pp. 52, 55, 62–69. Medalia identifies the Senate's "arms controllers" and their beliefs.

3. Anne Hessing Cahn, *Congress, Military Affairs and (a Bit of) Information* (Beverly Hills, Calif.: Sage Publications, 1974), pp. 16–19.

4. U.S. Congress, HFAC, Subcommittee on National Security Policy and Scientific Developments, *Hearings: Arms Control and Disarmament Agency,* 93d Cong., 2d sess., 1974, pp. 75, 114, 121, 123, 132.

5. U.S. Congress, HFAC, Subcommittee on National Security Policy and Scientific Developments, *Report: Review of Arms Control Legislation and Organization,* 93d Cong., 2d sess., 1974, p. 19.

6. Raymond Garthoff, "Negotiating with the Russians: Some Lessons from SALT," *International Security* 1 (Spring 1977): 13; *New York Times,* August 13 and August 14, 1970; and U.S. Congress, SFRC, *Hearings: Arms Control and Disarmament Act Amendments, 1970,* 91st Cong., 2d sess., 1970, pp. 14–15.

7. Dwight Eisenhower, *Waging Peace* (Garden City, N.Y.: Doubleday, 1965), p. 356.

8. U.S. Congress, HIRC, Subcommittee on International Security and Scientific Affairs, *Hearings: The Vladivostok Accord: Implications to U.S. Security, Arms Control, and World Peace,* 94th Cong., 1st sess., 1975, p. 128.

9. U.S. Congress, HIRC, Subcommittee on International Security and Scientific Affairs, *Hearings: Arms Control and Disarmament Act Amendments,* 94th Cong., 1st sess., 1975, p. 79; U.S. ACDA, *Documents on Disarmament,* 1967, pp. 402–405; U.S. Congress, SFRC, *Hearings: Arms Control and Disarmament Act Amendments, 1968,* 90th Cong., 2d sess., 1968, p. 7; U.S. Congress, SFRC, *Hearings: Arms Control and Disarmament Act Amendments,* 92d Cong., 2d sess., 1972, pp. 23–24; and John Lehman, address, in *Arms Transfers,* final report of senior conference, U.S. Military Academy, West Point, New York, 1976, p. 19.

10. Mason Willrich, "Factors Influencing U.S. Arms Control Policy," paper prepared for Fourth International Arms Control Symposium, Philadelphia, October 18, 1969, p. 15.

11. Harold K. Jacobson and Eric Stein, *Diplomats, Scientists, and Politicians* (Ann Arbor: University of Michigan Press, 1966), p. 448; and *Washington Post,* March 1 and March 4, 1963 (letters to editor).

12. John Newhouse, *Cold Dawn: The Story of SALT* (New York: Holt, Rinehart & Winston, 1973), p. 83.

13. *Congressional Record* 109, 88th Cong., 1st sess., May 27, 1963, p. S9483.

14. U.S. ACDA, *Documents on Disarmament,* 1966, pp. 329–330; U.S. Congress, Joint Committee on Atomic Energy, *Hearings: Nonproliferation of Nuclear Weapons,* 89th Cong., 2d sess., 1966, pp. 147–148; and Robert L. DeVries, "The Formulation of American Policy on the Control Provisions

of the Nonproliferation Treaty," Ph.D. dissertation, University of Michigan, 1974, pp. 62, 65, 86.

15. *Documents on Disarmament,* 1972, pp. 44–45.

16. PL 88-186; *Congressional Record* 109, 88th Cong., 1st sess., November 20, 1963, p. H22510, and U.S. Congress, HFAC, *Hearings: To Amend the Arms Control and Disarmament Act,* 88th Cong., 1st sess., 1963, p. 116.

17. Lack of information sometimes hindered Congress in other areas. For instance, Congress was unaware of the details of the 1974 draft agreements between Washington and Moscow on a threshold test ban. Lawrence D. Weiler, "The Arms Race, Secret Negotiations and the Congress," Occasional Paper 12, the Stanley Foundation, Muscatine, Iowa, 1976, p. 38.

18. U.S. Congress, HFAC, Subcommittee on National Security Policy and Scientific Developments, *Hearings: Chemical–Biological Warfare: U.S. Policies and International Effects,* 91st Cong., 1st sess., 1969, pp. 202–209.

19. *Documents on Disarmament,* 1973, pp. 333–339, 435–437; U.S. Congress, SFRC, Subcommittee on Oceans and International Environment, *Hearings: Prohibiting Military Weather Modification,* 92d Cong., 2d sess., 1972; U.S. Congress, SFRC, Subcommittee on Oceans and International Environment, *Hearings: Weather Modification,* 93d Cong., 2d sess., 1974; and U.S. Congress, HIRC, Subcommittee on International Organizations, *Hearing: Prohibition of Weather Modification as a Weapon of War,* 94th Cong., 1st sess., 1975.

20. U.S. Congress, SFRC, Subcommittee on Arms Control, International Law and Organizations, *Hearings: To Promote Negotiations for a Comprehensive Test Ban,* 93d Cong., 1st sess., 1973.

21. See U.S. Congress, SFRC, Subcommittee on Foreign Assistance, *Hearings: Foreign Assistance Authorizations: Arms Sales Issues,* 94th Cong., 1st sess., 1975, pp. 51–60, and U.S. Congress, SFRC, *Report: International Security Assistance and Arms Export Control Act of 1976–1977,* 94th Cong., 2d sess., 1976.

22. Clarence D. Long, "Nuclear Proliferation: Can Congress Act in Time?" *International Security* 1 (Spring 1977): 52–76.

23. Weiler, "The Arms Race," p. 12.

24. U.S. Congress, Senate, Committee on Armed Services, *Hearings: Military Implications of the Treaty on the Limitation of Anti-Ballistic Missile Systems and the Interim Agreement on Limitation of Strategic Offensive Arms,* 92d Cong., 2d sess., 1972, pp. 295, 369–370; U.S. Congress, HFAC, *Hearings: Agreement on Limitation of Strategic Offensive Weapons,* 92d Cong., 2d sess., 1972, pp. 25, 42; and Gerard Smith, "Arms Control to Improve American Security," address before the National Security Industrial Association, Washington, D.C., September 14, 1972.

25. U.S. Congress, SFRC, Subcommittee on Arms Control, Oceans, and Inter-

national Environment, *Hearings: United States/Soviet Strategic Options,* 95th Cong., 1st sess., 1977, pp. 7–39, and HFAC, *Hearings: Arms Control and Disarmament Agency* (n. 4 above), p. 139.

26. U.S. Congress, SFRC, *Hearings: Warnke Nomination,* 95th Cong., 1st sess., 1977, p. 37, and U.S. Congress, SFRC, *Hearings: Nomination of John F. Lehman, Jr., to Be Deputy Director, ACDA,* 94th Cong., 1st sess., 1975, pp. 2–4, 9–11, 47, 57, 63–70.

27. HIRC, *Hearings: Arms Control and Disarmament Act Amendments* (n. 9 above), pp. 11, 23.

28. The Case amendment episode had one positive spinoff. Subsequently, ARPA became even more cooperative. SFRC, *Hearings: Arms Control and Disarmament Act Amendments* (n. 9 above), pp. 36–40, 42–43, 62–64; U.S. Congress, SFRC, *Report: Foreign Relations Act of 1972,* No. 92-754, 92d Cong., 2d sess., 1972, pp. 90–91; *Congressional Record* 118, 92d Cong., 2d sess., May 30, 1972, p. S8563; and Medalia, "U.S. Senate" (n. 2 above), p. 217.

29. *Congressional Record* 119, 93d Cong., 1st sess., January 9, 1973, pp. S303–S304; Hubert H. Humphrey, *Report on The U.S. Arms Control and Disarmament Agency,* for the Military Spending, Arms Control and Disarmament Committee of the Members of Congress for Peace through Law, April 9, 1973; U.S. Congress, SFRC, *Hearings: Nomination of Fred Charles Iklé of California to Be Director of the United States Arms Control and Disarmament Agency,* 93d Cong., 1st sess., 1973, pp. 3, 31; and U.S. Congress, Senate, Committee on Appropriations, *Hearings: Departments of State, Justice, . . . Appropriations for Fiscal Year 1974,* 93d Cong., 1st sess., 1973, p. 932.

30. HFAC, *Hearings: Arms Control and Disarmament Agency,* p. v; U.S. Congress, HFAC, *Hearings: Arms Control and Disarmament Act Amendments,* 93d Cong., 2d sess., 1974, p. 42; and HFAC, *Review of Arms Control Legislation,* pp. v, 1.

31. U.S. Congress, HIRC, *Report: Arms Control and Disarmament Act Amendments of 1975,* No. 94-281, 94th Cong., 1st sess., 1975, pp. 5–7, 10, 14–15.

32. U.S. Congress, HFAC, *ACDA Report: The International Transfer of Conventional Arms,* Committee Print, 93d Cong., 2d sess., 1974, pp. CRS-2, 16.

33. HIRC, *Report: Arms Control and Disarmament Act Amendments of 1975,* p. 7.

34. *Arms Export Control Act of 1976* (PL 94-329), sections 25 and 36(b).

35. U.S. Congress, HIRC, Subcommittee on International Security and Scientific Affairs, *Hearings: Foreign Assistance Legislation for Fiscal Year 1978,* Part 2, 95th Cong., 1st sess., 1977, p. 161.

36. U.S. Congress, Senate, Committee on Government Operations, *Hearings:*

Export Reorganization Act of 1976, 94th Cong., 2d sess., 1976, pp. 565–566, 702, 765–766, and *Congressional Record* 124, 95th Cong., 2d sess., February 9, 1978, pp. H908–H919.

37. *Washington Post,* March 1 and March 4, 1977.

38. Subsequently, Nitze apparently retreated from this position. U.S. Congress, Senate, Committee on Armed Services, *Hearings: Consideration of Mr. Paul C. Warnke to Be Director of the U.S. Arms Control and Disarmament Agency and Ambassador,* 95th Cong., 1st sess., 1977, p. 183, and *Congressional Record* 123, 95th Cong., 1st sess., March 9, 1977, p. S3741.

39. Senate Committee on Armed Services, *Consideration of Mr. Paul C. Warnke,* pp. 5, 31, 85.

40. *Ibid.* pp. 17 ff.

41. *Ibid.,* pp. 7, 16, 98, 116–137, 163.

42. *Ibid.,* pp. 12, 231–232, and SFRC, *Warnke Nomination,* pp. 44, 97, 116.

43. *Congressional Record* 123, 95th Cong., 1st sess., March 4, 1977, p. S3539, and *Washington Post,* March 14, 1977. In June, several senators were appointed "congressional advisers to SALT." *Congressional Record* 123, 95th Cong., 1st sess., June 28, 1977, p. S10949.

44. *Congressional Record* 123, 95th Cong., 1st sess., May 3, 1977, p. H3941.

45. *Congressional Record* 123, 95th Cong., 1st sess., June 16, 1977, p. S10016.

46. U.S. Congress, House of Representatives, *Conference Report: Arms Control and Disarmament Act Amendments of 1977,* No. 95-563, 95th Cong., 1st sess., 1977, p. 6.

47. U.S. Congress, SFRC, Subcommittee on Arms Control, Oceans and International Environment, *Hearings: Threshold Test Ban and Peaceful Nuclear Explosion Treaties,* 95th Cong., 1st sess., 1977, p. 36. The Senator's concern about verification continued. His questions and comments on the subject comprised fully 25 percent of the entire 1978 hearing before the Senate Foreign Relations Committee on ACDA's budget authorization. U.S. Congress, SFRC, *Report and Hearings: An Act to Authorize Appropriations Under the Arms Control and Disarmament Act for the Fiscal Year 1979,* No. 95-843, 95th Cong., 2d sess., 1978.

48. U.S. Congress, SFRC, *Report: Arms Control and Disarmament Act Amendments of 1977,* No. 95-193, 95th Cong., 1st sess., 1977, pp. 40, 46–47, 55–56, and *Washington Post,* May 6 and June 25, 1977.

49. *Congressional Record* 123, 95th Cong., 1st sess., June 16, 1977, p. S10017.

50. U.S. Congress, HIRC, *Report: Authorization of Appropriations Under the Arms Control and Disarmament Act, Fiscal Year 1979,* No. 95-1048, 95th Cong., 2d sess., 1978, pp. 13–16. The first report to Congress under section 37—to which this group took exception, without specifying its objections—concluded: "The anticipated SALT TWO agreement is adequately verifiable." U.S. Department of State, Bureau of Public Affairs,

SALT ONE: Compliance, SALT TWO: Verification, Selected Documents No. 7, 1978, p. 12. Later that year a panel of conservative congressmen did enumerate objections and concluded that "Independent verification of several important aspects of SALT II will not be possible." It also erroneously cited Warnke as having stated that "our cancellation of the B-1 should be followed by a similar type of arms restraint by the Soviets . . ." Representative Bob Carr (D–Mich.) contacted Warnke directly about this alleged statement. Warnke denied describing the B-1 cancellation in these terms and he definitely did not consider it an act of restraint. U.S. Congress, House of Representatives, Panel on the Strategic Arms Limitation Talks and the Comprehensive Test Ban Treaty, Intelligence and Military Application of Nuclear Energy Subcommittee, Committee on Armed Services, *Report: SALT II An Interim Assessment,* 95th Cong., 2d sess., 1978, pp. 6, 29, 44.

Chapter 14: Arms Control Impact Statements

1. U.S. Congress, HFAC, *Report: Amending the Arms Control and Disarmament Act,* No. 93-904, 93d Cong., 2d sess., 1974, pp. 4, 9.
2. *Ibid.,* pp. 10–11; U.S. Congress, SFRC, *Report: Arms Control and Disarmament Act Amendments,* No. 93-836, 93d Cong., 2d sess., 1974, p. 3; U.S. Congress, HFAC, Subcommittee on National Security Policy and Scientific Developments, *Hearings: Arms Control and Disarmament Agency,* 93d Cong., 2d sess., 1974, pp. 155–156; and *Congressional Record* 120, 93d Cong., 2d sess., April 24, 1974, pp. H3097–H3107.
3. U.S. Congress, HFAC, Subcommittee on National Security Policy and Scientific Developments, *Report: Review of Arms Control Legislation and Organization,* 93d Cong., 2d sess., 1974, pp. 36–37; U.S. Congress, HIRC Subcommittee on International Security and Scientific Affairs, *Hearings: Arms Control and Disarmament Act Amendments,* 94th Cong., 1st sess., 1975, pp. 29–30; and U.S. Congress, HIRC, *Hearings: Arms Control and Disarmament Agency Authorization for Fiscal Year 1976,* 94th Cong., 1st sess., 1975, pp. 4–5, 8.
4. HIRC, *Hearings: Arms Control and Disarmament Agency Authorization,* pp. 10–12, and U.S. Congress, SFRC, *Hearings: Warnke Nomination,* 95th Cong., 1st sess., 1977, p. 42.
5. U.S. Congress, *Conference Report: Foreign Relations Authorization Act, Fiscal Year 1976,* No. 94-660, 94th Cong., 1st sess., 1975, pp. 25–26.
6. Individual legislators envisaged additional, secondary purposes: involving ACDA and Congress in the weapons research and development process; giving the Foreign Relations and International Relations committees jurisdiction in the weapons acquisition process; and, though only one or two of the more liberal legislators held this view, consciously holding ACDA hos-

tage by positioning it in such a perilous way that it would be extremely dependent upon congressional support.

7. George Berdes, "Congress's New Leverage," *The Center Magazine,* July–August, 1976, p. 80.

8. Excerpt from the Arms Control and Disarmament Act, as Amended (PL 94-141, as amended by PL 95-338):

Arms Control Impact Information and Analysis

Sec. 36. (a) In order to assist the Director in the performance of his duties with respect to arms control and disarmament policy and negotiations, any Government agency preparing any legislative or budgetary proposal for—

(1) any program of research, development, testing, engineering, construction, deployment, or modernization with respect to nuclear armaments, nuclear implements of war, military facilities or military vehicles designed or intended primarily for the delivery of nuclear weapons,

(2) any program of research, development, testing, engineering, construction, deployment, or modernization with respect to armaments, ammunition, implements of war, or military facilities, having—

(A) an estimated total program cost in excess of $250,000,000 or

(B) an estimated annual program cost in excess of $50,000,000, or

(3) any other program involving technology with potential military application or weapons systems which such Government agency or the Director believes may have a significant impact on arms control and disarmament policy or negotiations, shall, on a continuing basis, provide the Director with full and timely access to detailed information, in accordance with the procedures established pursuant to section 35 of this Act, with respect to the nature, scope, and purpose of such proposal.

(b) (1) The Director, as he deems appropriate, shall assess and analyze each program described in subsection (a) with respect to its impact on arms control and disarmament policy and negotiations, and shall advise and make recommendations, on the basis of such assessment and analysis, to the National Security Council, the Office of Management and Budget, and the Government agency proposing such program.

(2) No request to the Congress for authorizations or appropriations for—

(A) any program described in subsection (a) (1) or (2), or

(B) any program described in subsection (a) (3) and found by the National Security Council, on the basis of the advice and recommendations received from the Director, to have significant impact on arms control and disarmament policy or negotiations, shall be transmitted without a complete statement analyzing the impact of such program, either as an individual program or an aggregation of related programs, on arms control and disarmament policy and negotiations.

Any classified arms control impact statement must be accompanied by an unclassified version.

(3) Upon the request of the Committee on Armed Services of the Senate or the House of Representatives, the Committee on Appropriations of the Senate or the House of Representatives, the Committee on Foreign Relations of the Senate, or the Committee on International Relations of the House of Representatives or the Joint Committee on Atomic Energy, the Director shall, after informing the Secretary of State, advise

such committee on the arms control and disarmament implications of any program with respect to which a statement has been submitted to the Congress pursuant to paragraph (2).

(c) No court shall have any jurisdiction under any law to compel the performance of any requirement of this section or to review the adequacy of the performance of any such requirement on the part of any Government agency (including the Agency and the Director).

9. U.S. Congress, Congressional Research Service, *Analysis of Arms Control Impact Statements Submitted in Connection with the Fiscal Year 1978 Budget Request,* Joint Committee Print, 95th Cong., 1st sess., 1977, p. 6 (hereinafter cited as *CRS Report,* 1977), and U.S. Congress, HIRC, *Report: Arms Control and Disarmament Act Amendments of 1975,* No. 94-281, 94th Cong., 1st sess., 1975, pp. 10–11.

10. U.S. General Accounting Office, *Statements That Analyze Effects of Proposed Programs on Arms Control Need Improvement,* ID-77-41, October 20, 1977, pp. 8–9, 41 (hereinafter cited as *GAO Report,* 1977); *CRS Report,* 1977, p. 4; and HIRC, *Report: Arms Control and Disarmament Act Amendments of 1975,* pp. 6, 11.

11. *GAO Report,* 1977, pp. 7–8. See HIRC, Subcommittee on International Security and Scientific Affairs, *Hearings: The Arms Control and Disarmament Agency Authorization for Fiscal Year 1978,* 95th Cong., 1st sess., 1977, p. 66, and PL 95-338.

12. *GAO Report,* 1977, pp. 5–6, 40, and *CRS Report,* 1977, p. 6.

13. *GAO Report,* 1977, pp. 6–7, and *CRS Report,* 1977, p. 7.

14. HIRC, *Report: Arms Control and Disarmament Act Amendments of 1975,* p. 12.

15. HFAC, *Hearings: Arms Control and Disarmament Agency* (n. 2 above), p. 44, and HIRC, *Hearings: Arms Control and Disarmament Act Amendments* (n. 3 above), pp. 77–78.

16. HIRC, *Arms Control and Disarmament Act Amendments,* pp. 32–33, 76–77.

17. *CRS Report,* 1977, pp. 368–377.

18. *Ibid.,* pp. iv–v, 4–5, 27.

19. *GAO Report,* 1977, pp. 11–13, 40–41, and HIRC, *Hearings: Arms Control and Disarmament Agency Authorization for Fiscal Year 1978,* p. 22.

20. *GAO Report,* 1977, p. 17.

21. HIRC, *Hearings: Arms Control and Disarmament Agency Authorization for Fiscal Year 1978,* pp. 8, 30.

22. *GAO Report,* 1977, p. 15.

23. *Ibid.,* pp. 22–23, 27, and HIRC, *Hearings: Arms Control and Disarmament Agency Authorization for Fiscal Year 1978,* pp. 29–30.

24. "Arms Control and the 1976 Presidential Election," *Arms Control Today* 6 (October 1976): 2.

25. SFRC, *Hearings: Warnke Nomination* (n. 4 above), p. 42.

26. HIRC, *Report: Arms Control and Disarmament Act Amendments of 1975* (n. 9 above), p. 13.
27. *GAO Report,* 1977, p. 28.
28. HIRC, *Hearings: Arms Control and Disarmament Agency Authorization for Fiscal Year 1978,* p. 23.
29. *GAO Report,* 1977, pp. 28–29, 39–41.
30. *Ibid.,* pp. 40–41, and *CRS Report,* 1977, pp. 20–21.
31. U.S. Congress, Congressional Research Service, *Report: Additional Arms Control Impact Statements for Fiscal Year 1978,* 95th Cong., 1st sess., 1977, p. 23.
32. *Ibid.,* p. 3, and *Washington Post,* June 28 and July 6, 1977.
33. U.S. Congress, *Fiscal Year 1979 Arms Control Impact Statements,* Joint Committee Print, 95th Cong., 2d sess., 1978, pp. iii–iv.
34. *Ibid.,* p. 170.
35. For various assessments of the ACIS process see Robert Metzger and Paul Walker, "Legislating David into Goliath: Arms Control Impact Statements," paper delivered at the International Studies Association Convention, February 1978; U.S. General Accounting Office, *Improved Procedures Needed for Identifying Programs Requiring Arms Control Impact Statements,* ID-78-48, 1978; Robert Butterworth, "The Arms Control Impact Statement: Gauging the Effects," in *Reformulating American Strategic Doctrine and Policy, Policy Studies Journal,* Spring 1979; U.S. Congress, HIRC, *Report: Evaluation of Fiscal Year 1979 Arms Control Impact Statements: Toward More Informed Congressional Participation in National Security Policymaking,* Congressional Research Service, 95th Cong., 2d sess., 1979.

Epilogue: The Carter Administration and Paul Warnke: A Further Look

1. *Washington Post,* October 11, 1978.
2. This was substantiated by two high-level sources, neither of whom would specify the issue(s) involved.
3. See, U.S. Department of State, press conference of Paul C. Warnke, October 30, 1978, p. 16.
4. However, it appears that in mid-June 1978 Carter altered his position so as to permit very low-yield (far less than 1 kiloton) experimental testing. Several factors reportedly influenced this decision: a feeling that it would be difficult to gain Senate approval for a complete ban while the controversial SALT II accords were pending; an active anti–test ban lobby that raised the specter of Carter's being "soft on national security"; and a variety of familiar reservations on the part of some leading nuclear physicists. Walter Pincus, "U.S.

Sees No Early Nuclear Test Ban Accord,'' *Washington Post,* August 9, 1978, and William Kincade, ''Banning Nuclear Tests: Cold Feet in the Carter Administration,'' *Bulletin of the Atomic Scientists*, November 1978, pp. 8–11.

5. Spurgeon Keeny, Jr., ed., *Nuclear Power: Issues and Choices* (Cambridge, Mass.: Ballinger, 1977).

6. U.S. Congress, HIRC, *Hearings: Proposed Sales to Israel, Egypt, and Saudi Arabia,* 95th Cong., 2d sess., 1978, p. 53, and *Washington Post,* November 23, 1978. The State Department's views on the Korean transaction were mixed. Ultimately, however, Vance, like Brown, favored the sale.

7. At his last official press conference Warnke was asked to give ''some feeling as to how this [SALT II] treaty will fare in the Senate.'' He replied, in part that it would ''do a lot better than I did [Laughter].'' U.S. Department of State, press conference of Paul C. Warnke, October 30, 1978, p. 11.

8. One government official offered the following explanation: ''In the late 1960s when Warnke was in DOD he was one of the few Pentagon critics of the Vietnam war. Hence, on the Hill, he had several old friends and old enemies who remembered this earlier era. This colored his relationships.'' While Jackson's opposition to SALT II was well known, his first formal public statement of disapproval came in a speech delivered on November 20, 1978, before a meeting of NATO parliamentarians in Lisbon. *Washington Post,* November 30, 1978.

9. Carter had first offered the post to former NATO Commander General Andrew Goodpaster, but he declined the offer.

10. *Washington Post,* October 21, November 9, and November 16, 1978; and Alton Frye, ''ACDA's General: Time for Strategic Withdrawal,'' *Washington Post,* December 6, 1978. Compare, U.S. Department of State, ''Special Briefing on SALT Two,'' by George M. Seignious, December 13, 1978, pp. 2–3.

11. One week after assuming the directorship, General Seignious announced his wholehearted support for SALT II. U.S. Department of State, ''Special Briefing on SALT Two,'' p. 3.

12. Warnke may have been alluding to ACDA's persistent image problem when he said, ''But the one conclusion I've come to is that arms control just doesn't come naturally. It's a very unnatural act.'' U.S. Department of State, Warnke press conference, p. 1.

13. Public opinion, of course, is fickle and frequently contradictory. For example, a Harris Survey released on May 22, 1978, showed that 71 percent of those polled favored détente, while 75 percent supported a SALT II accord. In December 1978 an Associated Press–NBC poll showed 75 percent support for SALT II. However, an AP–NBC poll in October 1978 found widespread concern that the United States was militarily weaker than the Soviet Union, and two-thirds of those polled said that Moscow cannot be trusted to live up to agreements. Divining linkages between fluid and conflicting public attitudes and, say, congressional voting patterns is a risky enterprise.

Index